Critical Voices in School Reform

School reform of one kind or another is a priority for education systems the world over. Yet the voices of students – those most affected by, and most pivotal to, the success or failure of any program of school reform – are rarely heard on this topic. This is the first book to look at school reform from the perspective of the students. Such a youth-centered approach to studying school reform provides valuable insight into how students experience changes in school structure and classroom instruction. The studies included in this collection focus on reform initiatives aimed at overcoming persistent patterns of racial, class and gender inequality. The authors combine the theoretical aspects of research with its practical applications, making this an invaluable resource for teacher educators, classroom practitioners, researchers and policy-makers.

Critical Voices in School Reform: Students Living Through Change is divided into two parts. Part one describes and analyzes programs of reform that turned out contrary to the intentions of adult reformers, illustrating the – often unspoken – tension between adult and student perspectives on school change. Part two looks at reform initiatives that were able to harness student energies and thereby improve student engagement in school life. These reforms, which were finely attuned to the needs and interests of students, offer clear, valuable guidance to those trying to create more equitable school experiences. A concluding chapter draws together the themes and insights gained from looking at school reform through a student-centered lens and offers suggestions for more relevant and lasting reforms.

Beth C. Rubin is assistant professor in the Graduate School of Education at Rutgers, the State University of New Jersey. **Elena M. Silva** is Director of Research for the American Association of University Women.

Critical Voices in School Reform

Students living through change

Edited by Beth C. Rubin and Elena M. Silva

RoutledgeFalmer
Taylor & Francis Group

LONDON AND NEW YORK

First published 2003 by
RoutledgeFalmer
11 New Fetter Lane, London EC4P 4EE

Simultaneously published in the USA and Canada by
RoutledgeFalmer
29 West 35th Street, New York, NY 10001

RoutledgeFalmer is an imprint of the Taylor & Francis Group

© 2003 Edited by Beth C. Rubin and Elena M. Silva

Typeset in Palatino by
HWA Text and Data Management, Tunbridge Wells
Printed and bound in Great Britain by
MPG Books Ltd, Bodmin

British Library Cataloguing in Publication Data
A catalogue record for this book is available from the British
Library

Library of Congress Cataloging in Publication Data
A catalog record for this book has been requested

ISBN 0–415–30267–6 (hbk)
ISBN 0–415–30268–4 (pbk)

To our mothers,
Lois Rubin and Mary Silva,
for all of their love, encouragement, and support.

B.C.R.
E.M.S.

Contents

Contributors

Anthony M. Collatos is a doctoral candidate in urban schooling at the University of California, Los Angeles and a research associate with UCACCORD and the Institute of Democracy, Education and Access at UCLA. His research focuses on creating critical spaces within urban schools to increase learning opportunities and college access for urban youth.

Anthony De Jesus is a research associate at the Center for Puerto Rican Studies at Hunter College (CUNY). His interests include Puerto Rican and Latino education. Prior to earning his Ed.D. from the Harvard Graduate School of Education he was a social worker in the Boston Public Schools.

Ilana Seidel Horn is an AERA/OERI postdoctoral fellow at Stanford University. In fall 2003, she will be an assistant professor of education at the University of Washington, Seattle. Her research interests center on issues of teacher learning, teacher community, and equity in secondary mathematics classrooms.

David Lee Keiser is an assistant professor in the Department of Curriculum and Teaching at Montclair State University. His research interests include school-university partnerships, including professional development schools; the persistence of the achievement gap; culturally responsive teaching and teacher preparation; and mindfulness within teacher education.

Ernest Morrell is an assistant professor of Teacher Education at Michigan State. His work examines the relationships between language and literacy practices in sociocultural contexts and innovative classroom practices that increase academic and critical literacies among urban youth. Prior to entering the academy Morrell taught high school English for six years.

Pedro A. Noguera is the Judith K. Dimon Professor of Communities and Schools at the Harvard Graduate School of Education. His research focuses on schools' responses to social and economic forces within the urban environment. He has engaged in collaborative research with several large, urban school districts, and has published and lectured widely on topics including youth violence, race relations in schools, and the potential impact of school choice and vouchers on urban public schools.

Alicia P. Rodriguez is an independent educational researcher. Her research interests include the sociocultural context of education, identity formation, and educational reform. She received her Ph.D. in Educational Policy Studies from the University of Illinois at Urbana-Champaign.

Beth C. Rubin is an assistant professor of education at Rutgers, the State University of New Jersey. Her research examines students' daily lives in schools at the intersection of sociocultural context and classroom practices, with a particular interest in equity-geared school reform and critical social studies education. She taught high school social studies prior to earning her Ph.D. from the University of California, Berkeley.

Elena M. Silva is the Director of Research for the Educational Foundation of the American Association of University Women. Her research interests include racial, class and gender inequity, the social and cultural dynamics of school policy-making and reform, and youth voice and activism in school and community change projects. She received her Ph.D. in Education from the University of California, Berkeley.

Shana Stein is a social studies teacher at Montclair High School in Montclair, New Jersey. She received her Ed.M. in Social Studies Education at Rutgers, the State University of New Jersey. Her teaching in the Civics and Government Institute focuses on social reform movements, social activism, and race, class and gender in politics.

Jean Yonemura Wing is a founding member of the Berkeley High School Diversity Project and a former research associate at the Western Field Office of the Educational Testing Service. Her research interests include racial inequality, equity in school reform, Asian Americans in education, and implications of the global economy for US education.

Elisabeth L. Woody is a project director at Policy Analysis for California Education (PACE) at the University of California, Berkeley. She received her Ph.D. in Social and Cultural Studies in Education at the University of California, Berkeley. Her research interests include student experiences of school reform, gender and diversity issues, critical pedagogy, and educators' responses to accountability in public schools.

Foreword

Pedro A. Noguera

In the 1970s and 1980s, a number of powerful critical ethnographies were produced which opened the black box of schooling. Books by Rist (1972), Willis (1981), Eckert (1984), Metz (1978), Peshkin (1978) and Fine (1991) exposed the world of schools in powerful ways and provided new insights into how they worked and operated. Social theorists like Rousseau and Durkheim had made the case long ago that schools play a central role in reproducing the social order, but it was not until the doors of schools were opened through critical qualitative research that we were able to understand how this occurred. Through powerful up close and personal accounts of the lives and experiences of the central actors within schools – teachers and students – new insights into the workings of these important social organizations were generated and revealed.

This volume builds upon this important scholarly tradition and extends it with an investigation of the experiences of students, a group both under-studied and pivotal to any understanding of life in schools. It does so with new research carried out by a diverse group of scholars who have spent a great deal of time in schools and who know and understand how they work from the inside out. The insights generated from first-hand knowledge and from excavating the perspectives and voices of students in particular, provide a unique standpoint from which to understand the social processes that occur within schools. The attention to the social complexities of schooling presented in this book is important because it serves as the most effective means to combat common sense explanations of the way schools work and function in American society.

What we take for common sense is a significant obstacle in under-standing and changing how schools work. Having gone to school, there is a tendency for policy makers and the general public to assume we know how schools function and to take for granted much of what happens there. Without much reservation, too often we assume that the way schools determine winners and losers in the larger society is fair because it is based upon merit, talent and ability.

With a focus on equity and student experience, these studies should prove helpful in encouraging readers to question and re-think some of those assumptions. By examining how things work up close, and by listening to the voices of students, we will be better able to see the injustices that too often are inflicted upon children through the practice of schools and through educational policy. Hopefully, such revelations will prompt more of us to ask ourselves why they work that way. We may even be moved to consider how they might work differently to achieve more just and equitable ends.

Critical research cannot by itself transform schools but it can point to the areas and ways in which change is needed. As you read these chapters and look inside of the world of schools ask yourself why schools and the people in them function and act as they do. In asking ourselves why, we open the door to new ways of thinking about schools and the roles they play in our society. Given their importance as institutions of socialization and opportunity, such questioning is urgently needed.

Acknowledgements

We would like to acknowledge and thank the many people who offered us insight, encouragement and support throughout the creation of this book: the attendees of our symposium on the student experience of school reform at the 2001 Ethnography in Education conference at the University of Pennsylvania, and our discussant Jean Lave; Anne Haas Dyson; Judith Warren Little; Jabari Mahiri; Pedro Noguera; Barrie Thorne; William Firestone; James Giarelli; Katrina Bulkley; Carrie Lobman; Michelle Fine; Cecilia Martinez; the members of the UC Berkeley-Berkeley High School Diversity Project; our acquisitions editor at Routledge, Hywel Evans; and, most importantly, all of the authors included in the collection.

No less important was the patience and love of our family members, David Wish, Maya Rubin-Wish, and Brian Woodward, who put up with our lengthy phone conversations and extended absences.

Finally, we thank the students and teachers who shared their thoughts so generously with all of the researchers whose work is presented in this collection.

Introduction
Missing voices: listening to students' experiences with school reform

Elena M. Silva and Beth C. Rubin

> Without the voice of students, schools serve no purpose. They are nothing but institutions where adults run and tell you what you need to know in order to continue this tradition of, this cycle of "we have master's degrees and we know what's best for you so just shut up and deal with it."
>
> (High school senior)

What could students, who confront, resist, and affirm both the problems and reforms that characterize their schools, offer to the traditionally adult-dominated conversation about school change? Despite a small body of research emerging on the significance of "student voice" in school practices and processes (Cook-Sather, 2002; Shultz and Cook-Sather, 2001; Fielding, 2001; Rudduck and Flutter, 2000; Oldfather, 1995), embracing or empowering the voices of students is not a well-practiced approach to understanding or implementing school reforms.

Within a growing wave of reform in public schools, calls for and claims of "student-centered" goals and "student voice" initiatives pervade the process and practice of school reform efforts (Wasley *et al.*, 1997; Olsen, 2000). Yet, more often than not, the student perspective is often represented in fixed and uncomplicated terms that undermine the true agency and diversity of students and student experiences.

Why is the student perspective of reform important? Public high schools boast greater student diversity than ever before in the history of this country (Nieto, 1999; Garcia, 1999). At the center of this diversity are hundreds of thousands of students who experience a reality relatively unknown to the adults who govern their school experience. Students' daily lives in school take place amid the richly interwoven webs of friendship and romance, the heated pulls of emerging racial, ethnic and social identities, the demands and expectations of teachers and parents, and the constructions of academic competence. Particularly in schools confronting persistent problems of racial, class and gender inequity, the significance of students' experiences is neither a well understood, nor commonly explored factor in school planning and reform. Although presumably understood by adult educators, "the student experience" is often mistakenly couched in terms of a single, uniform and invariable experience. Accordingly, the role of the student as an active member of the school community and as an active agent in enacting or resisting reforms remains vastly underestimated.

A closer look at the student experience reveals a mosaic of daily choices and decisions that are remarkable both in their complexity and their significance to the schooling process. This recognition of student agency offers a dialectical view of schooling, a perspective on teaching and learning that acknowledges not only how school structures and processes shape students, but also how students shape the character of their schools and, in turn, shape their own environment and learning objectives.

The chapters in this volume describe the interweave between equity-geared reforms and the daily realities of adolescents' lives in school, pointing to both the complexity and promise of reform. Our hope is that this collection will provide the much-needed link between schools' efforts to achieve equity among students and students' efforts to find purpose, meaning and knowledge within schools.

Our aim is to reach a broad audience including classroom teachers, teacher educators, school administrators, educational policy-makers, and adult and student researchers in education who may find the voices and stories of these students useful in their own practice and decision-making. With this in mind, the empirical studies in this collection illustrate the ways that the multiple identities, social relations, and collective dynamics that constitute students' daily experiences of school are implicated in the processes of schooling and school change. For without attention to the student experience, we run the risk of reproducing policies and practices that ignore the social character of schooling and undermine the role of students as partners in shaping and changing their own educations.

Section and chapter descriptions

This book consists of two separate sections. The five chapters that make up the first part of the collection, "Difficult endeavors: the lived complexities of school reform," illustrate the richly nuanced view of school reform that emerges through student-centered research. These studies show how students' lives in school complicate the enactment of equity-based reform initiatives aimed at "all students," at times subverting the good intentions of the reform and reformers. The second part of the collection, "Deliberate aims: putting students at the center of reform," presents five studies of reform projects that take into account, build upon, and address the specific needs and concerns of those students at the bottom of the achievement gap. According to students, the reforms described in this part of the collection provided them with the targeted support and deliberate attention they needed to progress and remain in schools that they otherwise experienced as discouraging, even hostile.

In the first part of the collection we see reforms that, at times, were experienced by students in ways that were contrary to the intent of the adult reformers. Elena M. Silva, for example, explores the perspectives of a diverse group of high school students as they struggle to participate as partners in their school's efforts to close a persistent race- and class-based achievement gap. Silva's chapter, "Struggling for inclusion: a case study of students as reform partners," illustrates how the increasingly en vogue practice of inviting student participation can, even unwittingly, exclude the least powerful voices and maintain a hierarchy of power and privilege within the school. Even among students, this study demonstrates, certain voices and interests are privileged over others. In the end, the project of student-inclusive, equity-based reform proved problematic as the student group in effect reproduced the very divisions and inequities it set out to dismantle.

Beth C. Rubin's analysis of detracking in a ninth grade "core" program, "On different tracks: students living detracking reform at a diverse urban high school," builds on the idea that reforms directed at "all students" often present different opportunities to and are negotiated differently by students with different backgrounds, experiences and resources. Rubin's chapter follows the experiences of three girls through their first high school year, both within and outside of their detracked classes. Sasha, a high achieving European American student from an upper-middle-class background, found the detracked core, and high school itself, to be rich with opportunities for personal, intellectual, and artistic development, and found a peer group who supported her in these interests. Tiffany, a lower achieving African American student from a working-class background, struggled in her detracked English and social studies classes without academic or social support, and eventually gave up. Kiana, a biracial African American-European American girl from a middle-class family, experienced conflict in her detracked classes, as she struggled to both do well academically and forge a fulfilling social life in the racially polarized social and academic setting of Cedar High School. These students' experiences illustrate the complex interweave of students' social relationships, racial and ethnic identities, and academic preparation in the detracked setting, challenging the idea that detracking will automatically confer equity while, at the same time, contesting the view that detracking might harm higher achieving students.

Alicia P. Rodriguez' study of an Ethnic Studies class, an Asian American history class, and a Chicano/Latino Studies class at a diverse urban high school, " 'There's not really discussion happening': students' experiences of identity-based curricular reform," again draws upon student experiences to complicate the notion of reform. These programs, originally instituted in the 1960s and 1970s, are examples of "multicultural" curricular reforms that focus on a narrow view of ethnicity and race borne out of identity politics, old and new. Some of the courses were highly cherished, as indicated by the students, while others were seen as problematic. This chapter takes a critical look at the relevance and usefulness of "identity-based" courses, suggesting that much of these curricula imparts simplistic and one-dimensional understandings of cultural difference and systems of power. Proposing that perhaps these courses on their own are not the solution or "equity pill" that they are often believed to be, Rodriguez argues for curricular reforms that offer a more complex analysis of young people's multiple identities and realities and which are supported by broader school-wide aims at equity.

Elisabeth L. Woody's study of single-gender academies in California, "Constructing and resisting a theory of difference: student experiences in California's Single Gender Academies," draws upon similar themes of identity and experience. Her chapter investigates how public single-sex schooling influenced students' experiences of gender, as well as how students used the single-sex environment to establish, maintain, and challenge ideologies of gender. The students in several of California's Single Gender Academies simultaneously resisted the use of gender as a static predictor of behavior, noting contradictions in their individual experiences. The chapter challenges assumptions of students' experiences of single-sex education, pushing educators to see the commonalities and complexities among girls' and boys' experiences.

In Ilana Seidel Horn's study of alternative assessment in a geometry classroom at a diverse urban high school, "Helping, bluffing, and doing portfolios in a high school geometry classroom," students and teachers held competing understandings of what was important in the classroom setting. While the classroom teacher (along with other alternative assessment advocates) intended to gain better and more accurate student assessments through portfolios, the students approached the portfolios with very different intentions and unexpected behaviors. Driven by overwhelming concerns for parent and peer approval, students found creative strategies to simultaneously "gain" good grades and avoid an overly academic reputation among their peers. Horn's analysis shows how the different – and often competing – agendas of a teacher and students can transform the intentions and effectiveness of authentic assessment tools. This transformation diminished the impact of the portfolio assessment on the teaching and learning of mathematics in the classroom.

By listening to the voices and experiences of students we learn, in the first part of the collection, that reform initiatives become more complicated when they leave the drawing board and are brought to life by students in schools. The second part of the collection presents studies of reform initiatives which seem to have been able to harness student energies, hook into their daily struggles and concerns, and engage them more profoundly in school.

In their chapter, "Apprenticing urban youth as critical researchers: implications for increasing equity and access in diverse urban schools," Anthony M. Collatos and Ernest Morrell explore a reform aimed to actively engage students as critics of school and society, while simultaneously developing their academic skills and increasing college access and opportunity. The authors describe their involvement in a four-year action research project designed to study and intervene in the trajectories of working-class students of color attending a diverse comprehensive high school in southern California. As students participated in a critical research-focused community of practice, they not only learned to navigate an oppressive school structure, they also became much more involved in school reform efforts. Collatos and Morrell discuss the implications of this action research project for high school students, as well as for educators, researchers, and activists interested in empowering youth as change agents in the struggle for urban educational reform.

Similarly, Anthony De Jesus, in " 'Here it's more like your house': the proliferation of authentic caring as school reform at El Puente Academy for Peace and Justice," describes how the El Puente Academy for Peace and Justice, a small innovative community high school in Brooklyn, New York, was able to create a learning environment and pedagogy that privileges marginalized students' social and cultural resources as an important foundation for academic achievement and community development (Rivera and Pedraza, 2000). The El Puente approach, De Jesus argues, incorporates "authentic caring" (Noddings, 1992) and "educación" (Valenzuela, 1999), nurturing the social ties and reciprocal relations pivotal to the academic success of the school's students. Creating a supportive, caring and culturally relevant community for students was critical to El Puente's success.

A sense of adult caring was also the fundamental strength of the small learning community investigated by Jean Yonemura Wing in "The color line in student achievement: how can small learning communities make a difference?" Wing found that students of color enrolled in a technology-focused small learning community (the Technology Academy) at a large, diverse urban high school in northern California were more likely to stay in school and do better academically than their peers outside of the small learning community setting. Indeed, this particular small learning community focused on serving students most at risk of school failure, and had strikingly impressive rates of retention, graduation, and acceptance to institutions of higher learning. Technology Academy students reported that they felt cared for by their teachers and had a sense of community and identity within the larger high school, aspects of belonging to a small learning community that the students felt were essential to their academic success.

In their chapter " 'We have a motion on the floor:' Montclair High School and the Civics and Government Institute," David Lee Keiser and Shana Stein probe the views of diverse students attending another small learning community, Montclair High School's Civics and Government Institute (CGI), on the experience of being part of a small learning community focused on fostering democratic participation. An internal assessment of the program revealed that the students felt challenged, cared for, and, eventually, well prepared both for college and for civic participation in a democratic society.

Finally, in " 'I'm not getting any F's': what 'at risk' students say about the support they need," Beth C. Rubin describes the MOST (Making Our Success Today) program, a support for "at risk" students, disproportionately low-income students of color, at a suburban high school with a reputation for academic excellence. Rubin describes how a committed teacher and instructional aide were able to support students' success through a mixture of serious daily assistance and the creation of a classroom setting which fostered a more fluid understanding of academic competence. In this chapter we hear from the students themselves what type of academic assistance was most helpful to them as they struggled to succeed in an atmosphere of raised expectations. That the most meaningful support for these students was surprisingly simple might cause us to pause and re-evaluate our emphasis on sweeping reform approaches.

Summing up

Turning a student-centered lens on school reform practices is powerfully revealing. When we attend to the ways in which equity-geared reforms are enacted, negotiated, and, at times, resisted by students, we learn a great deal about how we might more effectively create change in schools. Reforms that take students' needs and interests into account, these studies tell us, are more successful for diverse students. The "critical voices" speaking in this volume challenge adult-driven reform agendas, asking reformers to look more closely at the circumstances and texture of students' daily lives in schools when developing reform practices. For adults concerned with changing schools into more empowering, engaging, and equitable institutions where all students can thrive, listening to such voices is critical. We hope this book will be a small step in that direction.

Bibliography

Cook-Sather, A. (2002) Authorizing students' perspectives: toward trust, dialogue, and change in education. *Educational Researcher*, 31(4), 3–14.

Fielding, M. (Ed.) (2001) Special issue on student voice. *FORUM*, 43 (2), Summer.

Garcia, E. (1999) *Student Cultural Diversity: Understanding and Meeting the Challenge.* Boston: Houghton Miflin.

Nieto, S. (1999) *The Light in Their Eyes: Creating Multicultural Learning Communities.* New York: Teachers College Press.

Noddings, N. (1992) *The Challenge to Care in Schools: An Alternative Approach to Education.* New York: Teachers College Press.

Oldfather, P. (Ed.) (1995) Learning from student voices. *Theory into Practice*, 34(2).

Olsen, L., Nai-Lin Chang, H., De la Rosa Salazar, D., Dowell, C., Leong, C., McCall Perez, Z., McClain, G. and Raffel, L. (2000) *Turning the Tides of Exclusion.* Oakland, CA: California Tomorrow.

Rivera, M. and Pedraza, P. (2000) The spirit of transformation: an education reform movement in a New York City Latino/a community. In: S. Nieto (Ed.), *Puerto Rican Students in U.S. Schools.* Mahwah, NJ: Erlbaum Associates, 223–43.

Rudduck, J. and Flutter, J. (2000) Pupil participation and pupil perspectives: carving a new order of experience. *Cambridge Journal of Education*, 30, 75–89.

Shultz, J. and Cook-Sather, A. (Eds) (2001) *In Our Own Words: Students' Perspectives on School.* Lanham, MD: Rowman and Littlefield.

Valenzuela, A. (1999) *Subtractive Schooling: U.S.-Mexican Youth and the Politics of Caring.* Albany: State University of New York Press.

Wasley, P., Hampel, R. and Clark, R. (1997) *Kids and School Reform.* San Francisco: Jossey-Bass.

PART I

Difficult endeavors

The lived complexities of school reform

Chapter 1

Struggling for inclusion
A case study of students as reform partners

Elena M. Silva

Introduction

A recent wave of school reform literature provides an extensive discourse on ways to restructure, reorganize, and reassess the American high school (Carlson, 1996; Oakes *et al.*, 2000; Lee and Smith, 2001). Local, state and national reform agendas emphasize school reform initiatives that promote principles of shared decision-making, democratic governance, and student-centered change.[1] In response to this trend, school administrators are increasingly sanctioning the involvement of teachers, parents, and students in school change efforts. Yet while these calls for greater collaborative inquiry and action ostensibly include students and center on student learning and achievement, students themselves are rarely asked to participate in reform decision-making, development or implementation. To date, there is little evidence of student voice and participation within the increasing number of school reform efforts that claim their involvement (Kaba, 2000; Fielding, 2001). Consequently, students are treated as recipients of the educational product rather than partners in the educational process and reforms come and go without attention to the diverse opinions, perspectives and experiences of students.

    This chapter, in part, is a tribute to the practice of student inclusion in school decision-making and reform, particularly within the current efforts to restructure comprehensive, desegregated public high schools. However, the research grounding this philosophy complicates the simple notion that schools will be more democratic, equitable, and effective and students will be more empowered, engaged and successful simply by inviting students to participate in school reform.[2] This chapter begins with some background on the current trend toward shared decision-making and student inclusion in school reform. Next, it offers a case study of one group of students as they struggle to become full participants in their California high school's restructuring process. The experiences and perspectives of these students offer a window into the rhetoric and reality of including students as participants in the school change process.

A close look at these students' efforts sheds light on the complexities of what many reformers are calling a simple and necessary measure: extending a participatory reform approach to students. In fact, it is simple only in theory to extend power to the least powerful, to give voice to those who feel silenced, and to provoke the participation of those closest to dropping out altogether. Set in the context of a school struggling to overcome a tradition of racial and class inequality and division, this study challenges schools to do more than preach platitudes about the importance of student involvement and youth voice and go further than inviting students to melt into the traditional model of adult-generated, adult-driven reforms. Indeed, the perspectives of students caught in the haste, politics, and bureaucracy of the restructuring process remind us to carefully approach reform and distinguish between efforts that actually challenge unequal relationships of power and privilege and those that merely serve to reproduce them.

School restructuring and the rhetoric of shared decision-making

> Are we witnessing the emergence of something genuinely new, exciting and emancipatory that builds on rich traditions of democratic renewal and transformation? Or are we presiding over the further entrenchment of existing assumptions and intentions using student voice as an additional mechanism of control?
>
> (Fielding, 2001: ii)

School restructuring has become a guiding philosophy in many state and federal reform initiatives. These new reforms encourage a restructuring of school organization, governance and accountability, increasing school site control and flexibility while upholding national and state frameworks and guidelines. Unlike the vouchers and charters of the growing school choice movement, restructuring efforts boast the overarching goal of extending challenging curriculum and instruction to *all* students in increasingly large and diverse public schools. Within this, school districts and individual schools have embraced a series of popular strategies designed to promote more democratic and inclusive practices in schooling.

There are a variety of broad-based restructuring models, among them the Coalition for Essential Schools (Sizer, 1992), Comer Schools (Comer, 1992), Paideia Schools (Adler, 1982), and Success For All (Madden *et al.*, 1991),[3] that promote a flatter, less hierarchical organization with increased collaboration and site-based decision-making. Terms such as "collaborative inquiry," "shared decision-making" and "cooperative teaching and learning" are tenets within these models and have been borrowed individually and collectively by smaller district and school-based restructuring efforts. Accordingly, numerous state and local initiatives are focusing their attention on empowering the voices and participation of parents, teachers and students within the process of reform. In particular, calls for "student voice" in the inquiry, planning and decision-making processes of reform have become a popular addition to traditionally adult-driven school reform efforts.

In a study of California's school restructuring initiative,[4] Judith Warren Little found that shared decision-making as a new governance structure was a "fundamental tenet of most restructuring initiatives" in California. The study demonstrates more inclusive governance structures, a wider range of participants in schoolwide goal-setting, and the ubiquity of committees or task forces charged with specific aspects of schooling. However, the study also points to serious questions about whether these new decision-making structures really open up participation in decision-making (Little, 1996: 24). "In most cases," the report states, "the organizational structure described on paper provides only a partial map of the actual decision-making locations and processes (ibid.)."

The study continues:

> Students remain a nearly silent voice in school decision-making, even at the high school level. They are silent in two ways – first in their relative invisibility as participants in formal decision-making, and second in the relative infrequency with which information from or about students is made a part of decision-making. There are exceptions – for example, a high school that has organized periodic student forums and a "student voice task force" composed equally of staff and students – but such are few in number.
>
> (Little, 1996: 24)

The study further points to questions concerning access, equity, and the adequacy of social and academic support for students among these restructuring schools. Despite these shortcomings, a growing number of schools – in California and nationwide – are inviting the voices of students into the process of restructuring. What is the nature and outcome of these efforts to include students? How are students experiencing this increased "voice" in school change initiatives? The following case study explores the experiences of one group of high school students as they struggle to participate within their school's restructuring efforts.

Students as reform partners: the case of Berkeley High

> Of all the schools that I have ever been to before, B.H.S. is the most diverse, populated, and culturally rich and aware school. But the students lack something... a VOICE.
>
> (15-year-old BHS sophomore)

Berkeley High School has tremendous energy, most of which is generated by the 3,200 students who crowd the classrooms, hallways, courtyards and parking lots. The number and variety of elective classes and academic, social, and cultural organizations, many of which were initiated by students, is far greater than most high schools in the country. Berkeley students organize musical performances, participate in political action, host poetry slams, design murals, perform community service, win basketball championships, participate in university and community events, and hold part-time jobs all over their city. The buzz of student activity serves as a constant reminder to the school and community that students are alive and kicking at Berkeley High School. Yet while the vitality of the students holds great significance to the character of the school, it bears little weight on the way the school is operated, organized, or reformed.

Like many public high schools in California, Berkeley High School struggles with its own diversity. The school serves a student body all shades of California, from its hills and its flatlands, yet is plagued by its inability to serve these populations equally. Often, Berkeley is described as two separate schools: one serving the needs of academically elite students through extensive advanced placement programs, extra- and co-curricular clubs and activities, and college preparatory classes; and the other serving lower achieving students with fewer programs to meet their academic and social needs. These divisions are undeniably along lines of race, ethnicity and class, with large numbers of White, Asian American, and affluent students receiving the resources and accolades of high achievement, while less affluent, predominantly African American and Latino students, receive a less than adequate education and attain much lower levels of academic achievement.[5] The inequities exist among student grades, course placements, levels of attrition, disciplinary referrals, and the completion of college admission requirements.

In 1996, Berkeley High School was beginning a whole-school reform process, in part provoked by a 1996 report by the accrediting commission of the Western Association of Schools and Colleges (WASC) which outlined the need for a schoolwide, collaborative action plan. The WASC report made a series of recommendations to the school, including the increased participation of all stakeholders, the incorporation of student input into assessment of the effectiveness of teaching and learning, and wider involvement of the larger student body in the overall assessment of the school. That same year, the Diversity Project,[6] a collaborative project between the University of California-Berkeley and Berkeley High School, began to bring together teachers, parents, college students and professors to research the existing racial and class inequities at the school. The Project, emphasizing equitable access and outcomes for students, became an important part of the developing reform agenda at the high school. During the 1997–8 school year, Berkeley High School developed a draft strategic plan outlining a five-year timeline of objectives and strategies to restructure school organization, evaluation procedures, and pedagogical practices.

Although the draft plan was developed by a group of twenty-one teachers and administrators, outreach groups of students and parents were organized to discuss and debate various issues of school change. The forums and meetings held by these groups varied in success and the incorporation of student and parent ideas and opinions was negligible in the development of the plan's first published draft. In fact, although this draft states "the Strategic Planning Work Group provided school staff and students with opportunities to be involved in the planning process through presentations, meetings, materials, and forums," not a single student actually participated in the writing or discussion of this draft. Thus, the initial stages of the reform process at Berkeley began without any formal involvement of students.

Inspiring participation

In September of 1998, a new principal arrived at Berkeley High School, three months before the deadline for the school's next WASC accreditation report. She entered the position with great enthusiasm for change. Her new leadership, along with the impending WASC report, spurred a new sense of motivation and urgency for the completion of a final strategic plan and the inclusion of all parties in its development. Within a month of her arrival, she met with Diversity Project members to discuss the role of the Project in encouraging the involvement of students, parents, and a greater number of teachers in the assessment and development of the final plan. The student outreach committee of the Diversity Project, formed a year earlier to promote involvement among students on issues of equity and achievement, seemed a natural path to involving students in the plan assessment. Like other Project committees, the student committee was organized by a partnership between a graduate student and a BHS teacher, in this case myself and Maria,[7] an Ethnic Studies teacher. We also had the support of a local college student, Wanda, who had been active with BHS students since her graduation from the high school two years earlier.

The three of us were inspired by the new principal. Together, we agreed to recruit a group of students who would represent the racial and ethnic communities, social and academic peer groups, and various grade levels of Berkeley High students. With the help of other teachers, we identified students who would represent different perspectives on BHS: ninth graders; seniors; students from the leadership/student government class; students from the ESL (English as a Second Language) department; students from the previous year's Diversity Project student group; students with high grades and low grades; students from the affluent hills, and students from the surrounding flatlands. We organized our first meeting as a three-hour retreat at the local college campus, inviting seventeen students to participate.

Sixteen students showed up for the four o'clock meeting. In all, we were a group of twenty-two, including me, Maria, Wanda, two other Diversity Project members and the principal. Following a ten-minute icebreaker exercise, I introduced the "new" student outreach committee as "a new piece of the school's planning team." Wanda added to my words, speaking with confidence, poise, and the inflection of someone much closer in age to the students. "You are a very special group," she remarked, "You represent 'B' High. So ya'll gotta step up and make this thing fly. You need to represent the high school. Otherwise they'll do it without you."

By this point in the meeting, the students all seemed to be listening closely, as the principal began to speak. She spoke with authority and a firm sense of certainty as she told them that they are an essential part of developing a final plan. She smiled and nodded often as she declared that each of them has an obligation to use whatever talent they have for the greater good of the school. There is not a lot of time, she told them, but a lot of work to be done. "You are an important part of this," she explained, "You must share your ideas of what works and what doesn't, the understanding you've gained after however long you've been here, whether a freshman or a senior."

For the next three months during the Fall of 1998, inspired by the words of the principal and those of us working with the Diversity Project, the student committee met weekly to learn and assess the first draft of the strategic plan. Their primary goal for this semester, set by an agreement between me, Maria, Wanda and the principal, was to develop an understanding of the plan, including its structure and esoteric language, so that they could participate in meetings to review and revise the draft. Their experiences, set in the context of the already difficult reform process, offer a glimpse of the complexity of achieving diversity, unity, and a voice for students within the formal, adult-driven tradition of school decision-making.

The challenge of diversity

The experience of confronting and participating in the adult dialogue and process of planning and negotiation proved to be a formidable task for the student committee. Equally significant, however, was the committee's challenge to develop a group dialogue and process of their own. At a school struggling to confront and overcome racial and class inequities, in which extra-curricular activities and clubs are largely segregated along these lines,[8] the group embarked on a deeply meaningful project in its efforts to represent the diversity of the whole student body. From the start, there were gaps in representation[9] that over time grew even larger. Still, this group was more diverse than most of the co-curricular and extra-curricular groups at the school and faced the unpracticed work of simultaneously synthesizing and supporting their differences. Ultimately, the students developed some shared meaning and practice, but not without a long process of negotiating their different identities, communities, and levels of participation, and not without reproducing some of the same inequities and divisions they were a part of reforming.

Developing a common vision for the committee while still maintaining the inherent diversity among the group's individuals was an overwhelming challenge. Although a few students were friends or classmates, most of the students had little in common with one another. Notably, they did not even seem to share a common reason for their involvement with the committee. Several students expressed interest in the goals and objectives of the Diversity Project, specifically the creation of a more equitable and multicultural school. Some wanted to be part of changing the rules of the school. Others were tired of feeling ignored and wanted their voices to be heard by the adult administration. A few were seeking the opportunity to be leaders among their peers, and at least one student was simply interested in being involved in an interesting extra-curricular activity. While the students understood that they, as a group, needed to determine "the student perspective" on the plan, they plainly saw that their perspectives often varied, agreement was difficult, and consensus was rare.

Similarly, the students committed varying levels of time and effort. Of the original sixteen, three students dropped out over the course of the first three weeks, and two more over the next month. Others struggled to balance commitments to family, school, friends and work. In an effort to respect the students' efforts and time, and to encourage continued participation, Maria and I agreed to select eight students as leaders[10] and to pay them each a small stipend for their work on the committee. However, the designation of "leader" and the anticipation of a stipend played little, if any, part in the participation of the students. Two of the "leaders" only sporadically participated in the committee's work and one dropped out altogether. Four other students, not designated as leaders, participated regularly and committed a great deal of time and energy to the group. Their reasons for participation or non-participation on the committee varied and did not appear to be tied to a sense of obligation or compensation. Rather, high levels of participation seemed tied to peer acceptance of the group and its activities, free time after school, and either parental support or apathy.[11] Conversely, lower levels of participation seemed related to pressure from parents to focus on other activities such as schoolwork or family, time commitments to after-school jobs, or a sense of disconnection or unfamiliarity with the group members and activities.

Ironically, as the students examined and critiqued the school's sixty-page plan designed to address problems of student inequity, segregation, and detachment from school, the committee itself embodied these dilemmas. Despite attempts by Maria, Wanda and me to involve all students equally, those most involved with the group were already leaders and high achievers at the school. Moreover, it was impossible to ignore that these students were primarily White, female and middle-class. These students, with both greater economic status and higher levels of social and cultural capital,[12] were urged into leadership positions in the group while others were relegated to support positions. These students who recognized the arcane language of reform and were familiar with the adult processes of organizational decision-making were the obvious choices for leadership roles. They offered comments such as: "I can facilitate. My mother is the director of social services, so she talks about having to lead meetings like this all the time" and "You know what we need? We need to write a formal proposal outlining all of our ideas." These students, in their efforts to be helpful and supportive, would unwittingly strip responsibilities and the accompanying power from others. After one meeting, a student volunteered to type up the minutes only to be assured by another student, "No, that's okay. It'll be harder for you. I have a computer at home and I already have a template for minutes so I can easily do it."

This pattern of privileging certain voices was reinforced by all of the students, including those most silenced within the group. At another meeting, when the group was deciding who would present their issues to the principal, I suggested that Amy, the single ESL student left in the group, be one of the presenters. Almost all of the students agreed that this student did not have the language skills to present. Even Amy stated, "I'll mess up and say the wrong thing." When I commented that a lot of students at BHS had limited English skills and that she might be able to better represent the needs of those students, an African American student said, "That's totally true, but I think somebody like Sheila or Mark could really explain that better than Amy. Especially since it's the principal we're talking about. We don't want to go in there and sound stupid. No offense, I mean I couldn't do it either."

Indeed, as certain students were rising into leadership roles, others were dropping out – including a Cambodian ESL student, two African American male students, and a Latino student, leaving large gaps in the group's ability to understand and represent the whole student body.

> I can't help but notice that there is less and less participation from the students of color ... Lindsey, Kerry and Sheila [White females] are leading the group. Francisco is gone, Marcos [Black male] has transferred to an alternative school and Malcolm [Black male] is spending his time working with a different youth group, one that focuses on conflict resolution and racial diversity ... I wonder how much we seem like the "Diversity" Project anymore.
>
> (Author fieldnotes, 9/98)

Influenced by a larger school culture that divided along lines of race, class and in certain circumstances gender, the student outreach committee struggled to sustain itself as a space where students could cross boundaries and develop multiple identities. Despite great efforts to include a variety of students from the beginning, a stipend to encourage participation, and the underlying – although elusive – goal of racial and class equity, much of the diversity of the Diversity Project student group was lost along the way.

Practicing democracy

Despite the clear divisions and limitations of the group, the committee members were remarkably persistent in their task to cooperatively learn and critique the strategic plan. Although never developing into a community of friends or even social or academic peers, the group unquestionably developed into more than a mere assembly of individuals. Evolving into a sort of "community of practice" (Wenger, 1998), they developed ways to connect, exchange, and produce ideas with respect to, rather than in spite of, their varying perspectives. They adopted common routines, slogans and ways of understanding the arcane language of reform, and created a rhythm of negotiating within the group and responding to the outside mandates of the reform process.

The students gathered weekly, meeting for three hours or longer, to pick through the sections of the plan and pull out the parts most pertinent to them as students. Armed with highlighters and markers, the students circled, underlined, and rewrote strategies, crossing out goals like "implement an expanded and enhanced co-curricular summer enrichment program" and replacing it with "improve summer school." Discovering the meaning beneath each long, complicated explanation in the plan empowered the group and, at times, added to the sense that the administration was conspiring to keep them out of the process. At one point, a student scoffed at a goal that declared that the school would "implement co-curricular activities within and across cultural groups that will empower students and help them establish their voice." Six students turned to the same page, pointing and laughing sarcastically at the "additional investment" required to achieve this: zero.

The differences among students, so apparent in some ways, were minimized when stacked against the adult administration. Indeed, part of the committee's practice was motivated by a strong "us" versus "them" sentiment. During one of the first group meetings, a student commented on the disingenuous objectives of the administration. "What kind of influence will we really have?" she asked. "I mean, they want us to sit here and 'be a part of this all' but are they even going to listen to us? It seems like a front to me. Like they just want to be sayin' 'oh, we're so in touch with the students at our school.' "

The students spent a fair amount of time throughout the six-month period discussing the ways in which they had been, and were continuing to be, left out of the process. Together, they considered the degree of their power, influence, and value in this planning process. Along with this came cynicism, lack of trust, and a puzzling combination of confrontation and insecurity. A series of strategic planning meetings that, according to the principal, were supposed to take place one month after the students began their work and were to discuss the development of the existing plan into a final draft, were the source of both motivation and disappointment for the students.

Throughout the process, Maria, Wanda and I liaised between the students and the principal. We would tell them when meetings were scheduled and, more often, when they were postponed. We would meet with the principal regularly, and I would send emails every week or so, updating her on how far along the students were and discussing what our next steps should be. In exchange, she would give us updates on the planning process: who was meeting when and where, and what decisions were being made. At times it seemed that we were fully included. Other times, it felt as though we were merely a whisper among the voices of the administration, teachers, and "professional educators" brought in to assess the plan. At one point, after two months of studying the plan, we had to tell the students that there was no time for the strategic planning meetings, only a chance for them to meet with the principal, prompting the response:

> They just decided that and didn't even ask us? Are we even part of this process? I mean, it's like they asked us to do this and they're just doing it their own way anyway. That is so messed up. I'm sorry, that is, like, hella wrong. They can't do that. Can they do that?

Another student replied,

> Yeah, they can do whatever they want. But I say, if they're not going to meet with us, we should, like, type up everything we've said and give it to them. Like in a big binder with our main points highlighted and in big bold type.

In an effort to support both their justified anger and their motivation to act, we encouraged the development of a proposal. A written document, we felt, could not be ignored nor put aside in the interest of time. During the next several meetings, the committee's process focused on the development of a proposal to present the major issues of student concern to the principal.

Although it was agreed that the proposal was crucial in voicing their concerns, the committee's process to decide on the main points for the proposal was notably difficult. The students struggled to determine the fairest decision-making procedure, emphasizing the importance of being "democratic" but unsure of how to achieve this. The committee's fifth meeting centered on a debate over this process:

JIMMY: Well I think we should do it democratically. Like, majority rules.

TAMILA: Okay, but what if I'm not here, or what if I gotta bounce early. Then I don't get a say in it? Is that what you're saying?

KERRY: I think everyone needs to be here or else we can't decide something.

JIMMY: That's ridiculous. We're never all here. Amy and Anita and ... what's that guy's name – he was here the first meeting?

CARL: His name's Malcolm. But I don't really see how we're still calling him a part of this. I mean he and those two girls, they're not even around at all. Are we supposed to include them because they're on the list?

DARI: Can I say something? I think people like Malcolm and Anita should not even be invited to be part of the vote. We're the ones who are here and doing the work. We're the ones who understand what's going on, so we should make the decisions.

JIMMY: Well, we're just saying our opinions, really. I mean, we're not like making decisions for the school. We can't represent all the students, we can only speak for ourselves. So whoever's here votes, and majority rules. That's the way it's done.

Struggling with notions of democracy, inclusion, and fairness, the students agreed that only those who were present at the time of a decision and who voiced their opinion would be counted. Those who were absent or silent would lose their right to vote. Challenging the students to be careful and critical in their decision-making, Maria asserted, "Think about it. True democracy is when the least powerful have voice. Is that what we're doing?" I proposed a second meeting to continue the discussion and give everyone time to consider the meaning and practice of "democracy." The students, however, declined the second meeting ("we don't really have the time")[13] and stuck with their initial decision.

Ironically, the group's decision to count only the votes of those present at meetings utilized the school's process as their model, one which the students regularly criticized. At various points during the strategic planning process, the students claimed the process was structured to exclude them as meetings were often scheduled for inconvenient times and occasionally rescheduled without their knowledge. Only weeks after the students agreed on their own decision-making process, Dari asked with a combination of shock and rage, "WHAT?! [The administration] just decided that? ... We weren't even there. That's not fair." Meanwhile, the students' own process was established based on "the way it's done," treating participation as a privilege for those who demonstrated the most commitment.

Supporting the process

Even when motivated by small successes, the process for integrating student voice into the formal reform process was confusing and frustrating. Maria, Wanda and I tried to direct the group's efforts while simultaneously giving them autonomy to represent student voice in their own way and through their own perspectives, rather than ours. Still, our roles were complex and the process of supporting the students while cooperating with the principal's vision for reform proved to be difficult.

Throughout, our primary concern was whether the students were being given the skills, knowledge and opportunities to express their views. Much of our time in the beginning months was spent getting students to attend meetings and teaching the students the words, terms and strategies they were confronting while reading the draft strategic plan. We discussed and practiced meeting strategies, assigning roles of facilitator, recorder, and timer during many of our sessions. Meanwhile, the three of us were also trying to keep abreast of what meetings were taking place, when and where, and who was to be involved in them. Yet meetings seemed to be scheduled at the last minute and decisions made without time or intent to inform everyone. The process for developing a final plan seemed to continually change, forcing us to relay new messages to the students on a regular basis. Expressions of "I don't know what's going on" were common among the students, contributing to a growing sense that the group was being slighted by the administration.

The principal, in particular, began to represent the adult administration, even the school as a whole. Having attended the first student meeting and encouraged the students to participate in the process, she was an essential element in motivating or discouraging the students' efforts. When arranging a student meeting with the principal proved to be more difficult than expected, the students began perceiving the formal process of reviewing and revising the plan to be progressing without them. Their frustration surfaced at a meeting during which the students discussed the significance of their involvement. They expressed both a sense of defeat, and a sense of determination and persistence:

> What's the point? I mean, if we don't ever get the chance to meet with anyone, no one is gonna hear us. It's just a huge waste of time.

> Did you say it was a waste? No, it's not! We've done so much! We have the proposal and everything. [The principal] asked us to do this and it's hecka important. We are the only ones representing the students on this. If we don't do this, there won't be any student voice at all and they'll just reform, reform, reform without us.

The students agreed to go to the principal the very next day during their fifth period, a free period for many of the students, to present their fully developed proposal. The principal was impressed and praised the students' hard work. The next day she announced that a planning meeting would indeed take place and was scheduled for the following Thursday. The meeting would be an all-day engagement to discuss and develop the final plan for the next school year. The students, although pleased with their success in presenting their proposal, were unsettled by the idea that the plan would be reviewed and revamped over a one-day period. They immediately began to ask questions about the meeting. "When and where will it be held?" Dari asked. Jimmy immediately noted that "all-day" meant during school, "Wait a minute. How long will it be, and how will I get out of class to go to it?" "I have a Physics test." Tamila added, "I can't miss Math," and Sheila pointed to transportation issues, "It's at school, right, because I have no way to get anywhere otherwise."

Equally concerned that the students would not be able to attend the meeting due to transportation and class scheduling issues, we expressed the issue to the Diversity Project team and in an email to the principal. Whether in response to our issues or other matters, the meeting was scheduled for the community theater of the high school and the students were to be excused from school, but permitted to go back and forth to classes from the meeting. Among the students, there was a fleeting sense of victory. They would finally have a chance to express their opinions to a sizable group of teachers and administrators in a formal arena. Yet, with the meeting scheduled for the next morning, a sense of serious urgency quickly replaced celebration:

> We have to be there. If we're not there, then we lose our chance, we lose our only chance after all this. Who all can be there? Come on, ya'll. We gotta represent!

The broken mic

The morning of this long-awaited meeting, I met three students outside of the school's community theater ten minutes before nine o'clock. Together, we entered the meeting room, a lime green room with poor lighting and four rectangular tables pushed together into a larger conference-like setting. At 9:15, when the meeting began, there were seven students present and only five of over twenty adult teachers and administrators. Shortly after, three more students and a handful of teachers arrived. The students' presence in the room was prominent and several teachers, unaware of the student committee or its work, whispered questions to each other. One teacher said hello to the students, smiling. Another teacher asked who they were and if they were going to stay for the meeting. "Oh that's really nice," she commented when one student told her about the group's work and participation.

The students and I sat together on one side of the room. They were confident and ready to discuss what they had learned over the past nine weeks. Fully prepared with copies of the plan and their proposal, the students immediately began asking questions as the meeting began. They were direct and specific to particular sections and goals of the plan. Raising their hands before speaking, they made comments and asked questions like "We are particularly concerned with Section I which deals with Counseling Goals. Are we going to discuss this?"

The teachers and the meeting facilitator in particular appeared rushed and impatient with the students' attention to detail. Unlike the students who were ready to finally discuss every issue in every section of the plan, everyone else in the room seemed to want to get through the revision process as quickly as possible. By the second hour, the students had been told by teachers and the meeting facilitator: "This isn't the time to discuss those issues," "We don't have time to go into detail," "We discussed this last year. I'm not sure if you're understanding the issue," and "I know you students spent a lot of time and know the plan really well, but if we could please hold questions, we really need to move forward."

The meeting was centered around categorizing the various sections of the plan and then breaking into groups to discuss the specific issues in each section. Ironically, although they had each spent months developing sections of the plan, many teachers had not yet had the opportunity to read the entire document and needed time to go through the plan before making decisions. The students had already been through this process during their own meetings, and were quick to notice, with a sense of both triumph and concern, that their questions had been silenced because they were ahead of the process. At one point, Kerry leaned over to me, passing a note that read, "We are *sooo* much more prepared than they are! We've already done all of this!" to which she added in a whisper, "But they're acting like we don't know what we're talking about!"

Despite growing frustration, the students remained in the meeting all day, presenting their ideas verbally and handing out copies of their proposal. At times they were praised by the principal and teachers for being so prepared, articulate, and knowledgeable about the plan. Several teachers took the time to speak individually with the students, asking questions about what they thought and why. Still, although the students might have been empowered by their success at the meeting, they later expressed discouragement and irritation at the teachers and administration. "They ignored us," said Dari. Jimmy followed with, "They weren't even prepared and they weren't willing to listen to us. They picked up the copy of our proposal, stuck it somewhere, and just went ahead and decided what to do. I coulda yelled the whole time and they wouldn'ta heard me. They already had a plan all thought up."

After the meeting, the issues they had discussed for months became secondary to the idea that they were being ignored. The students expressed feeling silenced, undervalued and controlled by the teachers and administration. They expressed feeling powerless and unimportant in the process. The insistence by me, Maria and Wanda that they had mastered a sixty-page document, attended meetings within and outside of the school, and developed a proposal mattered very little in comparison. Our weekly meetings centered not on issues of change, nor on issues of equity or diversity, but on how to be heard.

With this in mind, the students agreed to attend an upcoming conference on Student Voice and to present a session they entitled, "The Broken Mic." In this, they described to an audience of forty students and teachers their experience over the past four months. Together, they summarized their version of what happened:

KERRY: … Last year a group of teachers put together a plan to reform the school and hopefully correct its problems …

SHEILA: So we were asked to go through the plan and look at issues that were important to us. So we put in all this time – like hours every week.

DARI: And ya'll need to understand. The wording of the plan, it was not straightforward or to the point. They were very wishy-washy so we had to break it all down and put it in our own words. Like what we thought was cool or not so cool. And they said it should be short and sweet. So we did up the proposal. And here it is! So this is the before [holds up 60-page plan] and this is after [holds up two-page proposal]!

SHEILA: And this is where our title comes in. The Broken Mic. After all we did, they had this big full-day conference with us and staff and administration and some head facilitator guy. There's this big table and we're all sitting around trying to make our points, thinking they're gonna hear us and they're gonna make changes. But you know, after all that, we were given the chance to go to this meeting, handed the mic, and it was like it was turned off. Like when you tap a mic and you're like … 'one, two, three … testing' but nothing came out. It was dead. Broken.

The conference was full of other student groups confronting similar difficulties, oscillating between positive sentiment toward an administration that tries to involve them, and negative feelings about a process that never fully includes them. They are excited to be taken seriously, and enraged that they are not. They are certain about their opinions, and certain that the school should be considered "theirs" and not the teachers', administration's or even the community's. They also are sure that they cannot do it alone. They depend on formal structures and adult leadership. They are caught in the ultimate adolescent dilemma: wanting both autonomy and support. Returning to the initial inquiry of this chapter, we must ask ourselves if it is possible to legitimately involve students in the governance and reform of their school.

Conclusion

A final five-year strategic plan for Berkeley High School was adopted by the school board in February, 1999. In the memo announcing the final plan, the Associate Superintendent of Instruction states, "The plan is thorough, fiscally sound, and reflects the feedback and thinking of students, staff, and the community." The plan does reflect a few of the central issues that the students highlighted in their proposal. Still, for those involved in the process, it is difficult to ignore how minor the student influence was after so much effort. Moreover, the presentation of the plan as one which "reflects the feedback and thinking of students" seems an unfair representation of how and to what extent students were really involved.

Perhaps more important is the fact that the students do not feel as though they made an impact. A month later, when I got a copy of the memo mentioned above, I brought it to one of our student meetings to discuss. I made ten copies, hoping that at least eight students would show up (by this point interest had waned and participation was low). Only four students came to the meeting that Friday. Our small group of seven, three of whom were adults, sat on a table in Maria's room discussing the three-page memo that sadly seemed to sum up the results of months of hard work. A sense of defeat was highlighted by Carl's comment:

> I don't even care if the plan includes some of our ideas. They weren't our ideas anyway. We just highlighted which of their ideas we thought were most important. And, check it out, they approved a final plan and didn't even tell us. Did anyone here get a call? This is the first we're hearing about it, sitting in this room, six weeks later. And if you didn't force us to sit down and look at it, we never would've known. We were never a part of this.

What would it have been like for the student committee to be fully included? Would it take too much time, too much patience, and too much rearrangement of schedules? Or would it demand the serious consideration of alternative perspectives, some which might challenge the accepted structures, relationships, and notions common in the school? The student outreach committee was forced to confront notions of diversity and democracy in their group, seemingly reproducing the definitions they observed of the adult processes. They forgot about those who dropped out and they limited voice to only those who were present and assertive. They were led by people, myself included, who wavered between fighting for student voice and justifying excuses for student exclusion, who were caught between advocating for rapid necessary reforms and acknowledging the necessary time and effort for true democratic participation.

In retrospect, I am glad the students do not feel as though they were part of the reform process, because in truth they were not. I wonder what would have happened if the students had felt validated and included. Would they have learned to trust the politics of school, to support notions of "striking a balance," granting concessions, compromising beliefs, and reinforcing the powerful and privileged as elements of a necessary and efficient bureaucracy? On a personal level, I wonder if I inadvertently persuaded the students to support these notions anyway. I wonder if I could have done more to help the students better understand and critique, rather than just prepare, for the process of reform. I wonder how much more time, how many more meetings and phone calls it would have taken for Maria, Wanda and me to secure a fuller and more meaningful space for the students to voice their concerns and feel heard.

Involving students is just one part of the incredibly large and complex task of restructuring Berkeley High School. Yet the lessons of the student outreach group point to implications for teachers, parents, and others who are on the periphery of decision-making. Schools need to find a way of incorporating genuine participation, that which allows for challenges, conflict, and real change. Meanwhile, reformers continue to advocate for collaborative decision-making, student-centered change and a process of shared inquiry. Along these lines, Deborah Meier affirms the power of students' ideas. She writes,

> There's a radical – and wonderful – new idea here ... that all children could and should be inventors of their own theories, critics of other people's ideas, analyzers of evidence, and makers of their own personal marks on this most complex world. It's an idea with revolutionary implications. If we take it seriously.
>
> (Meier, 1995: 22)

Henry Giroux further asserts that schools exist to prepare democratic citizens. He stresses the need for the expanded practice of real democracy in schools, stating: "Public schools need to be justified as places in which students are educated in the principles and practices of democracy, not in a version of democracy cleansed of vision, possibility, or struggle" (Giroux, 1992: 15).

The significance of students' ideas and opinions should indeed be taken seriously. However, the realities of involving a representative group of young people in a democratic process that has never been modeled for them, nor encouraged their participation, are complex and extend far beyond a school's intentions or invitations for student inclusion. If our goal is more democratic and equitable schooling, we must recognize when we compromise or contradict these practices ourselves, when we get caught up in politics, and when we find rhetoric more appealing than reality. It *is* more difficult to involve students; it requires not only a willingness to invite and include students, but also a commitment to teach them about the pushes and pulls of both democracy and bureaucracy. It is possible, of course, that we may not want to or feel that we are able to genuinely include student voice and opinion, especially in today's increasingly large and diverse high schools. However, if we are going to promote principles of shared decision-making, democratic governance, and student-centered change, and sanction the involvement of parents and students in school change efforts, then we must do so with genuine resolve. We must offer students realistic space and time to be a part of the process, recognizing that students need support and encouragement to participate in this type of activity, particularly if they do not experience school or its activities as inclusive or worthy of their time. We must provide students with the skills and awareness of the process, and we must assure them constantly that their perspective – as much as it may seem unsophisticated and untrained – is significant and valuable. For without student perspective we miss the true character of the high school experience and we risk reproducing policies that undermine the role of the student in shaping and changing the culture and climate of their school.

Notes

1 The Coalition of Essential Schools and the US Department of Education New American High School (NAHS) initiative both advocate for strategies that promote collaborative reform efforts, partnerships between schools and community and student-centered learning.
2 The research for this chapter is based on one of three years of observation, interaction, and dialogue with a group of students organizing to participate in the reform process at their high school. My role with the student group was as one of three adults organizing and supporting the group's efforts to become involved in school change efforts, a position that allowed for close contact and familiarity with the students.
3 See Carlson, R.V. (1996) *Reframing and Reform: Perspectives on Organization, Leadership, and School Change* for a description of the various restructuring models.
4 Senate Bill 1274 (1990) introduced a five-year program for 150 California schools to demonstrate the effects of school restructuring. The School Restructuring Study was a three-year investigation to assess the ways in which SB 1274 enabled schoolwide change that measurably affects student learning.
5 These divisions are not without exception. For example, while a large number of Asian students are highly successful, many Asian students (particularly Southeast Asian and Pacific Islanders) are low-income and low achieving.

6 My research at Berkeley High was a part of the larger research and reform efforts of the Diversity Project.
7 All names are pseudonyms.
8 In 1996–7, the Diversity Project conducted a study of racial separation in school-sponsored activities and clubs and found that, although technically "integrated," the school remains segregated in its social, academic/career, and athletic circles. The student committee, although not yet in existence at the time of this study, would be classified as academic/career, in which only one of nineteen clubs had a demographic reflective of the school population.
9 Our selection of students was a hurried and imperfect process that relied heavily on the identification of students who would represent ethnic, racial, gender and age diversity. Likewise, we also sought students who we were able to contact, either in class or through other teachers or students.
10 We selected leaders based on our observations of students during the first several weeks. We tried to select students who were not necessarily expected leaders, intentionally not choosing the three students who already represented the school as student government leaders nor the one student who served as a school board representative.
11 Several students who were highly active in the group referred to parents who "don't care," "don't know," or who have their "own problems." It seems possible that these students were accustomed, perhaps preferred, to have their time occupied by activities away – physically and otherwise – from their parents. Interestingly, these students were some of the most resolute and influential of the group, perhaps due to a strong sense of independence.
12 Social capital refers to the power and resources that students gain through social networks; cultural capital refers to the power and resources that students gain through having an awareness and mastery of the tastes, preferences, and behaviors of dominant culture (Bourdieu, 1973).
13 Sheila, 10/98 meeting notes.

Bibliography

Adler, M. (1982) *The Paideia Proposal: An Educational Manifesto.* New York: Macmillan.

Anderson, G.L. (1998) Toward authentic participation: deconstructing the discourses of participatory reforms in education. *American Educational Research Journal*, 35(4, Winter).

Bourdieu, P. (1973) Cultural reproduction and social reproduction. In: R. Brown (Ed.), *Knowledge, Education and Social Change.* London: Tavistock.

Carlson, R.V. (1996) *Reframing and Reform: Perspectives on Organization, Leadership, and School Change.* New York: Longman Publishers.

Comer, J.P. (1988) Educating poor minority children. *Scientific American*, 259(5, November): 42–8.

Fielding, M. (Ed.) (2001) Special issue: student voice. *Forum*, 43(2).

Fine, M., Weis, L. and Powell, L.C. (1997) Communities of difference: a critical look at desegregated spaces for and by youth. *Harvard Educational Review*, 67(2, Summer).

Garcia, E. (1999) *Student Cultural Diversity: Understanding and Meeting the Challenge.* Boston: Houghton Miflin.

Giroux, H.A. (1992) *Educational Leadership and the Crisis of Democratic Culture.* University Park, PA: University Council of Educational Administration.

Johnson, J.W. (1997) *The Struggle for Student Rights: Tinker vs. Des Moines and the 1960s*. Lawrence: University Press of Kansas.

Kaba, M. (2000) They listen to me ... but they don't act on it: contradictory consciousness in decision-making. *High School Journal*, 84(December): 21–35.

Lee, V.E. and Smith, J.B. (2001) *Restructuring High Schools for Equity and Excellence: What Works*. New York: Teachers College Press.

Little, J.W. (1996) *The SB 1274 School Restructuring Study: What Are We Learning?* An Interim Progress Report. University of California, Berkeley.

Madden, N.A., Slavin, R.E., Karweit, N.L., Dolan, L. and Wasik, B.A. (1993) Success for all: longitudinal effects of a restructuring program for inner-city elementary schools. *American Educational Research Journal*, 30(1): 123–48.

Meier, D. (1995) *The Power of Their Ideas: Lessons for America from a Small School in Harlem*. Boston: Beacon Press.

Noguera, P.A. (1995) Ties that bind, forces that divide: Berkeley High School and the challenge of integration. *University of San Francisco Law Review*, 29(Spring).

Oakes, J., Quartz, K.H., Ryan, S. and Lipton, M. (2000) *Becoming Good American Schools: The Struggle for Civic Virtue in Education Reform*. The Jossey-Bass Education Series. San Francisco: Jossey-Bass Publishers.

Sizer, T.R. (1992) *Horace's School*. Boston, MA: Houghton Mifflin.

Wasley, P.A., Hampel, R.L. and Clark, R.W. (1997) *Kids and School Reform*. San Francisco: Jossey-Bass Inc. Publishers.

Weis, L. and Fine, M. (Eds) (1993) *Beyond Silenced Voices: Class, Race and Gender in United States Schools*. Albany: State University of New York Press.

Wenger, E. (1998) *Communities of Practice: Learning Meaning and Identity*. Cambridge: Cambridge University Press.

Chapter 2

On different tracks

Students living detracking reform at a diverse urban high school

Beth C. Rubin

Beth: What's your hardest class do you think?
Tiffany:[1] History. It's so boring and I feel so stupid ... I hate history.

There are times I just want to slap some of my friends ... I'll be like "Why do you act so ignorant? We are being oppressed because of the fact we're black and you're making us look bad." Because they'll just say stupid things and I'm like "Save that for when you're with your friends and you want to act stupid. Don't have me looking bad because of you."

(Kiana)

It's a life thing ... You always learn in school. That's kind of the way it is. But [what] you're going to remember is going to be all the relationships. All the different people you worked with and how to work with those people. You're going to carry that a lot longer than you are how to find the area of a triangle or something.

(Sasha)

Introduction

"Tracking," the sorting and grouping of students by perceived ability and the corresponding curriculum differentiation that results, is a widespread practice in the United States. Many educational researchers link tracking to the reinforcement and perpetuation of inequalities in educational attainment along race and class lines (e.g. Oakes, 1985; Slavin, 1988; Mehan *et al.*, 1994). Recognizing tracking as a potential barrier to educational equity, a number of schools have attempted to "detrack," consciously organizing students into academically heterogeneous classrooms. It seems simple. Tracking creates inequity; therefore *de*track to reverse this inequity. This chapter suggests the matter is not quite so simple.

This chapter follows three girls,[2] classmates in a detracked ninth grade English-History core[3] program, through their first year at Cedar High School. As Kiana, Tiffany, and Sasha entered the ninth grade, each brought with her a particular set of home resources and responsibilities, a circle of friends, and previous schooling experiences. In the racially and socio-economically divided context of Cedar High, the classroom-based reform of detracking both provided opportunities for these students to have powerful learning experiences together and threw the disparities among them into stark relief. As the opening quotations indicate, although Tiffany, Kiana, and Sasha physically inhabited the same space, detracking was a distinct experience with distinct results for each of the three girls.

The twofold premise of detracking – that it is beneficial for students with diverse ethnic, racial, and academic backgrounds to mix socially in a classroom, and that the raised academic standards the reform provides will help create a more equitable educational foundation for all kids – is an admirable one. Yet, when we take a close look at the daily experiences of diverse students in a detracked classroom, we see that it is not quite so easy to mix students socially in a racially and academically polarized school context, and that raised expectations must be accompanied by targeted support. By considering the experiences of Kiana, Sasha and Tiffany we gain an intimate perspective on detracking through the eyes of those very students targeted by the reform, and perhaps a better understanding of how detracking might most successfully be implemented.

Advocates and critics: the polarized discourse of detracking

Although the United States public school system was built on the ideal of equal education for all, children are separated and sorted within our schools by tracking. The correspondence between school tracking and structural inequalities in our larger society has been well documented, with many researchers arguing that tracking plays a crucial role in the creation and perpetuation of social inequality (Oakes, 1985, 1986, 1992; Slavin, 1991, 1995; Mehan, 1992; Mehan *et al.*, 1994; Goodlad and Oakes, 1988). African American, Latino, and low-income children of all ethnicities are over-represented in low tracks and vocational programs, and in integrated schools, tracking often resegregates students by race and class (Oakes, 1992; Noguera, 1995). Furthermore, students in different tracks do not receive the same quality of education (Page, 1987; Oakes, 1985). The consequences are a system that is demoralizing and de-motivating for the children, usually poor and of color, who end up in the lowest tracks (Murphy and Hallinger, 1989; Gamoran, 1992).

Detracking reform stems from the critiques of tracking outlined above. Like the subject of tracking, however, a topic that seems to easily raise the ire of both critics and proponents, the question of detracking is usually answered with a retreat into opposing camps. Critics and advocates dominate discussion of detracking in the educational literature. Critical pieces (e.g. Allen, 1991; Feldhusen, 1991; Kulik, 1991; Scott, 1993; Brewer *et al.*, 1995; Gallagher, 1995) proffer quantitative data, most commonly test scores, to support claims that detracking disadvantages high achieving students and that tracking allows teachers to target curriculum to student needs. Advocacy pieces (e.g. Slavin, 1991, 1995; Oakes, 1993; Pavan, 1993) either counter the claims of the critics with their own quantitative sources, or provide anecdotal evidence of detracking's success as school reform. Advocates have also provided a wealth of prescriptive writing, recommendations for implementing detracking which range from classroom strategies to institutional restructuring (e.g. Wheelock, 1992; Page and Pool, 1995; Oakes, 1992; Marsh and Raywid, 1994; Cone, 1992).

The most nuanced and methodologically rigorous research on detracking focuses on community and school conflicts over the issue (e.g. Yonezawa *et al.*, 2002; Wells *et al.*, 1996; Oakes *et al.*, 1997; Cooper, 1996). These interpretive studies portray detracking as a highly contested institutional reform. From these studies of school and community discourse, we know that the implementation of detracking at a school brings many power dynamics to the fore, especially in racially and socioeconomically diverse communities. Detracking touches upon deeply seated beliefs about the relationships between class, race, and academic competence. This literature, however, offers little insight into teachers' and students' experiences *inside* of the detracked classroom. There has been little systematic research conducted on actual detracking practices (Mehan, 1996), and none that focuses on how detracking is experienced by the students it was designed to help.

My research and teaching[4] in detracked classrooms has led me to a "critical advocacy" position on detracking. The ethnographic research on which this chapter is based points towards a more complex analysis of detracking as a reform policy, leading away from a position of simple critique or unquestioning advocacy. How *do* diverse students experience detracking in their daily lives in school? What happens when kids who have very specific, and racially defined, ideas about who is a good student and who is not, with whom they can be friends and with whom they cannot, find themselves called upon to work together in the blurry social and academic context of a detracked classroom? The following pages explore the experiences of three students as they make their way through a year of detracking, leading us, hopefully, toward a fuller understanding of what might be needed to make detracking work.

Studying detracking reform at Cedar High School

The site for this study was Cedar High School, a large urban high school in a western state serving over 3,000 students. Cedar High School is both racially and socioeconomically diverse with a student population roughly 40 per cent European American, 40 per cent African American, 10 per cent Latino and 10 per cent Asian American. Race and class were closely linked, with European American students tending to come from middle- and upper-middle-class families, and African American and Latino students mainly coming from working-class or poor backgrounds. Asian American students came from families with a variety of socioeconomic backgrounds, with students from immigrant families tending to be poor and working class. There was a striking achievement gap between students of color and European American students at this school.[5]

In 1992, a new principal boldly pushed through detracking reform at the ninth grade level, eliminating all ability tracking in English classes, partnering ninth grade English and World History classes into "core" pairs, and reducing class size in these classes to twenty. This was the most systemic and far-reaching reform ever to be implemented at Cedar High. The idea was to provide all students with a higher level curriculum in these subjects, to deepen the content by forging interdisciplinary connections, to help ninth graders transition to high school by providing a smaller unit within the school, and to combat the social divide between African American and European American students by consciously integrating them at the ninth grade level. A reform, in short, directed at the very problems that marked the social and academic landscapes of Cedar.

Mr Apple, an English teacher, and Mr James, a social studies teacher, taught Tiffany, Kiana and Sasha's detracked core classes. The two teachers, both European American men, had chosen to work with each other and shared a preparation period, and thus had an unusually close working relationship for a core team at Cedar. Both men were deeply committed to implementing detracking and other reforms to improve education and decrease the achievement gap at Cedar, and both were experienced at working in the detracked setting. This choice was intentional, as I wished to study a "best case" scenario of detracking rather than an effort doomed to failure by inexperienced or unconvinced teachers.[6]

Straddling the "bad split": students living detracking reform at Cedar High

I noticed Tiffany, Sasha, and Kiana on my very first day of observation in Mr Apple and Mr James' detracked ninth grade English-History core program. It was the second week of school, and all three girls had already gained enough peer and teacher recognition that I quickly learned their names by quietly watching the class. As I interviewed each girl, observed her in class, and shadowed each through her entire school day I was won over by the open reflectiveness with which each of the three approached my questions, and touched by the excitement and sense of possibility that each felt at the beginning of her first year of high school. The three girls were different from each other in many ways, but similarly articulate, vibrant, and thoughtful.

Yet Tiffany, Sasha, and Kiana were to have very different experiences of Cedar High during their ninth grade year. For Sasha, a higher achieving white[7] girl from an upper-middle-class background, Cedar, and the detracked core, turned out to be rich with opportunities for personal, intellectual, and artistic development. She quickly found a peer group to support her eclectic, yet academically recognized, interests, and was frequently singled out by her teachers as an exemplary student. For Tiffany, a lower achieving African American student from a working-class background, her ninth grade year brought frustration and difficulty, particularly in her detracked classes. She struggled with both the assignments and her fellow students in the detracked core, and, by the end of the year, no longer participated or completed work for those classes. Kiana, a biracial African American-European American girl from a middle-class family, experienced conflict in her detracked classes, as she strove to both do well academically and forge a fulfilling social life in the racially polarized social and academic setting of Cedar High School. Her school performance was sometimes outstanding, sometimes lackluster, and her early hopes of being able to move easily between friends with various racial backgrounds were dashed.

The paths of these three girls in a sense represented three different paths through the high school. Sasha's path, involving high level courses, many electives, and, eventually, a large number of advanced placement courses, was predominantly taken by Cedar's European American students, a higher income group. A large portion of Cedar's African American students, who were predominantly from working-class backgrounds, took Tiffany's path, with remedial courses, few electives, and non-completion of the state's public college and university requirements. Mr Apple named this academic polarization along race and class lines the "bad split," an evocative term hinting both at the depth of the division and the sense of shame felt about it by Cedar's many progressive teachers. This was, of course, the division which detracking reform was intended to interrupt. The following student portraits focus on Tiffany, Sasha, and Kiana's experiences of detracking.

Tiffany: doing well with a 2.0?

Tiffany's day

In September of her ninth grade year, Tiffany told me about her daily life. "I'm kind of like the person that runs everything in the house," she told me, with a hint of pride in her voice. Living with an ill mother and the infant daughter of a friend of her sister, Tiffany's daily routine involved juggling tasks and responsibilities not faced by many adults. As she described to me,

> [I] wake up every morning and get the breakfast ready and the lunches ready. I take my niece to school, help my sister get ready for work, take the baby and leave the baby with my sister's best friend. I get my mom ready for dialysis and all that ... I have to get her dressed and get her cleaned up ... it's like Mondays, Wednesdays, and Fridays ... And after school when I come home I have to wait for my mom to come ... then I get on the bus to go get my niece and on the way I pick up the baby. Then I come back home and then my brother'll be home on his lunch break and then after that he leaves for work again. Then my grandma and grandpa start coming home.

This situation did not leave Tiffany much time for completing homework. "I do it when I can," she told me. "When the kids are sleeping and when my older sister comes home and my mom, I can do some of my work, but not all of it." Sometimes, when she was just too exhausted, she would "start it and get in the middle of it, then I'll start getting sleepy and fall asleep."

Although Tiffany's detracked core classes were college preparatory, the rest of her course schedule did not put her on a college-bound trajectory, as we can see in Table 2.1.

Despite her participation in the detracked English-History core, Tiffany's math, science, and language choices put her on a distinctly non-college bound path. Integrated Science 1 would not lead her to the double period laboratory science classes that were necessary to complete the requirements for the state college and university system. By not taking a language in her ninth grade year Tiffany was also putting herself at a disadvantage in trying to fulfill these requirements. Still more troubling, by enrolling in pre-

Table 2.1 Tiffany's first semester schedule

Period	Class	Racial demographics[1]
1		
2	Afro-Haitian Dance	Mixed
3	English	Mixed
4	World History	Mixed
5	Ethnic Studies	Mixed
6	Integrated Science 1	Predominantly African American
7	Pre-Algebra	Predominantly African American

Note:
1 "Mixed" – students from no one racial/ethnic group make up 70 per cent or more of class; "Predominantly" – students from one racial/ethnic group make up 70 per cent or more of the class.

Algebra, Tiffany was precluding being able to reach the higher levels of mathematics available at Cedar.

The story behind how Tiffany arrived at this particular course schedule was telling. Although she had already taken and passed pre-Algebra while in middle school Tiffany had chosen to take it again because, as she told me, she did not want to be in the class with the "big kids." She also did not want to have to repeat pre-Algebra at the end of high school as her brother had done. She explained,

> Because, see, my brother, when he came he didn't go to pre-algebra. He went to pre-algebra in middle school, and then he went to algebra here, and he never went to pre-algebra here, so he needed to go to pre-algebra this year because it's his last year. So he's like "This is really easy."

As unlikely as this seemed, Tiffany insisted that this is what had happened, and neither counselor nor parent had stepped in to remedy the situation. She also had a misconception about her science class, telling me that she was in "Health Academy science," when the teacher informed me that the class actually was not in the Health Academy, a career oriented small school program. "I don't know why they think that," the science teacher told me, "this is just regular science."

Tiffany's day was also notable in the switch between racially mixed and predominantly African American classes. This had two implications. First of all, because her main social group was African American, she often felt more socially isolated in her detracked classes. Also, the difference in academic expectation was notable between her tracked and detracked classes, reinforcing the all too common negative assumptions about the academic competence of African American students at Cedar. In Tiffany's low tracked science and math classes, as was true for the other low tracked classes I observed, expectations were notably low, with reading from the textbook and answering a few questions as primary modes of instruction.

Tiffany detracked

In Tiffany's detracked classes, the expectations were different. In her English and history classes, doing the reading and talking in class were important elements being considered a successful student by both peers and teachers,[8] and Tiffany struggled to contribute "appropriately" in both of these areas. She frequently came to class late, refused to sit where the teacher assigned her, and announced loudly that she had not completed the assigned reading. Her social goals often took priority over her academic goals, as she often moved to sit and chat with friends, passed notes in class, and sometimes left the room to meet friends from other classes in the bathroom.

In the detracked core, students were expected to participate actively in whole class discussions and group activities that were based upon having completed a reading or homework assignment. Since Tiffany often was unable to complete her homework and reading, she frequently found herself displayed to her peers in a negative light. Perhaps even more so than in a traditional classroom in which students sit in rows and listen to the teacher, amid the progressive pedagogy of the detracked core Tiffany's lack of preparation and personal difficulties were glaringly apparent. This was compounded by the assumptions that many students brought to the table. Kiana's observation that "My white friends, or the majority of them, do fairly well, whereas my African American friends, my friends of color, they're just doing really poorly" reflected a common, though usually obliquely referenced, sentiment.

These tensions and assumptions were particularly noticeable in group-work situations in the detracked core, especially when groups were pre-assigned by the teacher. Both Mr Apple and Mr James followed recommended group-work practices (e.g. Bigelow, 1992; Bower et al., 1999; Cohen, 1986) by constructing students' groups with an eye toward "balancing" race, gender, and academic skill level. While this might be a good idea in theory, when put into practice in the detracked core it was often all too obvious to students why they were placed in particular groups. Additionally, within Cedar's racially polarized social setting, these "balanced" groups often created tense social dynamics.

When Tiffany was placed in a group with three higher achieving European American students for a "group quiz" on Lord of the Flies, for example, her group mates assumed (perhaps correctly) that she had not done the reading. The three white students conducted the group as though Tiffany was not there, talking around her and not asking her to participate in any way, all the while laughing and joking with one another. When Mr Apple noticed the situation he suggested that Tiffany be responsible for a drawing that was part of the quiz. When her group mates continued to ignore her, Tiffany began to call out to her friends in other groups. Eventually, Tiffany asked if she could leave the room. In the hallway outside of the classroom she told Mr Apple, "They don't want me in their group. They don't think I'm smart."

This sense of herself as not "smart" in her detracked classes continued to develop as the year went on. In May, Tiffany and I discussed her experiences in her detracked core classes as compared to her low tracked math class.

BETH: If I asked Mr Apple to describe Tiffany to me, what do you think he would say?
TIFFANY: She's loud and she's interrupting. If he doesn't call on me and I'm sitting there the longest I just get mad and I start yelling.
BETH: Do you think you talk a lot in that class?

TIFFANY: I talk a lot to Christie.

BETH: Would you say thinking about the other students in class that you're at the top of the class or the middle of the class or bottom of the class in how well you're doing?

TIFFANY: Bottom.

BETH: Why?

TIFFANY: It depends on the class. On math class I say I'm on top because I'm like one of the smart kids.

BETH: I noticed in math that you're helping a lot of other kids.

TIFFANY: Yeah, because when our teacher gives us tests, whoever gets the lowest grade, that's everybody's grade. So everybody's like – that girl I told you [about]? Elizabeth? She's slow. So everyone's like "We're not going to get a good grade. We're probably going to fail because of her." I feel like if you're going to say that you should help her out so that we'll get an A. So I just try and help her out.

BETH: That's great. What's your hardest class do you think?

TIFFANY: History. It's so boring and I feel so stupid … I hate history.

As this conversation reflects, Tiffany's sense of herself as a student varied from class to class. While she felt Mr Apple saw her as "loud and interrupting," and placed herself at the "bottom" of that detracked class, in her low tracked math class she was "one of the smart kids." When I went with Tiffany to her math class I was struck by the difference in her demeanor from that in her detracked core classes. She entered the class early, engaged in some joking banter with the teacher, then picked up the "warm-up sheet" from a side table and got right to work. She finished the two warm-up problems quickly, and spent the next few minutes helping the students near her to finish their sheets. In this class, Tiffany was the expert, and she acted on this status by empathetically assisting others. Tiffany cared about her grades and her classmates in this setting.

Tiffany's detracked history class, as noted earlier, made her feel "so stupid." Mr James held high expectations for his students, and assigned a constant stream of interesting and challenging work. Most of the in-class activities were based upon out-of-class preparation, and reading and writing were a daily necessity. Work was cumulative, and once a student fell behind it was difficult to regain momentum. When I spoke with Tiffany immediately following a history test, she sounded angry but resigned:

He gave us a study guide and you could use the paper notes. But the stuff that he told us to study didn't seem like none of it was on the test. I was like "Oh well." [cynical and resigned] [I used] his notes and I did the study stuff that he told me to do, but I couldn't deal with it.

Despite her attempts at preparation, the curriculum remained beyond her reach and she was left with feelings of inadequacy and resentment.

Tiffany at year's end

By the end of the year, Tiffany's performance in her detracked classes had taken a downturn. Where Kiana and Sasha were able to use the progressive practices of the detracked core as a bridge between personal experience and academic engagement, by May, Tiffany seemed almost completely disengaged in both English and history. But although by most standards Tiffany, with a 2.0 grade point average, was doing poorly in school, she herself felt that she was doing exceptionally well. The context of Cedar High allowed her to accept her performance as adequate.

When Tiffany compared her grades to those of her closest friends, she seemed like a high achiever. "I think I'm doing better than some of my friends," she told me. "Some of them got a 1.83." None of her friends, she told me, was doing better than her academically; none of them had an "A" or a "B" average. Her grades were "way better" than her eighth grade grades. According to Tiffany, her family concurred with this assessment. "My mom's like 'Oh you're doing good.'" For Tiffany, in the Cedar context, she was doing fine.

Tiffany had high hopes for her future. "Now I'm starting to think about college and stuff," she told me. "That's the really main thing, is college now. I never really thought of college." What got her thinking about college, I asked. "My sister," replied Tiffany. "She's like, 'You know you got to start going to college. You're going to be going to college soon.' It's like 'Really?' She's like 'Yeah.'" But was Tiffany gaining the skills and building the transcript she needed to get into college? Neither her tracked nor her detracked classes seemed to be engaging, challenging, or supporting her academically. Testimony to the lack of institutional support at Cedar for the aspirations of a student like Tiffany was the fact that it was her sister rather than a teacher or counselor who pushed her to think about college. Within the Cedar context, Tiffany's low academic performance was seen as unremarkable, and the progressive practices of the detracked core did not seem able to intervene in this normalization of failure.

Sasha: a journey of personal growth and transformation

Sasha's day

At the beginning of the school year Sasha was excited to be at Cedar. Unlike her middle school, which was "a little teeny private school" with "surface people," Sasha was energized by Cedar's size, diversity, and wealth of options. "There's such a variety of people here," she told me, bubbling over with enthusiasm, "that I can find deep people where they actually have some insight into life and they actually know what they want to do

Table 2.2 Sasha's first semester schedule

Period	Class	Racial demographics
1	Spanish 3	Mixed
2	World History	Predominantly European American
3	English	Mixed
4	Photography	Predominantly European American
5	Communication Tech.[1]	Mixed
6	Geometry	Mixed
7		

Note
1 Communication Technology was a required course for students in the "small school" housing the detracked core program.

other than go to the store and get new lipstick. It's about diversity. It makes it a lot more interesting to be here and find interesting people."

Sasha's schedule, shown in Table 2.2, reflected her sense of herself as an "arts person," her parents' assistance in her navigation of the school structure, and her identity as a college-bound student.

This schedule, with second year Spanish, advanced math, an art elective, and college prep English and World History, put Sasha on a decidedly college-bound track.

Sasha's experience with her math class bears closer examination, particularly in contrast to Tiffany's math situation. Although Sasha had experienced difficulty in math at her private middle school, she enrolled in Geometry, an advanced class for a ninth grade student. Her parents hired a tutor to support her in this subject, and she was able to do well despite her misgivings. At one point early in the school year Sasha's parents, concerned that she was "not learning very well in math," had intervened on behalf of their daughter to try and improve conditions in her math class. As Sasha explained, "I actually had to have my mom help me because there were so many weird adults that talk to each other and talk to somebody else who gives a little bit away to the teachers who talk to us. So it's so complicated I had to have some help." By hiring a tutor for her, closely monitoring her progress, and making their presence felt at the school, Sasha's parents were able to turn a situation which could have been disastrous for another student – a difficult class, with an unresponsive teacher – into one in which she could be successful.

True to her description of Cedar's "variety of people," most of Sasha's classes were racially mixed. While in these classes, though, she tended to socialize mainly with European American peers. Although she loved "the diversity" of Cedar, she admitted, "I do hang out with a lot of Caucasians." She was "working on" developing a more diverse group of friends. "I have a couple of Latino friends," she told me, "but it seems like they really don't like me too much. I just don't seem to get along with them." She reported feeling "kind of ignored sometimes" by students of color, and seemed to gravitate toward European American peers.

Sasha's friends all did well in school. "In my central group we're all pretty much equal and try really hard to do well," she told me. "I don't hang out with people that really don't care because they're so different." During lunch and between class periods she and her friends strategized their class schedules for the upcoming years, discussed homework, studied for tests and quizzes, and completed school projects. Many of her friends in the detracked core were in her other classes as well, and she quickly developed an artsy, academically oriented social group.

Sasha detracked

For Sasha, the detracked core was of a piece with the rest of her school experience. It was an affirming space within which she could comfortably form social relationships and express herself intellectually. Her competence was continually affirmed during class. In English class, Mr Apple frequently read Sasha's written work aloud to the class as exemplars. "This is as true as it comes," he commented to the class, after reading them a short story Sasha had written. Sasha frequently received this sort of positive feedback in her detracked English class, affirming and developing her sense of herself as a good writer and an overall "artistic" person.

Sasha's academic competence was continually affirmed in history class as well, where, as described earlier, preparation was essential to participation. In history class, Sasha's cultural knowledge of school, her adeptness at being a student, stood her in good stead. Amid the progressive practices of the detracked core, which highlighted active student participation in meaningful (non-rote) activities, appropriate student engagement was particularly important. In such activities, consistent student engagement was a prerequisite for the teacher's ability to move the class along, cover main points, and progress to the next activity. Sasha played this role frequently, answering questions based on her preparation and personal knowledge, helping the teacher achieve his goals.

Sasha was able to interact with her teachers in the detracked core in ways that gained their attention and approval. Mr Apple reflected on this, telling me that Sasha was "really good" at appealing to him and forming a relationship with him through her dialogue journal. She wrote to him chattily in the journal, writing "you can call me 'Sash,' " and addressing him like a friend. This sort of journal entry made it easy for him to write a great deal in response, he said, and he felt he had to be careful that he did not "discriminate" in his journal responses. He contrasted Sasha with another student, Frankie, who wrote two lines in his journal, making it difficult for Mr Apple to get beyond, "Frankie, you have to write more," in his responses. Differences in cultural knowledge and interaction style meant that some students were positioned to get more and better quality feedback from the teacher, and Sasha benefited from this.

Sasha was a sought-after group member for the frequent group work activities of the detracked core. She was dubbed a "group maker" by Mr Apple, and mentioned by her peers as someone they would like to work with. In many group work situations, Sasha was able to balance her social and academic goals, laughing and joking with group members, but still getting work done, and thus avoiding the teachers' notice. In class she was able to sit near her friends without becoming distracted, as her friends were involved with taking notes, participating, and listening to the teacher as well.

Sasha at year's end

Ninth grade, for Sasha, was a journey of self-awareness and academic achievement, and the detracked core provided a nurturing setting for this growth. By May, spurred on by a thought-provoking assignment in English class – the "identity box" – Sasha had used the wide landscape of choices she saw as available to her at Cedar to reinvent herself. For this assignment, students had to create a box showing the inside and outside of their identities. "I was doing the inside and it was so much fun, then I got to the outside and I realized that they weren't matching at all." The inside was "colorful, and it had music and strange looking stuff," while the outside only had a few words, like "tall, boring, quiet." When she realized this, she said to herself, "I have to go and try to bring the inside to the outside."

These changes manifested themselves in her appearance, her actions, her choice of friends, and her convictions. "I have a bunch of punk style clothing, and I'm planning on dying my hair, so the outside, physical stuff is different," she told me. "I talk a lot more … People can't shut me up very easily." Her change in style went along with a new-found political consciousness, as she told me, "I'm very outgoing about what I believe and what I think about the whole Latin American thing." This transformation affected her future plans. After studying about Latin America in Mr James' World History class she decided, "I want to go down there and I want to help, and I don't have any problems telling people that. I want to take a lead and start to get the people to do something. I really, really want to go down to Latin America and try to help out there. I don't want to just be part of the program."

Self-knowledge and definition, political awareness, intellectual growth, and a sense of her own efficacy were important outgrowths of Sasha's ninth grade experience, and stemmed from her participation in the progressive practices of the detracked core. She finished the year extremely positive about both the academic content of the core and the experience of being in such a diverse class. "[What] you're going to remember is going to be all the relationships," she told me, "All the different people you worked with and how to work with those people. You're going to carry that a lot longer than you are how to find the area of a triangle or something." Rather than being ill-served by detracking, as detracking critics asserted would be the case for a student like Sasha, Sasha flourished in the detracked core.

Kiana: from "both" to "black," and the conflicts that follow

Kiana's day

At the beginning of her ninth grade year Kiana was full of excitement about being at Cedar. As an eighth grader she attended a small private school with only twenty-seven students. The few years prior to that had been rocky. When Kiana was in the intermediate grades her family moved from Cedarville to a predominantly European American suburb sixty miles north. For Kiana, whose mother was African American and father European American, the move had been difficult. "I went to several schools," she told me. "I had a lot of problems with racial issues. The diversity was horrible." They moved back to Cedarville before her eighth grade year. At Cedar, Kiana felt more at home. "I feel like I've been going to small schools for a big portion of my life and this is like *finally*. I needed a bigger social environment," she told me.

Cedar, in Kiana's view, was much more fun than her previous schools. Rather than being overwhelmed by the huge throngs of people, she thrived on the large numbers. She got a hint of how she would do at the school when she visited Cedar summer school for a day in the summer before her ninth grade year. "In just that one day I had so much fun, I was like 'Okay, I'm not nervous about Cedar at all.' Then the first day of school I came in and all my friends were like 'Aren't you nervous?' I'm like '*No*. I know it's going to be so much fun.' "

Kiana's reinvigorated social life was tied to Cedar's diversity. At Cedar, Kiana felt that, for the first time, she could be wholly herself as a biracial person in her relationships with her peers.

> I have never gone to a school that's so diverse … I had asked older students that had already attended Cedar High. "What's the diversity like?" and they're like "It's the ordinary thing but the black kids hang out with the black kids, the white kids hang out with the white kids and all that." Well, I'm both. So I came here and to some extent that is true but it's nothing like I thought it would be and I do have African American friends and Caucasian friends. I think that's good.

In this racially diverse atmosphere, Kiana felt she could finally be "into the social thing" that she said she had been "missing for so long" while a student at predominantly European American schools. About Cedar, she told me, "you couldn't get any more [social] than this, I don't think."

Doing well in school was very important to Kiana, who saw herself as a high achiever. Grades were Kiana's measure of how well she was doing, and she was very concerned with her grade point average. She ended the first semester with a 3.7, which did not meet her high standards. "I once had the best GPA," she told me. When I told her that I thought a 3.7 was quite a good average she told me, "I'm not that proud of it. I expect a lot from myself." Kiana's mother bolstered this academic persona. When Kiana came home with a 3.73, instead of congratulating her, her mother told her, "This is good, but I think you can do better." When she didn't do well she got "put on punishment," restricted to her house during her free time.

A look at Kiana's first semester schedule, shown in Table 2.3, gives us an insight into her daily experience of school.

Kiana's class schedule was relatively undemanding for her, made up, as it was, of several entry-level classes. In her Spanish 1 and Algebra 1 classes, Kiana stood out as particularly successful academically, and she found the work in these classes to be easy. The attitude of the other students in both of these entry-level classes was something of a shock to her. Her Spanish class, she told me, was filled with kids who "don't really want to learn." "People say the stupidest things," she told me, reflecting on her Spanish class, but the teacher "keeps everyone in check." She started out the year in a higher level of Spanish, but found that since she was on the tennis team she did not have time to do the homework in that class. When she tried to move down just one level (to Spanish 2) she found that the class was filled up, so she went into Spanish 1. It was okay, she told me, because "Hey, I'm getting A's." She excelled among her peers in Algebra 1 as well, and her math teacher told her she should apply to take Honors Geometry as a sophomore.

Kiana's detracked core classes and her Ethnic Studies class were racially mixed but her other classes were predominantly African American or predominantly students of color. This meant that the students in her easiest

Table 2.3 Kiana's first semester schedule

Period	Class	Racial demographics
I		
2	Afro-Haitian Dance	Predominantly African American
3	English	Mixed
4	World History	Mixed
5	Ethnic Studies	Mixed
6	Spanish 1/2	Predominantly Students of Color
7	Algebra I	Predominantly African American

classes – the entry-level classes mentioned above – were mostly students of color, while the detracked classes, which had higher academic expectations, were racially mixed. In terms of her induction into the social world of Cedar High, then, Kiana spent more time with African American peers in the context of entry-level classes.

Kiana detracked

For Kiana, her detracked core classes were the most intellectually stimulating part of her school day. Both her peers and her teachers in the core saw her as a good student. She thought Mr Apple and Mr James would describe her as "very articulate," and, indeed, this bore out in Mr Apple's description of her as an "ideal student." Kiana felt her "diverse" background was an advantage in these classes and helped her to better participate in class discussions. She told me,

> I think I have an advantage over most people because I'm so diverse. My mom's black, my dad's white. I have the weirdest family. My step-brother is disabled ... I've experienced a lot more than the average teenager, so when we have discussions it's like "I know about that. Let me say something."

The detracked class allowed Kiana room for the self-expression that helped her to bridge the gap between emerging self and school achievement. She found many of Mr Apple's English assignments to be enjoyable and relevant. One assignment she particularly liked was an essay about a time when she was self-reliant. "I wrote about an experience," she told me, "about my dad. I really enjoyed writing that paper and I felt like I really got into it and it's like a lot I wanted to say." She read this highly personal essay out loud, to the rapt attention of all her classmates.

I noticed, however, that she seemed to talk less in her detracked classes at the end of the year. "Maybe I don't feel as comfortable in his class," she told me. "Because of the people that are in his class. There's like no African American students." There were a greater number of higher achieving African American students in Mr Apple's other sections of ninth grade English, and when the two classes came together for activities, Kiana's participation blossomed.

For Kiana, the social aspects of class were in conflict with her academic goals. To have a satisfying and comfortable social life at Cedar, Kiana felt she needed to be part of an African American peer group. Yet the African American girls in her English class, Tiffany and Christie, had different stances towards school than she did. "Tiffany," she told me, "she's just like all fun and games. And I'm, like, my grade is important to me." Kiana felt that Tiffany's sense of herself as a student was very different from her own, telling me that "she [Tiffany] got an F on a test one time and she's like 'Oh, okay.' If I got that F I would be crying right now."

Kiana was in conflict, however. At the end of a particularly rambunctious World History class she told me, proudly, "We [the African American girls she was sitting with] like to talk. We just don't always talk about the right things." Balancing her unofficial social talk with the demands of the official curriculum was particularly difficult in content-dense history class. Kiana told me that sitting with friends was difficult in this class.

> Tiffany's sitting on my right, I'm in the middle and Jocelyn's to my left and they're just constantly "Will you give this to Tiffany?" It's just … in history he has us taking tons of notes and that's one of the things I have a hard time with. He'll be talking – having a discussion while we're supposed to be copying notes off the board – and I'm like trying to do both at the same time and I'm like "Wait, wait." But I'm learning how to do both. Then when somebody's asking me to pass something, I'm like: "No. Please let me do this."

Kiana's mother was concerned about her, worried that she would "fall between the cracks" under the influence of less scholarly peers, Kiana told me. Kiana hid aspects of her social life from her mother, such as the ribbing she took from African American girlfriends for being biracial. Her aware-ness of her mother's concern, however, weighed on her conscience, and if Kiana did fall behind in her classes she soon pressured herself to work harder until she was caught up. Thus despite the conflict between social and academic goals, Kiana was able to maintain her academic success in her detracked classes.

Kiana at year's end

Dynamics of race and friendship became more complex for Kiana as the school year progressed. At the beginning of the year, Kiana described herself as "both" black and white. By the end of the year, she told me, "It's hard for me because I'm half white and half black and I guess I just side more with my black side. But I don't think I really have a choice but to identify with it." She elaborated on this "choice" of racial identity, telling me,

> The thing is I have chosen though. It's not really me that's chosen it's more society. I think about it for my little brother, because he's mixed and he looks like he could be white. But, the thing is, he knows I'm African American. I don't even teach him "I am half black and half white." I teach him "I am African American. I am black." One day I heard him picking out colors and stuff and I said "What color am I?" He goes "You're black and I'm white." I was like "No, you're not white.

You're African American. You're a very light shade of brown but you're African American."

By the end of the year, her close friends at Cedar were almost exclusively African American. What would happen if she identified more with her "white side," I asked her. "My friends would kick my butt," she said, laughing. "I get teased about that [being biracial] all the time. All the time. Like 'Kiana's light-skinned.' Constantly. The fact that I have good hair. Just ridiculous stuff." The racially polarized social landscape at Cedar, along with a larger society unable to understand racial identity in a complex manner, contributed to Kiana's strong affiliation with an exclusively African American peer group by the end of the school year.

This affiliation had academic implications, as Kiana often found herself at odds with the academic orientation of her immediate peer group. Unlike most of her African American peers at Cedar, Kiana was from a middle-class background, and her mother was a lawyer. Many of Cedarville's middle-class African American families sent their children to private schools, to avoid placing them amid the taken-for-granted link between race and school performance in the local schools. Kiana's hope for building a social life that reflected her personal diversity, with both African American and European American friends, then, was made considerably more complex by the ways that race, class, gender, and students' social worlds intertwined in the Cedar context.

This was a source of disappointment, anger, and embarrassment for her, as she struggled to forge an identity as an academically successful African American student. "The thing that really disappoints me," she told me, "is the statistic that the majority of black students at Cedar are failing and doing really poorly. I find that with my friends. My white friends, or the majority of them, do fairly well, whereas my African American friends, my friends of color, they're just really doing real poorly."

She had thought about the causes for the achievement gap at Cedar. Kiana told me that the low academic achievement of many African American students was tied to racism. "I think it has to do with racism," she told me. "I think that with a lot of my teachers ... it's like black students have to prove themselves to certain teachers. The teacher won't take them seriously until you take that test. Like you have to prove yourself. They automatically assume I'm ignorant."

During the second semester of the year Kiana's grade point average took a plunge. She recounted this, telling me that,

> ... last quarter I got a really bad grade and it was like I was embarrassed
> ... The third quarter. My calculated GPA was a 2.66. Not only was I
> really disappointed in myself but I was embarrassed. That wasn't my
> actual GPA because Mr James made a mistake on my grading ... it's

like a 3.0 or something but still it's under a 3.5. That is like not good. Like a 3.3 and that's the worst I've ever had and I'm really not happy with it. And it is just a quarter grade and it doesn't go on my transcript or anything but still … I really disappoint myself.

Kiana's 2.66 on her third quarter grade report was acutely embarrassing for her, even though her friends thought she was crazy for being concerned about it. She told me, "I was like on the phone crying 'Oh my God I need to get my grades fixed,' because it was a 2.66, and my friends are talking about 'I would kill for a 2.66.' I was like, 'What are you talking about? Oh my God!' " Regardless of her friends' opinions, Kiana blamed herself for not completing her work and vowed to do better.

By the end of her ninth grade year, Kiana seemed to have become proficient at the complex juggling act faced by high achieving students of color at Cedar, maintaining reasonable levels of social and academic satisfaction. She was able to excel through the progressive practices of the detracked core, while at the same time building relationships with Cedar's African American peers in both her tracked and detracked classes. Her transcript, however, would not be as stellar as perhaps it could have been. Kiana did well in her less advanced math and foreign language classes, but did not have the same opportunities as similarly academically inclined European American students, like Sasha. While at times she experienced conflict between some of her friends and her academic aspirations, by the end of the year Kiana seemed well on her way to forging an identity for herself as a high achieving African American student.

Conclusion

In many ways, then, this chapter tells a story of the social and cultural reproduction of inequalities. While Sasha, a high achieving European American girl from an upper-middle-class family, was well-equipped to flourish at Cedar, both in her detracked core classes and beyond, Tiffany, a lower achieving African American student from a working-class family, attended the same school and many of the same classes with very different results. The institutional structure of Cedar High, the pedagogical practices of the detracked core, and the social capital (Bourdieu, 1977) brought by each girl to those interwoven sites all seemed to contribute to this reiteration of the very inequalities that detracking was designed to address.

It is both this simple and far more complex. Kiana's experience with detracking is an example of how detracking provides a desegregated space (Fine et al., 1997), albeit not without conflict, for a high achieving African American student at a high school which is socially and academically polarized by race. Were it not for the detracked core, Kiana's situation would conceivably have been much more difficult. Low tracked English and history classes would not have been challenging enough for her. Yet high tracked classes, dominated at Cedar by European American students, might have left her feeling as alienated as she had felt at her previous school as one of very few students of color. Although she was compelled to become something of a "border crosser," Kiana's academic talents were valued and nurtured in the detracked core, and her future goals were not compromised.

Detracked classes provided Sasha with a much broader school experience than she would have had in a completely tracked high school. She valued this aspect of detracking, as her words in the epigraph made clear. "You always learn in school. That's kind of the way it is," she told me, with the confidence of a student who has rarely doubted her own ability to succeed academically. Yet she sensed that there was more to be learned in school, something that had to do with human relationships in a diverse society or, as she put it, "All the different people you worked with and how to work with those people." Sasha's experiences hint at yet another complexity. While detracking critics often claim that detracking will harm higher achieving students, Sasha thrived in the detracked core. A racially and academically diverse classroom, at least in this case, does not seem to be incompatible with a creative and challenging curriculum.

Would a tracked classroom have been better for Tiffany, who struggled in the detracked core? Tracking sent a message to students of color at Cedar, high and low achieving alike. This message was heard clearly by Tiffany's good friend Christie, who told me, "tracking has a lot to do with race. Like in my pre-algebra class, it's all black kids in there." Yoshi, a multi-ethnic classmate of Christie and Tiffany, described Cedar before detracking as "a lot of the colored kids … in a lower track" and "all the white kids … in higher tracking." Detracking then, in some senses, embodied both a critique of race-linked tracking and a belief in the possibility that, as Christie put it, "people could turn around [in their academic work] at any old time." More was needed for Tiffany to be academically successful and reach her goal of attending college, but this, at the very least, was a prerequisite.

Tiffany, Sasha and Kiana's double-edged experiences in Cedar's tracked and detracked classrooms lead back to the "critical advocacy" position I briefly articulated at the beginning of this chapter. The experiences of these three girls reveal the naïveté underlying the presumption that placing racially and academically diverse students next to each other in a classroom setting will solve fundamental inequalities in how our educational system serves young people from different race and class backgrounds. Inequalities are reproduced within schools through a subtle process within which particular forms of knowledge are valued over others (Bourdieu, 1977; Morrow and Torres, 1994; Bowles and Gintis, 1976) both within individual classrooms and through institutional structures. Moving bodies around cannot in itself change this.

Yet this examination of student experiences with detracking leads to some concrete ideas about how this reform might provide a foundation from which to begin a challenge to these long-standing inequalities. There is much that could be done, both within detracked classrooms and beyond, to strengthen the impact of detracking reform. Within the detracked core program, greater academic support might have allowed Tiffany to be a fuller and more successful participant in the many whole-class and group activities that typified the core. Instruction in the "culture and language of power" (Delpit, 1988), and targeted academic support (Rubin, this volume) can assist students in meeting raised academic expectations. This should be obvious. Sasha's parents did not hesitate to send her to a tutor to support her work in an advanced math class. Yet lower achieving students are often not given the support they need to reach higher expectations, and are, instead, sent to lower tracked classes.

Research also indicates that for students of color, developing a critical perspective on societal inequalities can greatly assist them as they struggle to achieve academically without sacrificing their sense of identity (Mehan *et al.*, 1994; Morrell and Collatos, this volume). Such an approach might have bolstered and informed Kiana as she struggled to bridge the gap between her social and academic worlds. Finally, a more "culturally relevant" approach (Ladson-Billings, 1992; De Jesus, this volume) might have allowed both Tiffany and Kiana to connect more deeply with the curriculum and instruction in the detracked core.

I would also suggest, however, that the success of detracking is dependent on making cultural and structural changes in the larger school setting. School priorities, when analyzed, may prove to be bound up in the needs of particular groups to the detriment of other groups. At Cedar, for example, the emphasis on providing a private preparatory school type of education for high achieving students enrolled in a myriad of advanced placement, honors, and specialized courses, may have been at the expense of providing a high quality education for less academically sophisticated students. Looking after the needs of students like Tiffany might result in a very different set of school priorities, including a redistribution of resources to fund smaller classes, personalized academic support, and more substantive advising.

The success of detracking is also linked to the ability of a school's adults to foster a change in social relations among students from different race and class backgrounds. Most high schools take a hands-off attitude toward students' social worlds, yet, as is suggested by this look into the three girls' daily lives, this aspect of student life is deeply connected with the academic realm. Creating smaller schools-within-schools to explicitly foster community among diverse students, holding meaningful orientation activities for ninth graders, and reconsidering how the social spaces of the school are structured for student interaction are all means by which social divisions among students from different race and class backgrounds might be made more permeable.

Finally, this chapter hinted at the wide disparity in enrichment or out-of-school opportunities for students from different socioeconomic backgrounds. A comparison of Sasha's private tutor for Geometry and her unpaid internship at an animation studio set up for her by her mother with Tiffany's lack of such opportunities, demonstrates this gulf. Networking with local businesses and organizations to provide after-school opportunities, and the provision of tutoring support for low-income students so they can successfully complete difficult courses are a few possible ways to remedy this inequity. A summer school designed to accelerate achievement, preparing more students to take advanced math, science, and computer courses, might encourage a shift in enrollment patterns in these courses and mitigate the effects of economic privilege. Such changes would not only ease the disparities in the detracked setting, but would go further still by providing greater access to advanced coursework for all students.

The aforementioned conclusions arose from a study that put students at the center of data collection and analysis. A youth-centered approach to studying school reform reveals a different slice of the school reform experience, allowing us access to the ways in which students, in their daily lives, experience changes in school structure and classroom instruction. It can reveal, as it did in this study, that students sometimes experience school reforms in ways that are in conflict with the goals of reformers. Interviewing teachers, analyzing test results, or conducting large-scale surveys would not have led to such findings. Weaving the experiences of students into the study of school reform can point the designers and implementers of school change in new and unexpected directions, directions that may hold promise for the intended beneficiaries of that reform – the students themselves.

Notes

1 Names of students, teachers, school and community have all been changed.
2 The research for this chapter is drawn from a year-long ethnographic study of a detracked ninth grade English-History "core" (see note 3 for definition of "core") program at Cedar High School. The entire data set includes interviews with students and teachers, classroom observations completed over the course of a school year, and field notes from shadowing five diverse focal students throughout their school days. This chapter focuses on a sub-set of that larger data set, the experiences of three of the five focal students: Kiana, Sasha and Tiffany.
3 "Core" refers to the pairing of English and History classes so that two groups of students share the same teachers for both classes, usually scheduled one following the other. This enables the teachers to plan some common activities and projects, to combine the classes into a larger class for a longer time block, to discuss common students, and to plan an integrated or aligned curriculum.

4 In my six years as a public high school social studies teacher I taught primarily in detracked classrooms.
5 This achievement gap was seen through differences in grade point average, in college readiness, and in levels and quantity of courses taken. It is important to note, however, that despite these patterns of inequality, there were many academically successful students from poor and working-class, immigrant, and minority backgrounds.
6 In a study of the ninth grade core program conducted by a university research team, teachers complained of a lack of training for teaching heterogeneous groups and not enough time to plan integrated curriculum. The majority felt that social goals of integration were achieved through the detracked program, however, and supported its continuation.
7 It was necessary, in this study, to write about or indicate "attributes" of individuals that I believe to be constructed within social settings rather than innate or essential. There is an inherent conflict between my view of race/ethnicity, gender, and academic positioning as contingent and constructed, and the use of such labels to describe individuals. That being said, it would not be possible to understand the significance of particular settings, interactions, and outcomes for the individuals in this chapter without having some reference point with which to mark these aspects of identity. Achievement level, which I report as "lower achieving" or "higher achieving," is based on teacher assessment, student self-assessment, and my observations over the course of the school year. Race/ethnicity is recorded as it was self-reported by the participants.
8 Substantiated by interview and observational data.

Bibliography

Allen, S. (1991) Ability-grouping research reviews: what do they say about grouping and the gifted? *Educational Leadership*, 7(1–2): 75–94.

Bigelow, B. (1992) Getting off the track: stories from an untracked classroom. *Rethinking Schools*, 7(4): 1, 18–20.

Bourdieu, P. (1977) Cultural reproduction and social reproduction. In: J. Karabel and A.H. Halsey (Eds), *Power and Ideology in Education*. New York: Oxford University Press.

Bower, B., Lobdell, J. and Swenson, L. (1999) *History Alive! Engaging All Learners in the Diverse Classroom*. Palo Alto, CA: Teachers Curriculum Institute.

Bowles, S. and Gintis, H. (1976) *Schooling in Capitalist America*. New York: Basic Books, Inc.

Brewer, D., Rees, D. and Argys, L. (1995) Detracking America's schools: the reform without cost? *Phi Delta Kappan*, 77(6): 442–4.

Cohen, E. (1986) *Designing Groupwork: Strategies for the Heterogeneous Classroom*. New York: Teachers College Press.

Cone, J. (1992) *Untracking AP English: Creating Opportunity is not Enough*. Berkeley, CA: National Center for the Study of Writing and Literacy.

Cooper, R. (1996) Detracking reform in an urban California high school: improving the schooling experiences of African American students. *Journal of Negro Education*, 65(2): 190–208.

Delpit, L. (1988) The silenced dialogue: power and pedagogy in educating other people's children. *Harvard Educational Review*, 58(3): 280–98.

Feldhusen, J. (1991) Susan Allen set the record straight: response to Allen. *Educational Leadership*, 48(6): 66.

Fine, M., Weis, L. and Powell, L. (1997) A critical look at desegregated spaces created for and by youth. *Harvard Educational Review*, 67(2): 247–84.

Gallagher, J. (1995) Comments on "The reform without cost." *Phi Delta Kappan*, 77(6): 216.

Gamoran A. (1992) Synthesis of research: is ability grouping equitable? *Educational Leadership*, 50(2): 11–13.

Goodlad, J. and Oakes, J. (1988) We must offer equal access to knowledge. *Educational Leadership*, February: 16–22.

Kulik, J. (1991) Findings on grouping are often distorted. *Educational Leadership*, 48(6): 67.

Ladson-Billings, G. (1992) Liberatory consequences of literacy: a culturally relevant instruction for African American students. *Journal of Negro Education*, 61(3).

Marsh, R. and Raywid, M. (1994) How to make detracking work. *Phi Delta Kappan*, 76(4): 314–17.

Mehan, H. (1992) Understanding inequality in schools: the contribution of interpretive studies. *Sociology of Education*, 65: 1–20.

Mehan, H. (1996) *Constructing School Success: The Consequences of Untracking Low Achieving Students*. Cambridge: Cambridge University Press.

Mehan, H., Hubbard, L. and Villanueva, I. (1994) Forming academic identities: accommodation without assimilation among involuntary minorities. *Anthropology and Education Quarterly*, 25(2): 91–117.

Morrow, R. and Torres, C. (1994) Education and the reproduction of class, gender, and race: responding to the postmodern challenge. *Educational Theory*, 44(1): 43–61.

Murphy, J. and Hallinger, P. (1989) Equity as access to learning: curricular and instructional treatment differences. *Journal of Curriculum Studies*, 21(2): 129–49.

Noguera, P. (1995) Ties that bind, forces that divide: Berkeley High School and the challenge of integration. *University of San Francisco Law Review*, 29(3): 719–40.

Oakes, J. (1985) *Keeping track*. New Haven: Yale University Press.

Oakes, J. (1986) Beyond tracking. *Educational Horizons*, (65)1: 32–5.

Oakes, J. (1992) Detracking schools: early lessons from the field. *Phi Delta Kappan*, 73(6): 448–54.

Oakes, J. (1993) Reply: untracking evidence is there for the taking. *Educational Leadership*, (51) 2: 81.

Oakes, J., Wells, A., Jones, M. and Datnow, A. (1997) Detracking: the social construction of ability, cultural politics, and resistance to reform. *Teachers College Record*, 98(3): 482–510.

Page, J.A. and Pool, H. (Eds) (1995) *Beyond Tracking*. Bloomington, IN: Phi Delta Kappa Educational Foundation.

Page, R. (1987) Lower-track classes at a college-preparatory high school: a caricature of educational encounters. In: G. Spindler and L. Spindler (Eds), *Interpretative Ethnography of Education: At Home and Abroad*. Mahwah, NJ: Lawrence Erlbaum Associates, 91–117.

Pavan, B. (1993) Reply: Scott fails to discredit nongradedness. *Educational Leadership*, 51(2): 85.

Scott, R. (1993) Untracking advocates make incredible claims. *Educational Leadership*, 29(4): 79–83.

Slavin, R. (1988) Synthesis of research on grouping in elementary and secondary schools. *Educational Leadership*, 46(1): 64–77.

Slavin, R. (1991) Are cooperative learning and "untracking" harmful to the gifted? *Educational Leadership*, 48(6): 68–71.

Slavin, R. (1995) Detracking and its detractors: flawed evidence, flawed values. *Phi Delta Kappan*, 77(3): 220–1.

Wells, A. and Serna, I. (1996) The politics of culture: understanding local political resistance to detracking in racially mixed schools. *Harvard Educational Review*, 66(1): 93–118.

Wheelock, A. (1992) *Crossing the Tracks: How "Untracking" Can Save America's Schools*. New York: New Press.

Yonezawa, S., Wells, A. and Serna, I. (2002) Choosing tracks: freedom of choice in detracking schools. *American Educational Research Journal*, 39(1): 37–67.

Chapter 3

"There's not really discussion happening"

Students' experiences of identity-based curricular reform

Alicia P. Rodriguez

While schools at all levels have relatively recently rebuilt themselves to address the increasing diversity of US society, Franklin High began steps in this direction long before other institutions. During the late 1960s, 1970s, and again in the 1990s, Franklin High instituted identity-based/"multicultural" curricula in response to the demands of students who believed they were underrepresented in the academic curriculum. Hence, Afro-American Studies, Chicano/a Studies, Women's Studies, Asian American Studies, and Ethnic Studies courses were offered at Franklin High. These courses and programs were intended to fill large holes in the standard curricula and also help improve the achievement of traditionally underserved students, namely, African Americans and Latino/as.[1] These programs were seen as possible remedies to the low self-esteem and achievement of these students. A general Ethnic Studies course that dealt with all of the ethnic groups in the US was made a requirement for graduation. Women's Studies and the remaining ethnic studies courses, such as African American Economics, African American Literature, Asian American History, and Introduction to La Raza History, were electives. The genesis of these programs began in 1969 during the fervor around identity politics with the creation of the African American Studies Department, and some of the programs have been revived and reformed in the current second wave of identity politics around issues of multiculturalism, difference, identity, and cultural diversity.

While students initiated the reform movements that led to these programs, the programs have not since been re-examined. The courses remain almost in the same form as they were conceived in the 1970s. Based on a one-year ethnographic study of an Ethnic Studies, Asian American Studies, and Women's Studies class, this chapter examines what students thought of these programs, the correspondence between the curriculum and students' senses of identity, and how the programs related to the achievement gap at this institution. The students who are the focus of the study comprise a broad range of ethnicities (White, African American,

Chinese American, Mexican American, African American/Mexican American, Ethiopian, Indian, etc.), ages, and social class backgrounds. From the point of view of the students, the study asks us to consider how schools can address the multiplicity of human diversity through curriculum without both stereotyping and over-emphasizing difference.

For the most part, the students considered the courses to be potentially rewarding and relevant to their lives; however, some felt that the complexity of their identities was not represented in the course content. Students were most critical of the Ethnic Studies class for its simplification of important issues and tendency to perpetuate ethnic stereotypes. As for the impact of the programs on achievement, most students found that the ethnic programs did not bolster the achievement of African American and Latino/a students; that is, learning about one's ethnic/racial group does not always boost self-esteem and achievement. One would think that such programs would not only heighten the self-esteem of students of color, but would also encourage their academic success and intellectual engagement. Rather, it appears that some of these courses were not having a positive effect on the academic performance and aspirations of students of color. They are examples of "multicultural" curricular reforms commonly seen throughout the nation's schools that focus on a narrow identity politics and ignore the issues of student engagement, academic performance, intellectual learning, and critical thinking.

The school site and the identity courses

Demographically, Franklin High looks like many large urban high schools. Of the 3,124 students at the time of this study (1998–9), 40 per cent were White, 36 per cent were African American, 10 per cent were Latino, 10 per cent were Asian American, 3 per cent were interracial, and 1 per cent were of other ethnicities. The majority of the White and Asian American students came from middle class and above families and the majority of the Latino and African American families came from lower middle class and below families. Franklin High is the only public high school in a northern California city of 100,000 people. Consistently, 85 per cent of graduates have gone to college, many with Advanced Placement (AP) credit. The school was and remains the epitome of "the shopping mall high school" characterized by Powell, Farrar, and Cohen (1985) where students self-schedule and vie for choice teachers, drop and add courses almost at will, bypass course requirements with their parents' help, and can enroll in one of several academies/small schools if so desired. During the 1998–9 school year, the school offered almost 200 courses. The courses ranged from the traditional, such as, Geometry, English, United States History, and French, to the untraditional, such as, African American Journalism, Contemporary

La Raza History, Documentary Video Production, Ecoliteracy, Kiswahili, and The Bible as Literature. AP classes were 85 per cent White and Asian American and the lowest tracked classes were 85 per cent African American and Latino. Furthermore, the grades of D and F were three times higher among African American and Latino students than among Whites. The result of this tracking and racial disparity in achievement was the perception that while there were numerous options available to students, the options were dependent on one's race and class background and other factors, such as high educational expectations from parents and others, that are related to high academic achievement.

Throughout the 1998 Fall semester I spent at least three days a week observing two of Ms Thompson's[2] Ethnic Studies classes. I also interviewed Ms Thompson and students from one of her classes. The students represented a broad range of ethnicities. Ms Thompson is a young African American teacher who had been teaching at Franklin High since 1997. Ethnic Studies was a graduation requirement that is usually taken freshman year. I held individual interviews that were audiotaped with seven students from one of the classes (five females and two males). Two students were Chinese American,[3] one was Chinese, one was African American, one was White, one was Mexican American, and one was Egyptian American/ White.

During Spring semester 1999, I spent on average three days a week in Ms Simmons[4] Women's Studies class, observing, participating, and inter- viewing students. Women's Studies is an elective that is usually taken by upperclassmen. Ms Simmons is a young White teacher who was in her first year teaching in Franklin High. All but one student in the class was female. I interviewed eleven students from the class, including the only male. The group was fairly ethnically diverse: three Whites, three African Americans, two Ethiopians, two biracial students (White/Mexican Ameri- can and White/Haitian), and one Mexican American. Also during the Spring I spent two to three days a week in Ms Chen's[5] Asian American History class. Asian American History is an elective that is mostly taken by upperclassmen and Asian American students. At the time I was observing the class, all of the students were of Asian descent, except for one White, one African American/White, one Latina, and one Latina/ African American student. Ms Chen is of Chinese/Japanese ancestry. She is a veteran teacher who had been teaching for more than ten years and had been teaching Asian American History since the second year of its re- emergence.[6] Unlike Ethnic Studies, the Asian American History class was tailored to upperclassmen. I interviewed nine students from the class (five males and four females). Three students were biracial (African American/ White, Mexican American/African American, and Japanese/White), two Chinese American, one Chinese, one Indian, one Laotian, and one Viet- namese American.

The mixed roles of identity courses

Ethnic Studies was a much maligned course that many students were critical of:

> Ethnic Studies is just a weird class. Since Franklin High is one of the only schools that has that, isn't it? It's not required for colleges, but we still have it. And it is required for graduation. Like, I would not have felt comfortable expressing an opinion in that class, I don't think. Because being a freshman, like, I'd just come to Franklin High and there's all these people who, like, seniors who'd been there and they could really just dominate the conversation. So that was kind of a wasted class. That's just a not very well run thing at Franklin High, even though it's a requirement. I remember one assignment. We were talking about stereotypes. But instead of, like, breaking them down, she was, like, "O.K., name a bunch of stereotypes you've heard." And then it just, like, degenerated into a class and race warfare in the class. And we didn't, like, break them down. We just sort of, like, said them. It didn't work at all ... There's not really discussion happening, because you don't feel comfortable, like, actually discussing things.

Students, like the one quoted above, expressed again and again how many of the identity courses at Franklin treated complex concepts like race and ethnicity in very simplistic ways, thus not advancing the conversation on identity in ways that resonated with their lived realities. For many, living with diversity and the prejudices that come with it was a given and not unusual. Furthermore, they did not see that learning about race, diversity, and discrimination changed the attitudes of the majority of students. As an Asian American female saw it,

> I think with, like, the classes and everything, that people get to address their identity and people get to learn about the struggles of other people of color, or of people of color in general. I think that's a definite plus, because it's these things that'll help people get ahead that'll feel less alienated or less excluded. I think that the reason why I felt like sometimes race is too much is because that even though we learned about the stereotypes, it sometimes seems like that people aren't really listening in class, that they're not really getting it. Because people are still getting shoved in the halls [because of racism] ... First of all, I notice a lot of people are, like, "Ah, god! Whatever! Ethnic studies!" I think it's because it's almost like they're forced to take it. Because if they want to graduate, they have to take it ... I'm not sure what they really feel, but my opinion is that the reason why they're not just getting the message, don't care anymore, whatever, is because, like, like, all

their lives living here and being surrounded by different people, and so they're kind of, like, it's a natural thing. Like, "Yeah, whatever, you know. Yeah. We're people of color. So?"

The previous criticisms of Ethnic Studies were echoed by many of the interviewed students. Issues of race and racism were the centerpiece of the class, yet discussed so superficially that serious study of the concepts did not occur. As a student I interviewed said, "Everything was touched on the surface. We didn't really go deep into anything." A White male senior believed that there was a tendency to use simplistic binaries to teach about issues, such as discrimination and social history, that are more complex than they are constructed by the teacher:

What always happens is there's, like, a bad guy and a good guy. Or someone's being oppressed and someone's the oppressor. And there's never, it's never completely like that. It's not that clear cut. If it was that clear cut, these problems wouldn't exist in the first place. So, it's taking the easy way out, a lot of the time. And I think a lot of the kids, every kid deserves better than that.

While teachers of these courses meant well, one of the difficulties in teaching a survey course like Ethnic Studies is that there is the danger of treating histories and concepts superficially. Ms Thompson recognized this problem and acknowledged her lack of knowledge about different ethnic histories and felt that a year-long course would allow her to treat topics more thoroughly. She was not able to deepen the conversation on ethnicity as she would have liked. She believed that the course schedule placed limitations on the intellectual depth of the class. Ms Thompson and other Ethnic Studies teachers were told by the principal to make the class more rigorous because parents, students, teachers, and others had complained about the class. Many of the students I interviewed felt that the course should be more rigorous and less prone to the simplistic politically correct treatments. A year after the study, the course was overhauled.

While many of the American students were all too aware of the politics of ethnic identity in the United States, other students were unfamiliar with it. Many of the immigrant students I interviewed raised the concern that the American obsession with race and difference, as seen in the school, the media, and other public forums, is foreign to them. Because many of these students came from countries where they were the racial majority, they could not fully understand, until they had lived in the United States for several years, how race marked their identity. This was especially the case for the immigrant students of color. An Ethiopian female student in the Asian American History class explained her experience:

Race hasn't been that much important to me, because back home everyone is the same. Everyone looks the same. I mean, you never feel different from anybody, because everyone's the same. Just like everybody. Race is not the issue for anybody back home, but class is, kind of, is important. But here it's, like, race is also important and class is important and gender is important. When I first moved here I was, like, I saw everybody just like human because that's how we were seen back home, you know. People, like, don't treat you differently because your skin is light or dark or stuff like that … But I think the whole country kind of tries to give attention to all races and, you know, different cultures. So it's not really a huge deal. It doesn't matter, I guess.

As a Black female in US society, she understood what race meant. But she still maintained her Ethiopian identity and sensibilities above all else. Ms Chen attempted to incorporate multiple realities within the distinct Asian ethnic groups that she taught about, despite the homogenizing tendencies of the mainstream. Another student believed that one of the strengths of the Asian American History class was learning about the diversity between and within Asian groups and "what is an Asian American. How they are all perceived and how they actually are I think is very interesting." But, like the Ethiopian girl, he also believed that there were problems with the panethnicity of the Asian American label:

I think it's a stupid title. Let's say somebody from India compared to somebody from Japan is just as different as somebody from Germany as is somebody from South America, like somebody from Chile is so different from me, that the title "Asian American," I don't like it.

He recognized what many ethnic studies educators fail to recognize or teach; that there is much more diversity within ethnic and racial groups than is expressed in identity discourses.

The issue of cultural identification and the essentialism that often comes with identities such as Asian American, African American, Latino, and even "woman," for that matter, is ever present in the popular discourse around identity. Neither Franklin High nor scholars who tackle this problem have provided satisfactory tips for how to live with these constructs that are both helpful and harmful. Students felt that some of the identity courses tended to perpetuate unitary constructs of race and ethnicity that glossed over difference within racial groups and their experiences with race and ethnicity. Nevertheless, many found a course like Ethnic Studies to be valuable, especially if it were to be severely restructured and taught to upperclassmen rather than freshmen. In the next section I will discuss the politics of education at Franklin High and how, to a certain degree, the Ethnic Studies course and other similar courses promoted a politics of identity that had changed very little since the 1970s.

The passions of teachers and students: are they the same?

While identity politics tended to be dominant at the school, the numerous political/ethnic forums and protests did not consolidate most students into people who were committed to social justice issues and acted on their commitments. You did not see many student organizations or hear conversations among students that concerned social justice issues. Many multicultural education proponents who promote the social transformation component of multicultural education assume that students are just as concerned with social justice as their progressive teachers (see Giroux, 1992, 1994; Kanpol and McLaren, 1995; McLaren, 1997; Sleeter, 1991; Sleeter and McLaren, 1995). Rather, I saw much apathy from students who had teachers, like Ms Thompson and Ms Simmons, who were highly impassioned about social justice issues and attempted to motivate their students to be equally impassioned. Some students expressed criticism of the political passions of their teachers.

For example, some of the female students who took the Women's Studies course, taught by a teacher who was a self-proclaimed feminist, were resistant to labeling themselves "feminist":

> In one of my classes in English, it had a question to do with feminism and the girl was like, "I don't want to sound like a feminist or anything, but …" Like it was such a put-down. Like she was thinking, "don't think I'm a feminist, because I'm not, like, stupid."

Another Women's Studies student echoed the common fear of the feminist label:

> … when people talked about, like, feminism and women's issues, it seemed like I don't want to be part of that because I don't want to seem like I'm … It kind of felt bad to be trying to say that I'm a feminist because it seems kind of looked down on. There's kids in high school that are really, like, pro-feminism and really active and stuff. And it's not, like, whatever, you're just doing that, or it's not really important, but the class made me see that it sort of was. And that feeling wasn't my feeling. It wasn't like a natural response.

In probing her about whether she considered herself a feminist, she responded,

I don't really still even know what that means, sort of. But I'm definitely unhappy with how women are treated, and a lot of the problems. And if anyone said they were concerned about it, I wouldn't devalue them and I'd say I was [a feminist], a little bit now.

Both students were fearful of claiming a powerful identity for fear of what their peers would think of them. They implied that to their peers and maybe to themselves as well, being a feminist meant being a militant, a man-hater, and, perhaps, even a lesbian. None of those identities was popular among students.

Such resistance to a politically progressive identity may indicate that while the liberal ethic was prevalent at Franklin High, the more radical passions of many teachers may not have been shared by many or even some of the students. A Latina student I interviewed was particularly critical of her political Chicano/Latino Studies teacher:

She's really political, and to her that's being proud. And to be who you are means standing up and, like, fighting for, like, equality and things. But, I mean, I respect that about her, but to me that's not what it is to be proud. Like, you don't have to be political and, like, involved in issues and stuff. Just being who I am and being how I was raised is, like, that's good enough. She wants to get you mad about all the injustices and everything. But I'm not into that.

In some ways this student echoed the desires of the mainstream student who is socially aware but does not want to make any waves. They espouse the view, "Be proud of your ethnic background or your gender, but don't feel you always have to wear it on your sleeve." As a new Asian American student, who was also a political activist, described it,

I think Franklin High is a rare school. I don't know. It's hard to explain. There are a lot of people who are, like, they're so used to the liberal atmosphere that they're kind of sick of it. And there's a lot of other people that are, like, "Oh, Ethnic Studies. What a waste of time." But they still support Ethnic Studies. I think that they just think their class is a waste of time, but they support the whole idea.

A few years ago Ms Chen realized that she may have been influenced by the political progressivism of the institution and uncritically extolled the virtues of communism when teaching about Vietnam. A Vietnamese student made her realize that communism may look wonderful conceptually, but in reality it was imperfect and problematic. This made Ms Chen rethink how she taught about Vietnam and Asian American History in general.

In many ways, although the rhetoric that was prevalent in the hallways of Franklin High was politically progressive and very different from what one sees in most public schools in the United States, in the end, the city and its public high school had become like any other city that is socio-economically and ethnically diverse and struggling with the clashing desires for desegregation and social justice on the part of some political progressives and for economic mobility and stability on the part of struggling people of color. But some believed, namely Whites, that the rhetoric leaned towards pride for ethnic heritage, namely that of people of color, at the expense of Whites. In many ways the ethnic identity classes served as a safe space for students of color. As one student said,

> I would kind of get the impression that people were kind of, like, the reason why they signed up wasn't so much to really learn something, but just to kind of be surrounded and feel safe with people of their race.

Unfortunately, sometimes these courses built a safe place and promoted ethnic pride by contrasting the marginalized group in question to a dominant, oppressive White group.

Some White students felt that the ethnic politics prevalent in the school and curriculum were based on "White bashing." One student felt that Ethnic Studies was:

> ... a class that just was there so that Franklin could keep its reputation of being ethnically diverse. It seemed to me that it was kind of a White bashing class. I did learn more about other cultures, though, which was probably the purpose of the class.

Ethnic Studies was known as "White-bashing 101." This is what a White male senior from Ethnic Studies had to say about the forums on the oppression of people of color that they attended as part of the curriculum:

> I left all those with a really sour taste in my mouth. Just like, God, I learned a few just obscure facts and got this underlying message, not even subtle, it's really blatant. It's just like, "Whites are screwing you. Whites are the enemy – White government, White everything, White corporate America, just White males." I can't help but feel that those forums are just really doing a disservice to some of these kids, because you give them, you know, this victimology stuff. And you want to hear that. You want to hear that I'm having problems because of someone else, because you don't want to blame yourself.

Such a tendency to teach about cultural differences and systems of power in this simplistic way was something that many of the students I spoke with objected to. A Latina female senior from Ms Thompson's class said,

> When we talk about the immigration experience, it just talks about the negative things that they went through and everything. And, that kind of gets tiring, because, O.K., I know what they went through. Now tell me what good have they done. You know? I want to know how they've impacted this society and everything. What are the positive things? I want to know that. It's mostly negative things, complaining, or something, about how they're treated. You learn more of the bad part, the bad side.

The emphasis on negativity within the Ethnic Studies courses and people of color victimology were things that most students found problematic. This needs to be considered in evaluating these curricular programs that have been an institution within the school for decades but that were not having the intended effects of boosting self-esteem, achievement, and ethnic understanding.

Unlike the required Ethnic Studies class that was tailored for freshmen and thus lacked the depth that the upperclassmen desired, courses like Women's Studies and African American History tended to attract students who were already interested in the subject and had the sensitivities that these courses nurtured. As an Asian American female said,

> I think a lot of people who actually sign up for these classes are interested in them and they're already aware of the issues, kind of, so it's not really opening up minds, or opening up ideas to other people.

Others wanted more from the class. A White male senior in the Ethnic Studies class read the epic novel, *Roots*, in his spare time to supplement his knowledge rather than take an African American Studies class. He found that *Roots* had a greater impact on him than what he learned in class. In contrast, a Women's Studies student learned much in her class and was profoundly impacted by what she had learned:

> It's made me a lot more aware of certain things. Like that section we did on the media has made me a lot more aware of all of the things that go around me every day that I'd never noticed before. And, also, I'm a lot more aware of the struggles that women have gone through to get where we are today … Since it's meant for older people, it's a lot different, because everyone there is a lot more articulate and they express their ideas a lot more willingly and they all have great things to say.

The students suggested that because Women's Studies and Asian American History were tailored to upperclassmen and had a narrower focus (i.e. women and Asian Americans as opposed to all ethnic groups), these courses were more effective and less problematic than Ethnic Studies.

Effects of identity courses on achievement

> I think a lot of Black people in Franklin High, a lot of Black people in general don't have faith in themselves. They just don't. Like, oftentimes I'm in classes where there's me and, like, three other Black people, if even that. Usually in about four of my classes there's just one. And in these other classes, a lot of them don't have any faith in themselves. They just don't. They'll sit up there and be, like, "I don't know. I don't know. I don't know." A lot of Black people and a lot of Chicano people, they give up easily and they don't have faith in themselves and they don't feel the environment is inviting to them. They just don't. Most of the time when you're in a challenging class you're in a room full of White people, anyway. So you walk into the class and you're, like, "There's all these White people, and they don't talk like me. They don't look like me. They don't act like me at all."

In Ms Thompson's class, all but one of the students who failed the class were African American or Latino. The issue of Latino and African American students believing that it is not cool to be a bookworm because it goes against their ethnic identity is something that scholars have noted (Fordham, 1996; Fordham and Ogbu, 1986; Matute-Bianchi, 1986). However, considering some of the proud high achieving African American students I interviewed, this may not have applied to all high achieving African American and Latino students at Franklin. Ethnographic studies by Hemmings (1996) and Davidson (1996) show that there are African American and Latino high achievers who do not compromise their ethnic identity on their road to academic success. At every turn, they resist the message that because they are brown or black, they are expected to fail. Unfortunately, most Latino and African American students at Franklin High have succumbed to the low expectations. Based on the assessment of the student quoted above, the low achievement of many African American students came from giving up early and not taking on challenging situations.

An African American female senior from the Women's Studies class gave an explanation for the apathy among African American students and reasons why African American youth did not achieve as much as they could:

And now we can't even go and say, "Well, we're not learning anything about ourselves." You cannot say that. At Franklin High School you can't say that. 'Cause even AP classes there are Black people who are teaching some of the classes. We have "Patterns of Black Literature." I think that a lot of Black people in particular disconnect themselves from what they're learning and their actual life. They do not make the connection between the two. I think that Black people in general have lost or clouded their ability to think critically. Like in class, when we'll learn about the percentage of African Americans in jail or in prison, let's say, there would be Black people joking and laughing and not listening to what the teacher is saying when the teacher is directly talking about them. I think a lot of them lack the ability to think critically. They're not used to it. Not that it's not naturally there, because it's naturally there, it's just that they don't do it. And they don't sit there saying, "Damn, why did that happen?" I have no idea what to do about it, because all Black people are not in the same position. It's really easy to say Black people in a collective. But we're in such a diaspora that we're all in different positions as people and socially.

Another student of color, who is African American and Mexican American, echoed the above assessment, but suggested other reasons for the apathetic attitudes of Latino and African American students:

Maybe one of the reasons why they don't do well in the classes that are supposedly for them anyways, maybe one of the reasons is the study habits already that they had. You're not gonna get into a class and then be, like, "Oh, wow, I'm learning about all of this," and then organize yourself. You know? It's also what you're experiencing in your home, like, in your community. No matter what class you're taking, if you have to go home and worry about if your mother is going to be there or if she's gonna flash on you when you get home and start screaming at you for no reason or being, like, high. You know? Or if you're gonna get kicked out at night or how are you gonna get money to eat for the next day, which is a lot. Not everybody, of course, but a lot of people of color have to deal with different things, different circumstances. They have different circumstances that they have to deal with than most White people that are even taking the class. Like, they're taking it so they can be well-rounded people. Maybe it's the teachers and the curriculum. Maybe some of the teachers aren't good and motivating.

The above comment begs the question, are the identity courses relevant to the lived experiences of the students of color at Franklin High? If not, how can these curricula be altered to directly relate to the experiences of the students? The student also recognized that many students of color simply need to learn study skills and be given clear indications of what is expected to succeed academically. Educational reformers need to consider that rich curricula, as exist at Franklin High, need to be accompanied by academic and life skill lessons. Identity courses on their own are not the panacea, the equity pill that many believe them to be. They do not always raise the self-esteem and achievement of students of color. Many forces outside the home and experiences of persistent failure in school contribute to the despair and apathy that is so prevalent among African American and Latino youth.

Beyond the role of the teachers or the students of color in reinforcing notions of what students of color can and cannot achieve, students of color who took academically demanding classes where they were the minority faced a sort of achievement ceiling. In many respects this ceiling, whether real or imagined, was institutionalized, that is, it was a part of the structure of the curriculum and school. It is as if the Advanced Placement classes were coded as "White" and the ethnic-specific courses were coded as "of color." Students of color quickly learned that the Advanced Placement courses were not for them. As an Ethiopian student explained,

> I don't see that much crossing over. I don't, because I've been here [in the United States] for four years. If there was that kind of communi-cating, you wouldn't see, like, all of the Black students, most Black students taking not a lot of advanced classes. And at the same time you see all the White students taking a lot of advanced classes. Like, for me, I've had a lot of advanced classes. The class that I've been to there probably is, like, two Black persons, including myself, and I kind of feel left out in those classes. I don't feel I compete. Maybe, let's say, if the Black students and the White students were taking kind of the same classes, you'd probably see a lot of, like, you know, crossing over and stuff like that. I think the whole education plays a part in the school.

She explained how an advanced student like herself could lose confidence in her abilities in the White environment of an AP class. She also recognized the long-lasting relationship between race and achievement. She, like many students of color, found the road to achievement to be influenced by personal beliefs of ability and by the institutional barriers to achievement that are based on racial expectations.

Conclusion

According to the students, the Ethnic Studies course did not affect them greatly, perhaps because they lived in a highly politicized multicultural community and were already aware of the issues raised in the class. If anything, it is possible that the class may have reinforced where students were already at, so to speak, but did not make them question and radically challenge their identity and assumptions about identity. From what I observed, the critical social analysis of the many students quoted in this chapter was largely absent in many of the identity-based courses. Despite the criticisms of the identity courses, especially Ethnic Studies, students found some things of value in them, not the least being the elevation of social justice issues to a level of importance such that they became the basis of a class. The Asian American History and Women's Studies classes had more of an impact on students, perhaps because these courses were geared to upperclassmen and, hence, delved deeper into the issues. However, most of the students I interviewed felt that none of the classes they had taken had affected them personally and significantly.

Like detracking, which many consider to be the solution to the elimination of racial and social class patterns of academic achievement, a multicultural curriculum is also viewed as the solution to the educational marginalization of students of color. It is often assumed that multicultural curricula are the key to improving the achievement and achievement motivation of students of color because the curricula speak to their ethnic selves and, hence, boost self-esteem and achievement (Kanpol and McLaren, 1995; Nieto, 1996; Sleeter, 1991). However, as I have seen at Franklin High, this is not necessarily the case. Achievement among students of color still remains low despite the existence of these courses. One would think that a school like Franklin High, with courses and programs that exceed what is found in many colleges, would have achieved greater achievement diversity.

As the students commented, in order for identity-based curricula to have any positive impact on achievement they have to be supported by school-wide structures for success. As one student said, teachers are critical to such success:

> Our teachers are, most of them are idealistic and young and for that reason it's a bad thing sometimes because they don't really discipline you. You'll see this in test scores. We're very good at getting concepts. But you ask most students, you walk into any random class and you ask them, "What is the teacher talking about?" And they'll be able to explain the point and the gist of the class. But if you actually give them a test and ask them specifically, "what's this, what's this, what's this, what's this," they won't do very well. And that's kind of the result of the teachers being, like, "But are you getting the point?" The teachers are trying to make lessons that you digest and that you incorporate into your day-to-day thinking. History is not just history for them. History is how people should feel about themselves. And the kids get that, but they don't get the, "but I need to know the date of this."

As another student put it, a school that could learn how to "manifest each student's talents and feed them" would be ideal. Stanton-Salazar (1997) reminds us that school success "has never been simply a matter of learning and competently performing technical skills; rather, and more fundamentally, it has been a matter of learning how to decode the system" (p. 13), and "decoding the system" has always been more of a challenge to students of color than to White students.

Furthermore, as Ann Locke Davidson (1996) learned from the students who were involved in her study on the impact of sociocultural differences on school engagement, it is important to take

> ... a holistic rather than a particularistic approach to the democratiza-
> tion of school environments. Factors such as the patterns that emanate
> from academic tracking and the manner in which adults use power as
> they seek the attention of diverse pupils may work to strengthen or
> weaken conceptions about social differences, as well as subvert
> messages embedded within the explicit curriculum.
>
> (Davidson, 1996: 218)

When considering the role of curricula that attend to race, class, and gender issues, it has to be understood that there are limits to their effect. In a setting where expectations for school success are based on race and class, such curricula cannot be expected to single-handedly correct all of the ills, omissions, and failures of the school. But in concert with other structures for educational excellence, the benefits of such curricula are limitless.

For some students, the effects of such an education can be profound:

> Ethnic Studies is a class, but it's more of a feeling that you get. After
> taking that class I started to get that feeling. It makes me really sad
> when things are unfair and people are getting discriminated. Anything
> that has to do with people of color getting somewhere now really
> touches me, because it's never really been addressed for me. But also
> because people of color have been oppressed and that finally seeing
> some positive light on things makes me really happy. But also seeing
> really negative things makes me really sad that these things are still
> happening. And they're still happening because there's still stereotypes
> and there's still the structure that we have to fix.

A Women's Studies student gained the awareness of a shared reality with other women, simply due to the common experience of being a woman in contemporary society:

> I've never had a class like Women's Studies that made me realize that
> just 'cause I've never said it before, that doesn't mean that it didn't
> come from somewhere else, that it didn't come from an outside source.

Perhaps the most that can be expected from such courses is to raise the level of consciousness about social injustice and hope that some students will translate their knowledge into action, keeping in mind the limitations, institutional and otherwise, in the path toward change.

It can be argued that providing curricula on race, gender, ethnicity, and identity is good in itself, considering such omissions in mainstream curricula. It would be preferable to have these perspectives integrated throughout the curriculum. But given the resistance of many teachers to changing their curriculum, such stand-alone identity courses are valuable. As students explained, the general Ethnic Studies course discussed in this chapter was problematic, because depth was compromised over breadth and complexity over simplicity. But perhaps this was inevitable given that the course was intended for ninth graders and only one semester long. Nevertheless, many students I spoke with valued the intent of the course. Most of the Asian American History and Women's Studies students were intellectually challenged and personally affected by what they learned. This would be an achievement for any teacher – to profoundly impact the lives of students. When instituting educational reforms on behalf of race, class, and gender issues, schools may learn from students at Franklin High that a multicultural curriculum alone is not the panacea. But a good curriculum can help youth begin the process of self-awareness, cross-cultural understanding, and personal development.

Notes

1 Throughout the chapter, Latino/a is the preferred term used to describe Americans of Latin American descent, or Hispanic Americans. When appropriate, the specific binational term is used, such as Mexican American, Cuban American, etc. Recent immigrants who do not feel "American" or assimilated are identified with a specific Latin American national identity, such as Nicaraguan, Colombian, Puerto Rican, etc.
2 "Thompson" is a pseudonym.
3 In order to distinguish between students that identify themselves as being American or Americanized and those who are fairly recent immigrants, I attached the descriptor "American" to their ethnic identification.
4 "Simmons" is a pseudonym.
5 "Chen" is a pseudonym.
6 The Asian American Studies Program originated in the mid-1970s and was then phased out and re-emerged in the 1990s.

Bibliography

Davidson, A.L. (1996) *Making and Molding Identity in Schools: Student Narratives on Race, Gender, and Academic Engagement.* Albany: State University of New York Press.
Fordham, S. (1996) *Blacked Out: Dilemmas of Race, Identity, and Success at Capital High.* Chicago: University of Chicago Press.

Fordham, S. and Ogbu, J. (1986) Black students' school success: coping with the burden of "acting White." *Urban Review*, 19: 176–206.

Giroux, H.A. (1992) *Border Crossings*. New York: Routledge.

Giroux, H.A. (1994) Insurgent multiculturalism and the promise of pedagogy. In: D.T. Goldberg (Ed.), *Multiculturalism: A Critical Reader*. Oxford: Blackwell, 325–43.

Hemmings, A. (1996) Conflicting images? Being Black and a model high school student. *Anthropology and Education Quarterly*, 27(1): 20–50.

Kanpol, B. and McLaren, P. (Eds) (1995) *Critical Multiculturalism: Uncommon Voices in a Common Struggle*. Westport: Bergin and Garvey.

Matute-Bianchi, M.E. (1986) Ethnic identities and patterns of school success and failure among Mexican-descent and Japanese-American students in a California high school: an ethnographic analysis. *American Journal of Education*, 95(1): 233–55.

McLaren, P. (1997) *Revolutionary Multiculturalism: Pedagogies of Dissent for the New Millennium*. Boulder: Westview Press.

Nieto, S. (1996) *Affirming Diversity: The Sociopolitical Context of Multicultural Education*, second edition. New York: Longman.

Powell, A.G., Farrar, E. and Cohen, D.K. (1985) *The Shopping Mall High School: Winners and Losers in the Educational Marketplace*. Boston: Houghton-Mifflin.

Sleeter, C.E. (Ed.) (1991) *Empowerment Through Multicultural Education*. Albany: State University of New York Press.

Sleeter, C.E. and McLaren, P.L. (Eds) (1995) *Multicultural Education, Critical Pedagogy, and the Politics of Difference*. Albany: State University of New York Press.

Stanton-Salazar, R.D. (1997) A social capital framework for understanding the socialization of racial minority children and youths. *Harvard Educational Review*, 67(1): 1–40.

Chapter 4

Constructing and resisting a theory of difference

Student experiences in California's Single Gender Academies

Elisabeth L. Woody

Introduction

The last decade of educational reform is notable for the wide array of alter-native initiatives introduced in the public school system. Alongside the more nationally renowned charter school and voucher movements is a resurgence of interest in single-sex education. At this point, at least fifteen states have experimented with single-sex schooling, either in the form of all-girls or all-boys classes within a coed institution or as separate institutions. The Bush administration has recently brought national attention to the movement with a recent appropriation of funds to expand single-sex schooling in the public sector (Education Bill, 2002). In 1997, California's former Governor Pete Wilson introduced single-sex education into the public secondary school system through the funding of "Single Gender Academies," the largest experiment with public single-sex education to date. California's Single Gender Academies were proposed as a means to expand choice in the public sector and to address the perceived "different" needs of girls and boys (CA Education Code 58521).[1]

The recent interest in public single-sex education is perhaps all the more significant given the lack of conclusive data, with virtually no research conducted in public single-sex schools.[2] Indeed, the research conducted thus far reveals many more contradictions than patterns of commonality (AAUW, 1998). Existing research on single-sex schooling tends to employ quantitative approaches, using student outcome measurements (standard-ized test scores, grades, career aspirations) to assess its effectiveness as compared to coeducational environments (Lee and Bryk, 1986; LePore and Warren, 1997). While these measurements are important to consider, they provide little attention to the complexities of students' experiences. Until now, we have had little knowledge of social and cultural elements of students' experiences of single-sex schooling.

The introduction of the Single Gender Academies in California led to the use of gender as a category to define and organize students' academic and social lives. Gender became a marker of students' identity, and in many cases was assumed to be a reliable predictor of student behavior. Any school reform that highlights gender as a significant marker of identity must consider the implications of such a policy on students' lives. Girls and boys attending the Single Gender Academies were no longer merely "students," but were systematically defined by gender. How students respond to, interpret, and act upon those definitions is of central relevance to educators.

Relying primarily on student voices, this research challenges assumptions of gender in the context of public school reform, pushing educators to see commonalities in girls' and boys' experiences, as well as complexities among boys and among girls. In an effort to move beyond an analysis of gender differences, this research considers "gender practices" within the Single Gender Academies. As Eder explains,

> While studies of gender differences often imply more similarity within gender groups than actually exists, a focus on gendered practices helps us better understand the systematic processes through which both girls and boys are socialized to have distinct concerns, values, and styles of acting.
>
> (1997: 93)

Beyond simply a study of single-sex education, this research brings considerations of gender into discussions of school reform and has implications for raising awareness of students' gendered experiences across school contexts. This research was driven by an interest in how students' experiences were influenced by the event of public single-sex schooling, as well as how students used the single-sex environment to establish, maintain, and challenge ideologies of gender within the shifting contexts of their daily lives. Those contexts include institutional (including the structure and discipline of the schools), relational (including teacher-student and peer interactions), and individual (including students' personal ideologies and sense of identity).

Organizing students by gender presumed gender as the central element of identity in students' lives and promoted a dichotomous theory of gender in which boys' and girls' differences were made paramount to any commonalities. However, our conversations with students revealed far greater complexity, often challenging educators' assumptions about gender and single-sex education. Students challenged static notions of gender, actively constructing definitions of masculinity and femininity to suit the shifting contexts of their lives. Within the single-sex classrooms, for example, incidents of "girl talk" and "boy talk" allowed for a strengthening of gender identity in opposition to the other. Yet in discussions of personal experiences, students insisted on a more fluid definition of gender to accommodate a sense of agency and individual complexity. By listening to students in the Single Gender Academies, we learn that a public school reform based on a single aspect of identity may not accommodate the complex and often contradictory lives of students.

Project overview

In an effort to initiate public single-sex schooling in California, districts were invited to submit proposals for the creation of one girls' and one boys' academy within the same school site. Each district would receive $500,000 – a significant amount of money for a state-funded reform effort – for the start-up and continuation of the academies for two years, with the expectation that the academies would become self-sufficient after that time.[3]

The twelve resulting Single Gender Academies (six girls' and six boys' academies in six participating districts) represent the largest incidence of single-sex schooling within the public sector since the passing of Title IX in 1972.[4] Most recent efforts have been criticized and eventually shut down. California was quick to realize that any attempt to provide separate schooling would have to be offered equally to boys and girls. Therefore, the legislation explicitly called for "equal access to the schools," and required that for "all aspects of the curricula, the educational opportunity must be equal for boys and girls" (CA Education Code 58522).

The establishment of "equal" academies for boys and girls at one school site provided a unique dimension for research. Most single-sex institutions serve only males or only females, thus limiting researchers' ability to consider the experiences of both girls and boys within the same school.[5] This chapter draws on interviews with both boys and girls to provide a more complete understanding of student articulations of gender. The event of single-sex education also allowed for discussion of gender issues that might otherwise be a challenge in interviews with adolescents (e.g. Martin, 1996). Growing out of conversations about the single-sex environment, both boys and girls offered insight into issues of gender and sexuality. Students articulated an awareness of societal expectations for boys' and girls' behavior, as well as an awareness of the complexities of gender as exhibited in their own lives.

This chapter draws on one of the first comprehensive studies of public single-sex schooling in the US to date (Datnow et al., 2001). Qualitative data from over 300 interviews with students, teachers, administrators, and parents, conducted during three years of site visits, provide insight into adolescent articulations of gender within the context of single-sex public schooling.[6] This research adds the necessary layers of complexity to existing quantitative data, offering insight into assumptions of gender embedded within teaching and disciplinary practices, and in teacher and peer relations within the Single Gender Academies.

More importantly, this chapter offers a unique look at public single-sex schooling from the perspective of a diverse student population, both girls and boys. The school sites include a rural, predominantly white, lower-class community, a suburban middle-class community, and several urban Latino and African American communities. There was a significant amount of racial and socioeconomic diversity among students at each of the academies (see Appendix). This is a key difference between this study and other studies of single-sex education, which have primarily been conducted in private or Catholic institutions.

The following discussion provides an analysis of themes that emerged throughout each academy, across race, class, and community. The themes discussed in this chapter are all the more significant given their salience across sites, representing a diversity of voices and contexts. At the center of the analysis are students' voices, challenging us to consider the complexities of single-sex schooling as public school reform.

Structuring difference

The Single Gender Academies promoted a theory of gender which highlighted differences between boys and girls. Assumptions of difference can be traced to the language used in the State's initial call for district proposals. The Single Gender Academy Pilot Program was designed to serve "those pupils of each gender who because of their unique educational needs will benefit from single gender education." Further, the State explained, the Single Gender Academies would "be tailored to the differing needs and learning styles of boys as a group and girls as a group" (CA Education Code 58521). Not only were boys and girls presented as two separate groups, with separate needs, but those two groups were each seen as homogenous. Differences between boys and girls were highlighted, while intragroup differences were collapsed under the umbrellas of "girls as a group" and "boys as a group."

A "theory of difference" was further constructed through the teaching practices in the single gender classrooms. The physical separation of boys and girls led to a dichotomous understanding of gender, along with a heightened awareness of gender as a category to define students. Teachers who taught in both academies made comparisons between the academic performance and behavior of boys and girls, often to the dismay of students:

> They're always saying like why are you guys – like she's always comparing us to the guys ... I mean why she's comparing us to – if we're better at all these things and they're better at PE, I mean shouldn't she be happy or something?

At one school, a teacher called a meeting to tell the boys "how bad we are and that they're [the girls] doing a lot better than we are ... He was telling us that we have to get on the ball to keep up with the girls." Comparisons between girls and boys not only reinforced the assumption that boys and girls are inherently different, but also set up a dichotomy where girls were always "good" and boys were always "bad."[7] Students felt the comparisons between boys and girls were unfair, and more importantly, did not allow for shifts in behavior, as this boy explained: "We don't like that, just let us go the way we're going, and which, if we're bad one day, we might be good the next day." Students could not understand why their teachers insisted on setting up comparisons that created unnecessary competition between the sexes and did not allow for complexity among boys and among girls. Ultimately, a dichotomous framework of gender permeated the design of the academies, teacher expectations and classroom practices, and, inevitably, relationships among students.

Talking gender

Students, however, were not merely passive recipients of an institutional ideology, but played an active role in the creation and challenging of gendered assumptions. Girls and boys simultaneously constructed and resisted a theory of difference, in response to the shifting contexts of their lives. For example, patterns of discourse among students in the same-sex environments provided further justification for a theory of difference. Students recognized that the structure of the Single Gender Academies provided a certain freedom to discuss topics they felt were relevant only to boys or only to girls, where, for example, "we get to talk about what we want to because we're all boys." Incidents of what I call "girl talk" and "boy talk" are examples of "language routines," which Eder (1995) explains, "offered opportunities for adolescents to *collectively* create their own beliefs regarding gender and sexuality, or at least to challenge existing ones" (p. 151). Within the single-sex classrooms, students articulated a collective discourse grounded in the shared experiences of being all girls or all boys. Recognizing that this discourse only occurred in single-sex environments, students concluded that the bonds of shared interests were stronger among boys or among girls than between boys and girls.

It is important to note that the incidence of girl talk and boy talk was not entirely coincidental. As mentioned earlier, many teachers deliberately used the single-sex environment to initiate conversations that might otherwise not have occurred in a coed setting. At Pine, for example, girl talk was actually structured into the curriculum through the use of a program called Tribes. Accompanied by a workbook and a formal set of rules for discussion, "Tribes is like we talk about something real personal, and it doesn't go out of the room, and nobody discusses it." Clearly, this school felt a need to encourage such discussions with the girls; however, it was not made clear why a similar program was not implemented for the boys. Again, adults' assumptions about the specific needs and interests of boys and girls may have contributed to a heightened sense of difference between the sexes.

Not only were boys' and girls' interests assumed to be stereotypically different (e.g. boys were only interested in "sports and cars and stuff like that"), but they were perceived to be in direct opposition to each other, "because I think girls have a different mind than boys." Girl talk and boy talk strengthened students' sense of gender identity in opposition to the other:

I: Now, what about topics of discussion in class, um, tell me if there's any kind of conversation or discussion that would go on that would be specifically aimed at the fact that you're all boys?
ST: We won't talk about like hairspray "oh what kinda hairspray do you use," ... [everybody laughing] ...

Above all else, this boy defined boy talk as *not* girl talk, and girls similarly insisted that they would not discuss the same topics as boys. In her study of adolescent social structures, Eckert (1989) describes social divisions or "categories" which "represent ideologies and cultural forms that are variously adhered to by individuals and groups" (p. 18–19). An important element of Eckert's categories is their oppositional relation, as members of each category define themselves against the other. Similar to Eckert's "jocks" and "burnouts," academy students defined the categories of "boys" and "girls" through an oppositional discourse.

Students formulated a theory of difference based on patterns of mixed gender discourse as well. An underlying theme in students' discussions of boy talk and girl talk was that the Single Gender Academies provided a space where they did not have to compromise to accommodate the other sex. Following the logic that boys and girls held different interests, students felt their conversations were limited in coed situations. Girls in particular appreciated the chance to pursue gender-specific topics that would otherwise not occur in coed settings:

ST: I don't think that the guys would like it, you know, I don't think they're
    ...
ST: I don't think they would bring in speakers just for girls and talk about girls ...
I: Like if you had someone come in and she was like an astronaut, and she's a woman.
ST: No, they wouldn't be interested.
I: And she said, well, this is what it took for me to get to be an astronaut and there aren't a lot of women who are astronauts, but I'm an astronaut and this is how I did it. Do you think the boys would be like ...

ST: No, they would think it was so boring.
I: Would you be interested?
ST: Yeah.

Regardless of whether these girls thought a female guest speaker would be interesting, they recognized that the presence of boys limited their discussions, assuming that boys would never be interested in the same topics as girls. Ironically, while students perceived girl talk and boy talk to be oppositional discourses, I found a great overlap in the content and the purpose of those conversations. Girl talk and boy talk consisted primarily of discussions around personal issues, such as dating or family relations. Both girls and boys used the single gender discussions to solicit advice from teachers and to share concerns with peers, "to talk about things that were important to us, like our dreams, and stuff ... without being made fun of."

Students noted restrictions on cross-gender discourse based not only in a perceived lack of shared interests, but also due to experiences of discomfort. Both boys and girls expressed a strong sense of embarrassment around each other, often the result of teasing and verbal harassment in coed classrooms. Across all academies, students agreed that the single-sex classrooms provide the opportunity for discussions about "girl stuff" and "boy stuff" without fear of embarrassment or ridicule from the opposite sex:

> You're more open ... if you don't feel right about something you'll just say it, you won't be like ashamed of what a girl might think about it, like oh, he's dumb, you know, immature. You're more like, ok, you know, you tell how you feel.

The safety of the single gender classrooms provided further justification for student assumptions of gender differences as, again, the presence of the other sex was seen as a hindrance to open dialogue.

"They're just the opposite sex": relating to difference

Perhaps more disturbing than embarrassment were the feelings of distrust that boys and girls expressed about each other. Conversations between members of the same sex were perceived to be safer than those between boys and girls. The girls in this interview explained how they would not feel as comfortable sharing "personal stuff" in a coed situation, not only because of embarrassment, but also because they did not trust the boys to keep their secrets:

ST: 'Cause then you wouldn't be ... like you wouldn't be saying as much as personal stuff 'cause girls can understand better than boys, and if you said that in the boys, and you know, the boys would be like, eww.

ST: They won't understand, and then they would be like saying all to their friends, you know, about the girls.

ST: I have a lot of guy friends, but if I was to talk ... if I had a choice of talking to him about something personal, I wouldn't. I would never tell him.

ST: 'Cause they would like make fun of us and spread it around.

Boys' and girls' distrust of each other was largely connected to assumptions of difference. Embedded in these assumptions of difference were essentialist notions of gender. An exercise at Pine, for example, revealed an adherence to stereotypical definitions. We invited students to describe the qualities of men and women. While certain characteristics, like "intelligence," were shared, the lists describing men consistently included "strong," "plays sports well," "brave," and "big and buff." The lists for women included "pretty," "cute," "they like to keep their weight down," and "she's got to look fit." Students, in a sense, reiterated an institutional gender reasoning through an essentialist theory of difference.

Students felt that boys' and girls' differences precluded them from understanding, and thus respecting, one another on the same level as their same-sex peers:

Yeah. Because if a girl hears a rumor about you she's going to know how you feel because if that rumor was said about her she would feel the same way. So she wouldn't go around doing all this stuff. But then if a guy hears a rumor about a girl he'll go tell all his buddies and stuff because he doesn't really know how it feels to a girl to have something said about you like that.

Both boys and girls consistently told us that their same-sex friendships were stronger, based on a heightened sense of trust and shared experiences. The perceived inability to relate based on differences limited the potential of the opposite sex as a friend and confidante. Friendships between members of the same sex were perceived as "easier;" one boy spoke of the effort to engage a girl in conversation, whereas with another boy "it's like the conversation is already started. There's [no misunderstanding] or anything like that." Students throughout all academies agreed that platonic friendships were rare and indeed unlikely, as this girl explained:

'Cause I've never seen a case that a boy and a girl, they're not boyfriend, but they're like friends, really close friends, I never see them like walking ... I never see those kind of cases.

Students recognized that the structure of the Single Gender Academies limited opportunities to move towards a trusting relationship with the opposite sex, as this girl noted, "you could be missing out on good friendships with guys too." Instead, boy–girl relations were seen as a primarily sexual interaction.

Indeed, the rationale for the establishment of the Single Gender Academies did little to challenge boys' and girls' perceptions of the other as little more than a sexual partner. Administrators, teachers, and parents throughout the schools shared the belief that limiting interactions between girls and boys would reduce distractions. Significantly, they defined distractions primarily in terms of sexual interest, claiming that the middle and high school years were a time of "raging hormones." The assumption was that relations between boys and girls were first and foremost romantic or sexual in nature, and therefore hindered a focus on academic work.[8] The academies consistently sent students the message that boys and girls needed to be separated to prevent inappropriate sexual behavior. When asked, for example, why some of their peers did not finish high school, students echoed adult sentiments: "Because they got together with their girls and with their guys." Yet rather than encourage non-sexual friendships between girls and boys, the schools simply separated them.

Ironically, several schools actually perpetuated the perception of boys and girls as primarily sexual partners through occasional mixed-gender events. At the Pine site, for example, romantic relations were formalized in a school activity. While the school limited casual contact between boys and girls throughout the regular school day, concessions were made on Valentine's Day, when students were encouraged to write love notes to each other. Similarly, students at Evergreen were brought together for an evening dance. The notion that boys and girls are first and foremost sexual partners went unchallenged, leaving students little opportunity to build respectful platonic friendships with each other. By separating students in the classroom and limiting contact to social contexts, the academies further undermined boys' and girls' respect for each other as academic peers.

Central to students' belief that girls and boys could not be friends was an insistence that they were "just different." Such assumptions were largely grounded in an awareness of physical differences, perhaps more significant given the immediacy of puberty in their lives. When asked why she felt comfortable in the single-sex classroom, for example, this girl explained:

> Because girls have periods and have to have babies and stuff like that. They [the boys] don't know what we go through and we don't know what they go through so it's nicer to be around the person that knows what you're going through.

Students also pointed to the behaviors of girls and boys as a sign of their inherent differences. Drawing on daily experiences on the playground, these girls described the gendered boundaries of their activities:

ST: I've never seen during lunch like five girls playing basketball, only see a girl and other boys ... girls don't really play with each other athletic things, they just kind of walk around in groups, and stuff, boys are more like they play football with all boys [inaudible] I've only seen this one girl, she likes football, so she plays with them, but most of the time I never see any girls play anything with the boys, except for basketball, four square.

I: That's really interesting to me that like that the guys in their free time they play sports together, right. And girls in their free time they ... what did you say ...

ST: Walk around in groups.

ST: Talk. Sit on the benches and talk.

These girls described patterns of behavior that define what it means to be a girl or a boy, with little room for shared activities. Thorne (1993) writes of similar "borderwork" she observed on playgrounds, in which groups "interact with one another in ways that strengthen their borders" (p. 65). The girls above interpreted a lack of "border crossing" among their peers as an example of boys' and girls' inherent differences. Through patterns of discourse as well as peer interactions, students constructed a group gender identity. Cohen's (1993) interviews with urban adolescents reveal a discourse of difference in their efforts to make sense of racial identity in social contexts. Likewise, students in the Single Gender Academies employed oppositional self-definitions of gender, defining themselves within and against the other. Yet, as Cohen reminds us, adolescent percep-tions of identity, whether race or gender, hold enormous complexities.

"I really don't think it's the gender thing ...": students resisting stereotypes

While students often relied on a theory of difference when explaining group interactions in the Single Gender Academies, they were quick to resist generalizations when the conversation turned to individual agency. Students offered challenges to traditional gender stereotypes when they saw contradictions within their own lived experiences. Significantly, these challenges often contradicted their earlier comments about gender. The same generalizations about boys and girls that supported students' theories of difference were now dismantled when applied to themselves. Boys insisted on complexity among boys as a group:

There's a lot of guys that are a lot more feminine than regular guys.

Like there's some kids that I see walk around and talk to girls and like they kind of like bounce around kind of like a girl would. And they're a lot more shy or something like a girl.

and girls insisted on complexity among girls as a group:

ST: Girls are sensitive.
ST: Not all of them.
ST: Not all girls. Not all girls.
I: Explain that to me. What do you mean not all girls?
ST: Some girls are sporty. You know like me. They play basketball and they play football. I'm really sporty. I just like to play basketball, football.

Students recognized that stereotypical assumptions of gender, like "girls are sensitive," did not acknowledge girls' and boys' shared traits, nor did they allow for individuality.

Students also challenged many of the assumptions put forth by the Single Gender Academies. As discussed earlier, one common assumption was that the separation of girls and boys would reduce academic and social distractions. Yet, when asked about the level of distractions in the all-girls classrooms, many girls complained about noisy female peers, noting an increase in girls' talking in the Single Gender Academies. In a sense, girls subverted traditional expectations of gender by taking over the role of noisemaker, a role typically held by the boys. Decidedly, the single gender setting created an academic environment that eliminated certain distractions from the opposite sex and thus allowed many students to become more academically focused (Datnow et al., 2001). However, the absence of the other gender was not an isolated factor in the elimination of distractions. Students recognized that there will always be some amount of distraction, regardless of separation by sex: "I think that it doesn't matter what their sex is, there's always gonna be girls that play around and there's always gonna be guys that clown off, it doesn't really matter if you're a girl or a guy." Many students felt that other factors, including smaller class size and increased teacher attention, had greater influence in the success of classroom management in the single gender classroom.

Similarly, girls in the Single Gender Academies challenged the notion that all girls were victims, in the sense that they needed a "safe" space away from boys to encourage participation and raise self-esteem:

I: But now if you don't get to talk in class, like let's say the teacher asks the question and the boys that are rowdy and loud so they always get to answer. Then girls never get to answer the questions. And what do you think that does to you as students?

ST: It can like go both ways. It could make you stronger and make you like be stronger to get out your answer. You know become louder than the boys or it can make you draw backwards and you won't talk. You'll just sit there. It can go both ways.
ST: Yeah. I know some girls who would just try to be louder. It just depends on who it is.

These girls offer an important perspective on the issue of gender and classroom participation. While they acknowledge that some girls may be intimidated by louder boys, they know that not all girls will respond in the same way. More importantly, these girls remind us that gender is not always a predictable factor in classroom dynamics. When asked, for example, about gender as a factor in academic achievement, the following responses were echoed by students across all academies:

I: So do you think that boys and girls learn differently? Do you think there's any differences in the way you learn compared to the way the girls learn?
ST: It just depends on the person.
ST: You couldn't say. 'Cause some girls are smart and some girls can't hack it and there's a lot of guys that are smart too and some guys … [cross talk].
ST: It all depends on the guy.
ST: It just depends on the person as to who does better in class.

Indeed, students in the Single Gender Academies often felt that gender was not a useful predictor of behavior. Students' theories of gender clearly shifted according to context. While students may have relied on gender to explain relational behaviors and patterns of discourse, they resisted the category of gender as a single predictor of individual performance.

Students reminded us that gender is just one way that kids organize themselves. When asked, for example, if she felt less competition in the single-sex classroom, this girl replied, "Well it's still the same. If it's not boys and girls it's smart and dumb. Or eighth graders and seventh graders." At Evergreen in particular, students often relied on socioeconomic class as a more salient marker of identity. The boy whose parents owned the only store in town was consistently defined by his class status, "Well his parents own Smith's market over here and he's like spoiled. He's a snob." Just as this boy was ostracized for his apparent wealth, another girl was singled out as "weird" and unpopular due to her poverty and subsequent lack of hygiene. Given the rural poverty of that small community, any subtle discrepancies in wealth had far greater significance in establishing identity than gender. Girls' and boys' attention to gender identity was dependent on its relevance to the specific contexts of their lives. Ultimately, they resisted the limitations of gender as a sole marker of identity.

Reconciling gender and personal agency

While both boys and girls adhered to a theory of individuality when discussing personal issues, girls were especially quick to challenge the assumption that gender would be a negative factor in their future. Messages about femininity in the academies were complicated and created a situation where girls' lived experiences did not always fit with messages of empowerment. Girls and boys were told that women can do anything they want, following the assumption that the purpose of single gender education is to boost girls' self-confidence. However, girls were also made aware of the restrictions on their behavior, enforced through expectations about clothing and appearance as well as their experiences with sexual harassment. Current notions of femininity are at a crossroads in our society; popular culture is filled with images of "girl power," while the realities of teen pregnancy, sexual harassment, and gang violence tell quite a different story (Leadbeater and Way, 1996). As Kenway and Willis remind us,

> The popular feminist slogan, "girls can do anything" is premised on the principles of choice, free will and the work ethic. [T]he liberal fantasy that it is possible to do anything if you feel good enough, want to badly enough and work hard enough has ... little to do with the grim reality of many girls' lives.
>
> (1998: 148)

On the one hand, girls recognized the influence of gender on their lives; yet, on the other hand, they were told individual perseverance could overcome the limitations of gender. Girls received conflicting messages about gender from parents as well, as this Pakistani girl told us, "My father wants me to be a doctor, but my mother she says it's too much work for a daughter." It is precisely at this intersection, as girls struggle to reconcile the realities of their world with their belief that individual effort will prevail, that we find "gender recipes." In her work with Black adolescents, Taylor Gibbs (1990) notes their recognition of race as a category through which others perceive their identity. More importantly, they recognize the chasm between what she calls their "personal identity," or sense of self, and "racial identity." They cannot control how others perceive them in terms of race, and therefore must find a sense of agency within a personal identity. Similarly, academy students often rejected a gendered or racial identity in favor of personal agency. When asked whether any obstacles, including race and gender, stood in the way of future goals, students' responses were consistently individualistic:

I: Do you think there's anything in society that might stop you, any obstacles?

ST: There's nothing that really could stop me achieving my goals.

I: Your being a woman?

ST: Um, it's more up to me, if I want to achieve it or not, because it's my choice ...

Students either saw no limitations or they insisted that any gender or racial bias could be overcome through individual perseverance.

Significantly, the girls with the strongest awareness of racism and sexism attended the most diverse, urban schools, Palm, Oak, and Birch. These students were able to articulate how gender and race may influence their lives:

> Um, because most people ... they'll be like, oh well, since she's a girl, she can't do it or if because I'm half Black, oh since she's half Black, she's not gonna be able to make it, you know, because of her race, you know, that's how it would be.

When asked how she might overcome such assumptions, this student simply replied, " 'Cause you prove it." Indeed, it is not so much that these students were unaware of sexism and racism, but as one girl said, "I don't really think I'll let that stop me." Parents reinforced the belief that personal agency would prevail over societal biases, as one student explained:

> ... like my Mom, she says that sometimes people think that Chinese women like do sewing and stuff like that. Like do all the leftover work. Not like the really hard jobs. That's why my Mom wants me to get a good career and stuff and just show the world.

Yet despite this awareness, students saw limitations of sexism and racism as individual experiences, not as patterns of structural inequality.

It is important to understand students' adherence to individualism not as naïveté, but as a struggle to maintain a sense of agency in the face of simplistic categorizations of gender. Consistent with Phillips' (2000) recent study of young women's experiences of harassment and violence, academy students were eager to "believe in their own agency ... seeing agency and victimization as mutually exclusive" (p. 3). The danger, of course, is that girls are being told they can accomplish anything, with little practical advice to overcome hardships beyond "just show the world." Johnnetta Cole, former President of Spelman College, asks,

> So if we care about a gender analysis, where do our kids go to gender school? Where do they get the right information and examples? ... We need places for people to learn the lessons of gender and race and culture and their own humanity.
>
> (1993: 44)

Schools need to provide young people with a place to ask questions and receive honest answers. Efforts to empower students must be mitigated with a critical analysis of systems of oppression and an understanding of the challenges they may face on the path to their dreams.

Conclusion

Students adopted or resisted identities of gender in response to the shifting contexts of their lives. Student articulations of gender reflected a reproduction of essentialized definitions (often relying on conceptions of gender as solely a biological construct), while simultaneously insisting on the fluidity of gender and the universality of boys' and girls' experiences. While students employed a theory of difference to explain relationships, they relied on a theory of individualism when the conversation turned to personal experience.

Gender was a useful tool in constructing a relational identity, often in opposition. This was evident in their discussion of the relationships between girls and boys, as they considered the behavior and discourse of same-sex versus coed interactions. Segregated academic and social spaces created and legitimized student assumptions of difference. These notions of opposition were fueled by the perception that boys and girls have different interests, different physical attributes and exhibit different social behaviors. Specifically, the increase in girl talk and boy talk provided a justification for a theory of gender that made difference paramount. Incidents of girl talk and boy talk allowed kids to use conversations to create a group identity separate from the other, to maintain borders between them.

However, in situations of personal agency, students recognized the limitations of gender as a static category. Many institutional and pedagogical practices within the Single Gender Academies grew out of a reform policy that highlighted gender as the central organizing factor for students, and insisted on girls' and boys' differences. For example, many teachers took advantage of the academy structure to tailor their pedagogy to what they saw as the needs of girls or boys separately. Inherent in their differential classroom approaches were clear assumptions of gender, as one boy explained:

> OK. He favors the girls maybe a little bit more. He says, well, girls are always real talkative so I have to like ease up on them a little bit. But the guys, he has to be strict and teach us the basic things in life 'cause we're gonna be the ones going out and getting jobs and providing.

With little professional development around issues of gender and single-sex education, teachers enacted personal beliefs or popular notions of how best to teach boys and girls separately. Approaches to teaching boys reflected the assumption that boys need a disciplined environment. Teaching practices in the all-girls' classrooms were driven in large part by a theory of empowerment, following the assumption that the purpose of single gender education is to boost girls' self-confidence (Streitmatter, 1999).

Significantly, students resisted stereotypical assumptions about girls' and boys' learning. Instead, they articulated a theory of gender and schooling that moved beyond oversimplification:

> You can't blame it on genders, like girls are smarter than guys because that's not true. There are girls that are smarter than guys, but there's guys that are smarter than girls. So it's on the person, whatever you want to come and learn, you come and learn.

Students recognized that a school reform policy focused around gender did not allow for the complex and often contradictory realities of students' lives. One single factor is not a sufficient predictor of behavior, and often may not be relevant. As was often the case in the Single Gender Academies, a school organization based solely on one aspect of identity risks inaccurate generalizations and limitations on students' academic and social expression.

As schools continue to experiment with single-sex education and other reforms, it is critical that educators include students in the processes of policy design, implementation, and evaluation. Students can and should be included as valuable resources in the efforts to improve public education:

> The work of authorizing student perspectives is essential because of the various ways that it can improve current educational practice, re-inform existing conversations about educational reform, and point to the discussions and reform efforts yet to be undertaken ... Authorizing student perspectives introduces into critical conversations the missing perspectives of those who experience daily the effects of existing educational policies-in-practice.
>
> (Cook-Sather, 2002: 3)

This analysis of the realities of public single-sex schooling would be incomplete without an understanding of students' daily experiences in the Single Gender Academies. As this chapter demonstrates, a school reform policy grounded in a singular assumption of boys' and girls' needs does not allow for the complexities and contradictions of students' lives.

Appendix: characteristics of the Single Gender Academies in 1997–8

District	Location	Grades served/ type[1]	Student population	Approximate ethnic distribution[2]
Palm	Urban	Grades 7–12 Self-contained alternative schools.	60 boys; 30 girls Students had a history of truancy, gang violence, and substance abuse.	80% Latino 12% Asian 8% White
Evergreen	Rural	Grades 7–8 Schools within a K-8 school; $^2/_3$ of middle school students were in academies.	28 boys; 30 girls Students were very low income. Most relied on public assistance.	88% White 9% Latino 3% Native American
Cactus	Suburban	Grades 7–8 Schools within a K-8 school; $^1/_2$ of middle school students were in academies.	36 boys; 50 girls Students were a mix of upper-middle, middle, and low income.	65% White 14% Black 9% Asian 8% Latino 3% Pacific Isl.
Birch	Urban	Grade 9 (expanded to grade 10 in 1998–9) Schools within a high school.	18 boys; 22 girls Students were predominantly low income.	32% Latino 27% Black 12% White 14% Asian 10% East Indian 5% Pacific Isl.
Pine	Urban	Grades 5–8 Self-contained schools.	90 boys; 50 girls Students were low income and at-risk due to academic, health, and human service needs.	46% Latino 38% Black 18% Pacific Isl.
Oak	Urban	Grades 6–8 Schools within a middle school.	46 boys; 67 girls Students were predominantly low income.	32% Asian 27% Black 16% Latino 13% White 11% Other Non White

Notes
1 The extent to which each site was sex-segregated varied; students attending academies within a larger school had more opportunities for coed interactions during lunch and break periods than their peers at self-contained academies.
2 Some percentages do not add up to 100 due to rounding.

Notes

1 Wilson hoped that the academic and social benefits found for some girls and minority boys in private and Catholic schools (e.g. Hudley, 1997; Riordan, 1985; Lee and Bryk, 1986) would translate into public schools. Single-sex education was a means to address issues of low achievement by offering parents and students an alternative in the public school system.

2 This chapter draws on one of the first comprehensive studies of public single-sex education in the US (Datnow *et al.*, 2001).

3 Five of the six districts decided to close the academies, not coincidentally at the end of the two-year funding period. In most cases, administrators initiated the closures in the face of strong student, faculty and parent support for the academies. The demise of the Single Gender Academies resulted from a lack of district-level support, an absence of a strong theory as to why schools were implementing single-sex education, and high turnover rates among faculty and staff (Datnow *et al.*, 2001).

4 Legal restrictions to single-sex education in the public sector are largely based on Title IX. The law states: "No person in the U.S. shall, on the basis of sex, be excluded from participation in, be denied the benefits of, or be subjected to discrimination under any education program or activity receiving Federal financial assistance." This research is all the more significant given President Bush's recent proposal to loosen restrictions on Title IX in an effort to encourage single-sex schooling in the public sector (Federal Register, May 2001). While the outcome of this proposal is still uncertain, it has sparked considerable debate among school choice and gender equity advocates.

5 In a recent review of research on single-sex education, Mael (1998) finds a noticeable gap in the literature, namely in the lack of attention to the experiences of boys, as "the overwhelming preponderance of research has focused on females and female concerns" (p. 117).

6 Despite the closures, site visits continued through a third year, in an effort to explore students' transitions back into a coed environment.

7 Within the context of sex-segregated academies, boys were defined in opposition to girls, and, more often than not, as "bad" and in need of discipline. Despite an acknowledgement of complexities among boys in the Single Gender Academies, both boys and girls upheld hegemonic notions of masculinity through limited expectations of how boys should act. Ultimately, any efforts to challenge definitions of masculinity were tempered by a recognition of the inevitable privileges of being a boy. (See Woody, 2002 for further analysis of the implications of such comparisons on the construction of masculinity in the Single Gender Academies.)

8 The discourse of distraction that provided justification for the Single Gender Academies was an incomplete understanding of how kids disrupt each other, academically and socially. Adults' tendency to sexualize the experiences of kids caused them to overlook other types of distraction and harassment that exist in single gender and coed settings alike (Datnow *et al.*, 2001).

Bibliography

American Association of University Women (1998) *Separated by Sex: A Critical Look at Single Sex Education for Girls.* Washington, DC: American Association of University Women.

Cohen, J. (1993) Constructing race at an urban high school: in their minds, their mouths, their hearts. In: L. Weis and M. Fine (Eds), *Beyond Silenced Voices: Class, Race, and Gender in United States Schools.* Albany: SUNY Press.

Cole, J. *et al.* (1993) Raising sons. *Ms.* November/December: 34–50.

Cook-Sather, A. (2002) Authorizing students' perspectives: toward trust, dialogue, and change in education. *Educational Researcher,* 31(4): 3–14.

Datnow, A., Hubbard, L., Woody, E.L. (2001) *Assumptions and Realities of California's Single Gender Public Schools.* Final Report submitted to the Ford and Spencer Foundations.

Eckert, P. (1989) *Jocks and Burnouts: Social Categories and Identity in the High School.* New York: Teachers College Press.

Eder, D. (1995) *School Talk: Gender and Adolescent Culture.* New Brunswick: Rutgers University Press.

Eder, D. (1997) Sexual aggression within the school culture. In: B. Bank and P. Hall (Eds), *Gender, Equity, and Schooling: Policy and Practice.* New York: Garland Publishing, Inc.

Gibbs, J.T. (1990) Mental health issues of Black adolescents. In: A.R. Stiffman and L.E. Davis (Eds), *Ethnic Issues in Adolescent Mental Health.* Thousand Oaks, CA: Sage Publications.

Hudley, C. (1997) Issues of race and gender in the educational achievement of African American children. In: B. Bank and P. Hall (Eds), *Gender, Equity, and Schooling: Policy and Practice.* New York: Garland Publishing, 113–33.

Kenway, J. and Willis, S. (1998) *Answering Back: Girls, Boys and Feminism in Schools.* New York: Routledge.

Leadbeater, B. and Way, N. (Eds) (1996) *Urban Girls: Resisting Stereotypes, Creating Identities.* New York: New York University Press.

Lee, V. and Bryk, A.S. (1986) Effects of single sex schools on student achievement and attitudes. *Journal of Educational Psychology,* 78, 381–95.

LePore, P.C. and Warren, J.R. (1997) A comparison of single sex and coeducational Catholic secondary schooling: evidence from the National Educational Longitudinal Study of 1988. *American Educational Research Journal,* 34(3): 485–511.

Mael, F. (1998) Single sex and coeducational schooling: relationships to socio-emotional and academic development. *Review of Educational Research,* 68: 101–29.

Martin, K. (1996) *Puberty, Sexuality, and the Self: Boys and Girls at Adolescence.* New York: Routledge.

Phillips, L. (2000) Unpublished document distributed at the AAUW Gender Wars Symposium, Washington, DC.

Riordan, C. (1985) Public and Catholic schooling: the effects of gender context policy. *American Journal of Education,* 93(4): 518–40.

Streitmatter, J.L. (1999) *For Girls Only: Making a Case for Single Sex Schooling.* Albany: SUNY Press.

Thorne, B. (1993) *Gender Play: Girls and Boys in School.* Brunswick, NJ: Rutgers University Press.

Woody, E.L. (2002) Understanding masculinities in public single-gender academies. In: A. Datnow and L. Hubbard (Eds), *Gender in Policy and Practice: Perspectives on Single Sex and Coeducational Schooling.* New York: RoutledgeFalmer Press.

Chapter 5

Helping, bluffing, and doing portfolios in a high school geometry classroom

Ilana Seidel Horn

Introduction and overview

American students often leave high school with a fragmented and limited understanding of important mathematics (TIMSS, 1997). In response, educators have advocated dramatic changes in math teaching and learning over the past two decades (e.g. NCTM, 1989, 1995, 2000). Some strategies for reform have included: adoption of curricular materials that emphasize connections and meaning, teaching methods designed to foster sense-making, increased emphasis on classroom activities which allow for direct student engagement with concepts and problems, and a broadening of classroom assessment tools to promote active learning.

The present study focuses on this last reform strategy, changes in classroom assessment to promote active learning on the part of students. Because of its direct relationship to the mathematical values of the larger reform effort, classroom assessment has been an important site for change (Clarke, 1995; NCTM, 1995; Resnick and Resnick, 1992). The idea is that change in teachers' classroom assessment practices will induce changes in teaching practices. This, in turn, will influence students' mathematical learning.

The current study investigates the latter part of this model of assessment reform – the assumption that changing assessment practices will, indeed, influence student learning in mathematics. It provides a close analysis of a high school classroom in the beginning stages of implementing a non-traditional assessment tool, *mathematics portfolios*. Mathematics portfolios are collections of student work accumulated over a period of time. Students select samples of their work and typically organize these into *exhibitions*. The exhibitions often require an explanation from the student, either in the form of written or oral reflections on the sample work. Portfolios customarily are evaluated using a criteria-based system, often in the form of a grading rubric, in which a teacher specifies her expectations for the students' work.

Portfolios are a departure from traditional norm-based assessments in several ways. In contrast to paper-and-pencil tests, students have some choice in representing their learning and understanding. Instead of being evaluated on the success of a teacher-selected problem, students can provide evidence of their learning from the collection of work they have done over the semester. Thus portfolios provide a place for students to actively participate in their own assessment, as they must reflect on and examine their own learning. Also, portfolios recognize learning over time. While a student may not have understood a concept at the time a test was administered, he may later develop an understanding and have that "count" in the evaluation of his learning. Overall, portfolios demand students' multi-level engagement with their on-going mathematical learning.

I provide this generic – and idealized – description of portfolios to provide context for this study. It should be noted, however, that, across settings, portfolios vary tremendously in their form and meaning (Gearhart and Herman, 1998). This study suggests some of the causes for these variations in implementation, what Berman and McLaughlin (1978) call the "mutual adaptation" between an educational innovation and a particular implementation site. By taking the perspective that classroom assessment is a part of the cultural practices of schooling, this study examines how mathematics portfolios were lived out by students and a teacher in one classroom setting.

This study, then, tells a story of how schooling practices influenced the mathematics portfolio assessment reform strategy. As is the case in many American classrooms, the students and teacher in the classroom under study had developed ways of getting work done expediently with minimum engagement or risk (Doyle, 1983). Portfolio assessments, however, presume active engagement in learning. This gap between the ideal of portfolio assessment and the realities of classroom life left room for possible contradictions in the implementation of the reform.

The present analysis should be of interest to stakeholders in the current mathematics reform or alternative assessment reform efforts, as well as educators and policy-makers interested in the implementation issues of classroom-based reforms. The chapter is organized in the following manner. The next section contains a description of methods and of the case under investigation. The third section describes the student and teacher agendas in the mathematics classroom, the classroom practices that arose from these agendas, and how these practices transformed the meaning of assessments; followed by an account of the impact of these classroom practices on the portfolio assessment. In the fourth and final section, I discuss the lessons learned from this casestudy.

Background and methods of study

In the Spring of 1997, I studied the uses and meanings of alternative assessments in mathematics classrooms in a linguistically and culturally diverse urban public high school in the San Francisco Bay Area. The school's approximately two thousand students were about one-third Hispanic, one-third white, one-fourth African-American, with the remaining students Asian, Pacific Islanders, and Native Americans. About 15 per cent of the students were English language learners, and slightly over 25 per cent received free or reduced-price meals.

Along with another educational researcher, I worked with two teachers at the school, providing them with extended problem-solving activities to use in their classrooms. These extended problems were to be integrated with the existing math curriculum as "problems-of-the-week" (or POWs in math reform parlance) to provide the basis for the portfolios that we would develop in collaboration with the teachers. For our research, we used a combination of in-class observations, student and teacher interviews, as well as graded student work.

Although the department chair reported that the math department was "not tracked," students were sorted into differentiated curricular paths. In addition to a traditional college preparatory sequence, the school's mathematics department offered a sequence of applied mathematics in which students could fulfill their graduation requirements. The focal class for this study, a geometry class, was in the college preparatory sequence. The department also had a separate geometry class for ninth grade students, a choice made, according to the department chair, to protect these socially vulnerable students. The non-native English speakers were placed, as much as possible, with the department's one teacher certified to teach this population.

The focal class had twenty-two students enrolled. The text, *Discovering Geometry* (Serra, 1993), structured most of the curriculum along with some supplementary activities and the previously described problems-of-the-week. The class met daily in ninety-minute blocks. Students were seated in rows, next to assigned group mates. Typically, the class started with a review of homework, proceeded to a group activity, which was followed by a review or debriefing of the activity and an opportunity to begin homework. Occasionally, the teacher provided direct instruction, especially if students were having difficulty on a topic. Tests, group tests, and quizzes were administered on a weekly to biweekly basis, as were problems-of-the-week. Students were also expected to keep an organized notebook of their work.

Within the focal class, I chose a primary focal student, Candice,[1] an eleventh grade Japanese-American girl who was repeating geometry. Although she was not a typical student, Candice provided a helpful lens into the student experience of classroom assessments. Because her particular strategies for negotiating school were more exaggerated than those of her peers, she highlighted the tensions in implementing portfolios. She exhibited an amazing repertoire of strategies for weaving in and out of the official and unofficial worlds of the classroom, successfully mimicking on-task behavior while often being far off-task. She was a good tour guide of the classroom, showing me many of the constraints and affordances of its structure, pointing out all the places where assumptions broke down. In particular, Candice had developed numerous strategies for getting answers in math class that avoided actually learning or understanding. Since portfolios presume the existence of individual students' original products, I found myself wondering how a student with this particular strategy – which is highly adaptive in a traditional classroom (Doyle, 1983) – would present her learning in a portfolio. Finally, unlike a few students too cool to engage in the official classroom world, Candice worried about grades enough to do what it took to pass.

I could not focus on Candice, however, without focusing on her almost constant companion, Ramona, a tenth grade Chicana. Ramona employed many of the same strategies as Candice for avoiding the cognitive demands of work. She, too, was often off-task while posing as a compliant student. In many ways, however, Ramona served as a foil for Candice. Although they often turned in the same work, Ramona consistently received better grades than Candice. Ramona tended to participate in class discussions more, for one, and exhibited other teacher-pleasing behavior: Ramona was more organized than Candice; Ramona paid attention in class more often than Candice. Where Candice would frequently argue if the teacher put her name on the board for detention, Ramona would quietly cease whatever objectionable behavior had caught the teacher's notice in the first place. The teacher once described Ramona to me as a "good student" and described Candice as "flaky." Given the frequent sameness of their work along with the differences in their engagement in the official world of the classroom and in the teacher's view of them, observing Ramona alongside Candice helped me understand much of the complexity of classroom assessment.

For the first two months of my observations, Candice and Ramona were in the same group, along with Miguel, a tenth grader from Portugal, and Armando, a tenth grade Chicano.

The focal teacher, Marty, had ten years' teaching experience in public schools. She was very engaged in and committed to the profession of teaching, constantly seeking ways to improve her practice and optimize student learning.

Assessment practices in the classroom

Before the portfolios arrived, the classroom had its own established culture and practices. It turned out that some of these existing practices – particularly the ones around doing assessments – arose out of the students' and teacher's agendas and played an important role in doing the portfolios.

Agendas in assessment

To understand the existing assessment practices, I looked at the influences on and agendas held by the students and teacher in the classroom. First, I describe the influences on the focal students' agendas: *grades and parents, minimization of risk,* and *social and peer concerns.* Then, I briefly describe important influences on the teacher's agenda: *time, perception of students,* and *a concern for fairness.*

Student influences and agenda

Both Candice and Ramona expressed a concern about getting good grades. Candice wrote in her portfolio that she often felt worried in math class. During an interview, I asked her why:

> Mostly because I'm like pressured to do good. Like this semester I got a C plus or something. I could have got a B minus if I worked a little bit harder, and then I know I'm going to get in trouble with my parents and stuff.

Some student assessment practices underscored the importance of grades. First, the student practice of copying work was prevalent in this classroom, as shall be elaborated later. Ramona explained cheating in the classroom during an interview:

> [Kids cheat] to get good grades. I mean, no one wants to come home with an F. You know? An A. Or a B is good.

Additionally, students would often ignore class activities when there was no direct link to grades. For example, when the teacher finished reviewing a topic and solicited any lingering questions, a recurrent one was, "Is this going to be on the test?" When the answer was no, Candice would usually go back to whatever off-task activity she had been involved in.

Candice, in particular, found it difficult to engage in class activities. She described herself as someone who had to "move around. And I get off track and I think of something, like, 'Oh, what am I going to do this weekend?' " Observations confirmed her distractibility, as I watched Candice read clothing catalogs and teen magazines, fidget with school supplies and calculators, and even play a key chain video game (in silent mode) during class.

Candice did engage with some of the assignments, but not in ways that involved mathematics. For example, she had a penchant for decorating her papers. When she decided to get organized and have a notebook for the second semester, it materialized as a glittery-gray report folder with a clear cover. Candice had made an elaborate title page with her name written in capital, graffiti-font letters. She had pasted in two department store photos of herself and her friends, one in which they posed with the Sesame Street character, Elmo. On the left side of the cover, she had a cut-out picture of Chuck Norris doing a high kick. She explained her aesthetic reasoning to me:

> I hate carrying those big binders around and stuff. I'm just like lazy like that. And I have small backpacks. [*laughs; I laugh too*] Got to match my outfit or something. [*laughs*]

Candice made the notebook assignment fit her style – literally. Other times, she decoratively colored in diagrams on quizzes or made assignments into mini pop-up books. These decorative practices seemed to be her way of engaging in class assignments. They often represented sustained effort on her part, but they notably avoided significant engagement with academic content. In other words, she was highly involved in something more important in her adolescent world: a search for self-expression and exploration of style.

High school students' minimized engagement with academics is not atypical and has been described elsewhere (e.g. Labaree, 1997; Powell *et al.*, 1985). Doyle frames students' minimized engagement as a way of managing the "ambiguity and risk" of academic work:

> There is some evidence that students invent strategies for managing the ambiguity and risk associated with classroom tasks. [...] The picture painted here is one of caution: Students restrict the amount of output they give to a teacher to minimize the risk of exposing a mistake. In addition, restricted output can elicit assistance from others in a classroom.
>
> (Doyle, 1983: 184)

Minimized academic engagement is common among high school students, and in this classroom setting it proved to be an important influence on the assessment system.

Students' desire to engage socially with their peers strongly influenced their agendas. Candice admitted to doing her work quickly so that she could talk. She recognized that this was detrimental to her learning:

> I do that and then, at the end, I'm stuck. Because I know what I did but I don't fully understand what I did.

Despite her recognition of the deleterious effect of this habit, the social world continued to draw Candice away from the academic content of her work. Sometimes social engagement involved academically damaging displays of bravado. For example, Armando avoided working in order to impress his peers. On several occasions, Armando was overheard bragging that he never did homework and yet still received passing grades. This posturing was, in fact, a bit of a front: although he received a C minus for the semester, according to the teacher's records, he had earned some homework credit as well. Marty was cognizant of the social stakes involved in classroom participation. In reviewing the students' portfolios with me, Marty explained one student's failure to do a portfolio: "He won't do that kind of thing. It's beneath him [*laughs*]."

Students in the classroom, then, were strongly influenced by a concern for grades; minimized engagement with classroom activities; and social and peer concerns. These three influences shaped an agenda that required (1) doing work in such a way that insured good grades; (2) finishing work to get it done and avoiding engagement with activities; and (3) maintaining a constant awareness of peer judgments and evaluations. These components interacted to create a coherent student agenda, one in which engagement in the academic world was devalued in favor of engagement with peers.

Teacher influences and agenda

Marty frequently complained about the time crunch that resulted from the block schedule. The teachers were required to teach a year's course in (what used to be) a semester's time. Time was often given as a reason to not do things. The students added to her time bind by complaining that things were moving too fast. Ramona provided this response to the portfolio cover letter prompt: "*I think this math class would improve if:* 'we could go over things more carefully – if the teacher could take the time to explain things more carefully.'"

When we first met with the teachers, they made it clear to us that their students "don't do homework." Our in-class observations supported this general claim, and the reasons for this seemed entangled with many other issues. In fact, Ramona did tell the teacher in her introductory math autobiography assignment: "My weaknesses in school are me not being able to do homework. I don't like homework, but I'll do it if it means passing."

At the same time, Marty was a caring teacher and held many positive perceptions of her students, some of which affected the assessment practices in her classroom. For example, on several occasions, she told me that she had "good kids" who would "never cheat." I once stopped by her class to drop off some POWs while her students were taking a quiz. She came to the doorway to speak with me. I said that we could go inside and talk so that she could continue to proctor the test. "It's alright," she told me. "They're good kids. I trust them."

Marty valued being fair to her students. She was often flexible, bending official policies about deadlines, passing out extra worksheets, and curving her grades. Marty's concern for fairness would also come out when a student explained a problem to the class at the overhead. She would ward off taunts and teasing, imploring the class to give the presenter a chance. Candice lauded Marty for her fairness during an interview:

> Like, if I turned in something, if I wasn't here, you know, and I like turned something in late, she'll still accept it and give me extra, you know, just a little bit of points to help me out. You know? I mean, most teachers wouldn't do that. You know, "If it's late, I – I won't take it," you know?

The teacher was strongly influenced by a lack of time; what she perceived as underprepared and unmotivated – but basically good – students; and a concern for fairness. These three influences shaped an agenda that required (1) moving through activities in as timely a manner as possible; (2) developing strategies to engage students academically without having to confront the holes in their mathematical knowledge; and (3) maintaining a sense of fairness while fulfilling the first two parts of the agenda. All of these components were highly interactive and often in tension with one another.

The student agenda and teacher agenda often seem to interact and become mutually reinforcing. For example, the students' prioritizing of the social world over the school world reinforced the teacher's perception that the students were unmotivated. The teacher's concern for time created an obstacle to encouraging students to slow down on their work. At other times, the respective agendas created conflict and tension as well. The teacher's concern for fairness, for example, caused her to make many concessions in grading her students. The interaction of the participants' agendas made a dynamic environment for the portfolio assessments.

Impacts of agendas on classroom assessments

Given the agendas behind the students' and teacher's assessment practices, it is easy to see how homework, tests, and other assessments were not done by the book. Modifications happened. I call these modifications "gaps" – as in the gaps between the official ways in which assessment activities are accomplished (for example, as described by textbooks or in notes to parents) and the unofficial ways that arise as participants manage their agendas. Certain practices created and sustained these gaps. These practices were, in many ways, logical solutions to the problem of addressing the competing agendas while still getting some form of schooling accomplished. In the following sections, I will explain how the gap-creating practices of *helping* and *bluffing* manifested themselves in the classroom and how they arose in the interaction of the student and teacher agendas. I will follow the descriptions of each assessment practice with an account of how it shaped the portfolios in this classroom.

"Helping"

> It's up to you if you pay attention and, then, if you don't, well then, it's either you flunk the test or you decide to, um, get help from someone.
> (Ramona)

During an interview, Ramona acknowledged some of the choices that students faced in class: first, students could choose whether or not to pay attention, and, second, they could choose whether or not to flunk the test. Construing these as "choices" directly reflected the influences on the students' agenda – namely, minimized engagement and a concern for grades. Additionally, a choice to not pay attention did not necessitate flunking the test, which obviously would be harmful to a good grade. Students could use their peers to support their agendas by getting "help."

One of the places that this sort of helping occurred was during in-class tests. I once watched Ramona, Candice, Miguel, and Armando share quizzes during class. Ramona signaled to Miguel, who whispered an answer to her across the aisle. The teacher said, "What's the matter, Miguel?" "Nothing," he answered. Miguel then handed Ramona his quiz, which she began to copy. Marty headed toward their group, and Miguel whispered urgently, "Ramona!" Ramona put Miguel's quiz under hers until the danger (i.e. Marty) had passed. Armando then leaned over toward Ramona, eyeing me suspiciously. I looked away, burying myself in my notes. He took the quiz off her desk and copied it. Candice turned and looked down at Ramona's paper. They continued on like this until the teacher called time. Ramona protested, "No!" The teacher told Ramona to just turn it in. "But I want to get an A on it!" Ramona complained. She finally passed in the quiz.

"Helping" (or what might be called "cheating" in the official world of the school) was not isolated to Candice and her group. I saw many students around the room – even those who seemed more confident in geometry – exchanging papers and copying answers. One student noted in her portfolio cover letter to Marty, "Watch out for cheating on tests!" When asked about it during an interview, Ramona reported that cheating happened "everywhere" in the school.

In fact, the students had many strategies for getting work done without engaging in its academic content. Candice in particular had multiple means for obtaining answers, some of which I never observed but heard her discuss with Ramona. Early on in the semester, she told Ramona, "I have all my other stuff from my other geometry class. I had [another teacher] and they do the same thing." Candice understood schooling practices well enough to know that textbook-designed tests and activities were used across classrooms, and thus she reused materials (some of which had presumably been graded) from previous years. At the end of the semester, Candice was upset to learn that Ramona had earned a whole grade better than she. She told Ramona that she had earned a C plus, and Ramona puzzled, "How'd you get that? We did like the *exact* same things." "Thanks," Candice answered, "make me feel stupid." Under her breath she followed it up with, "Anyways, who got the tests for you?"

"Helping" and these other illicit means of getting work done were consistent with the students' agenda, with its influences of minimized engagement, a concern for grades, and concerns about the peer social world. As noted earlier, because of helping and its related practices, the choice not to pay attention in class did not require students to sacrifice their grades. In addition, there was an underlying social economy represented in the exchange of work, as socially low-status students purchased the favor of high-status students by sharing their work. Thus, the exchange of work also helped students to manage social and peer concerns.

While copying on individual tests seems to be a clear case of "cheating" in the world of school, the many collaborative activities in the classroom rendered other types of copying more ambiguous. Since group work sanctions some forms of sharing of work, and since doing work in Marty's class often involved getting answers without doing work, I asked Candice where the line between acceptable and unacceptable copying lay:

> [If] you know it well, I guess it's okay. Because what's the point of doing it over and over, you know, you already know it. So you can copy. But if you don't know what you're doing [...] you're stuck on one problem, you're all, "Forget it, I'll just copy," you know, maybe [...] it's not cool like that, you know.

In this view, individuals determine the ethics of copying, based on their own sense of what they know and understand. During my observations, I did not see copying limited to this special circumstance – although it became apparent that I have a different sense of what it means to "know" and "understand." This difference was instanced as I watched Ramona explaining an algorithm to Candice. She handed Candice her worksheet and later checked in with her, asking, "Do you understand it now?" Candice replied, "This is how I understand stuff." Ramona agreed, "I know, huh? Copying off other people." Given the limitations of Ramona's explanations (Candice: "How'd you get it?" Ramona: "You just look at it and it's hecka easy."), copying might have facilitated an understanding of the patterns in comparison.

This less illicit form of copying served to meet the students' agenda in a manner similar to the other types of "helping." It minimized their engagement in the academic work, completed the tasks well enough to receive credit for grades, and had the social component of sharing with peers.

Copying, although not officially sanctioned, was adaptive to the teacher's agenda. Because of her time-push, Marty did not have many assignments that required careful attention in grading, which might have tipped her off to the uniformity (a sign of copying) or the pseudomath[2] in some of the students' work.

Like most teachers, Marty felt the tension between her limited time and her ability to grade carefully. Also, the prevalence of "helping" and Marty's neglecting to notice it may have stemmed from the schematic processing that arose out of her perception that her students did not cheat. That is, she did not see the cheating because, in her mind, these were good kids who would not cheat. Her concern for fairness, and perhaps her perception of her students as unmotivated learners, led her to acquiesce to the types of copying she saw in the more ambiguous setting of collaborative work.

Helping and copying often created gaps in the official and unofficial purposes of many assessments: tests no longer represented individual students' work; worksheets were no longer opportunities for practice. Helping, more than anything else in this classroom, changed assessment artifacts from windows into student understanding of mathematics to refracting lenses. Taking any student product as a representation of individual mathematical competence became extremely problematic. At the same time, helping did not necessarily undermine the purposes of every assessment task. Students' collaboration would sometimes fulfill some of the goals of a classroom task.

"Helping" with portfolios

When our teacher/researcher team developed the portfolios, we developed a portfolio with three exhibitions: (1) evidence of progress, (2) toughest problem, and (3) best possible work. Each exhibition had a "reflection sheet" that asked students organizing and reflective questions. The first exhibition asked students to compare earlier and later work on the same topic to demonstrate and describe their improved understanding. For the second exhibition, students had to discuss a POW that was hard for them and what strategies they used to persist in working on it. The third exhibition required students to revise a POW and polish it to demonstrate their best possible work.

For her Best Possible Work section, Candice "revised" a problem called Pentagon Loops (or, as Candice called it, "Pentaloops"), which asked students to (1) find a geometric pattern using pentagon tiles given certain constraints, (2) observe related numerical patterns, and then (3) write an algebraic expression to describe the patterns. Candice's revision consisted of adding diagrams to her earlier solution. I asked her about her work during our interview:

LANI: [W]hat about the patterns over here? [*referring to the numerical patterns*] How did you get those?

CANDICE: And then it shows like how many of tiles did you use you just count it. And how many of edges inside you just count like one, two, three, four –

LANI: Mhm.

CANDICE: – the edges. And number of outside edges, you just count one, two, three all these edges. Total number of edges, I think the middle, and you add all the middle and inside.

[*Candice has basically restated the directions to the task.*]

LANI: Mhm. And then you came up with these patterns at the end?

CANDICE: Yeah.

LANI: And how'd you do that?

CANDICE: Um. [*smiles*]

LANI: Do you remember?

CANDICE: No. [*reads, muttering*] Describe the pattern ... find the nth term in each sequence. I don't – remember. It was probably like. How. [*reads, muttering*] I don't remember.

LANI: Do you remember how to do those nth term sequence things?

CANDICE: It's like how you solve a problem by using like n. Because if you like you can change the n. And to make it to equal always the same number.

LANI: So like for example, in this one, where it says ...

CANDICE: Six.

LANI: So it says ...

CANDICE: $2n + 4$. I mean, 2, 6 + 4? Something? 2, 8 + 4?

Candice's response indicated, at best, an unstable understanding of algebraic expressions. Although she seemed to have some notion of variable ("You can change the n"), she did not manage to evaluate the algebraic expression $2n + 4$ for particular values of n ("2, 6 + 4? 2, 8 + 4?"), omitting the multiplication between the 2 and the n. While the interview situation may have exerted some extra pressure, we had established a fairly comfortable and casual rapport. Additionally, the limitation of her algebra skills seemed apparent in other in-class observations as well, where she relied heavily on Ramona who was "good at algebra."

The teacher marked Candice down for the Best Possible Work exhibition described above. Specifically, Candice received 2 out of 5 points for "Revised problem communicates the mathematics clearly, including concise explanations and clarifying diagrams." The teacher underscored this with a handwritten comment: "Best Possible Work – *Write* an explanation of the pattern." Perhaps because of her lack of understanding of the algebra, Candice could not do so. In any case, the portfolio provided a site at which she became accountable for not communicating understanding; yet because Candice still managed to receive a satisfactory B on the overall portfolio, she did not analyze the lower score on this criterion so as to improve her performance in the future.

In another portfolio entry, Candice seemed to have used an answer of Ramona's that went undetected. In our interview, Candice told me that Ramona had "helped" her with the problem. Comparing Ramona and Candice's answers reveals the nature of this "help." As background, the task requires students to (1) figure out the rate at which a field is being harvested, (2) find the amount that remains to be harvested, and (3) calculate the time to harvest the remainder of the field. Ramona submitted this piece for her Toughest Problem exhibition. In writing, she explained her technique (I have highlighted in bold the sections that reappear in Candice's explanation):

> To start out, I took the length of the field and d[i]vided it into **10 mm sections**. There were **8 sections**, so I multiplied 15 by 8 and got 120. Since cutting 85 cm **equals a half hour**, <u>I added another half hour</u> since I had 120 cm. There I had 30 minutes. Then I **subtracted 85 by 120**, and I got 35, then I **added 11 because there were 11 squares left** over from where the tractor left off. Then I **added 11 to 35**, and I got **46 minutes**.

Ramona's markings on her diagram do not indicate that she partitioned the field in the way she described – nor do Candice's. Candice explained her solution to the Harvester Problem in her Toughest Problem exhibition:

> First I took the field and divided it into **10 mm sections**. In all I got **8 sections**. That **equal[s] 30 minutes**. <u>I doubled that</u>. The [sic] **subtracted 85 by 120**. Then **added 11 cause there was 11 squares left**. Then **add 11 + 35**. The answer was **46 minutes**.

In itself, Ramona's answer did not make sense with her diagram, although it could have explained a different partition of the field. Candice's rewording of Ramona's solution was revealed because, not only did she repeat Ramona's mistake of labeling the sections in millimeters instead of centimeters, she changed Ramona's "adding another half hour" (an unusual but possible way to think about the problem) to "doubling [30 minutes]" (see the underlined text above) – mathematically equivalent but inconsistent with the physical context of the problem.

The students' practice of "helping" was detrimental to the effectiveness of the portfolio assessment. Copying was a deeply entrenched practice in this classroom (and, according to Ramona, beyond) and it undermined the portfolio's validity as an assessment tool, as well as making it an ineffectual inducement for sense-making and understanding. Indeed, the question of ownership of work has posed challenges to other implementations of portfolio assessment (Gearhart and Herman, 1998), even when collaboration is sanctioned.

Bluffing about "what counts" in grading

The teacher's perception that the students lacked motivation was consistent with the students' minimized engagement with class activities. She knew to her advantage that the students were concerned about grades and employed a practice of "bluffing," allowing students to have a slightly distorted understanding of her grading system. Specifically, like many other teachers, she allowed students to have the impression that certain activities "counted" more than they actually did to encourage student involvement.

For example, during one class session, Marty reviewed some homework problems at the overhead with her class. A student asked her to go over problems seven and eight:

> Number seven and eight. Would someone like to come up and explain? [5 second pause] Number seven. [2 second pause] That's how you get your points, guys. I give you your class grade based on your participation. Number seven? Someone give me the definition of slope again.[3]

Ramona answered the teacher and eventually went up to the overhead to do the problem. This was not the only time that participation points lured the grade-conscious but socially self-conscious students from their reticence. In fact, the students frequently volunteered on the condition of receiving these points, their hands shooting in the air with the cry, "Participation points!"

In a conversation about assessment in her classroom, Marty told me that she gave students five participation points a day for things like presenting problems at the overhead. When I expressed awe at her meticulous bookkeeping, she confided that actually, she often just kind of guessed at the points. She told me, "The kids think it counts more than it does." As in many classrooms in which participation is linked to class grades, the teacher relied on her own professional judgment to assign a value to the quality of participation. Nonetheless, there was a deliberate gap between the official and unofficial meaning of participation points arising out of the practice of bluffing.

Bluffing suited the previously described influences on the participants' agendas. The teacher's time constraint made it difficult to actually carry out the system she had set up, while the students' minimized engagement – and their need to manage their images in front of their peers – precluded them from truly volunteering. The teacher thus used their perception of participation points to her advantage. When, in the above example, she sought a volunteer for problem seven, she relied on the lure of points to get the students to come forth. This strategy successfully addressed both the students' and the teacher's agendas: Marty could lure some of her reluctant students to engage with classroom activities, and the students could feel as if they were contributing to their grade in a socially acceptable way.

Bluffing with portfolios

In the case of the participation points, Marty allowed the students to ascribe an inflated meaning to the grades they received so as to engage them with classroom activities. With the portfolios, bluffing worked for a different purpose. Instead of inflating the *meaning* of the grades to the students, Marty used the criteria-based scoring rubric and, in the end, she inflated the *actual* letter grades in order to be fair.

In part, Marty felt on uncertain footing embarking on this new assessment. Ever-mindful of fairness, she did not want to penalize the students for her uncertainty. She ended up "curving" the grades so as not to "give anyone an F who at least handed it in." The criteria-based rubric and the open-ended nature of the exhibitions introduced a new level of ambiguity for the teacher. Although she had a habit of developing criteria while grading in order to be consistent, she could not find a satisfactory way to feel as if she were being consistent with the portfolios. To alleviate her concern, she applied the norm-based practice of grade curving to the criteria-based portfolio scores.

Nor did the students use the rubric criteria to make sense of their portfolio scores. Just as they did not understand the relative insignificance of the participation points, the students did not report an awareness of inflation of their portfolio grades. Since grades took precedence over learning in the students' agendas, Ramona was simply pleased with her A and Candice felt her B was reasonable since she had rushed through the assignment. Both of them reported feeling like the portfolio was "easy." By curving the grades, the teacher adopted a technique for fairness from a norm-based assessment system and applied it to a criteria-based assessment. This mismatch of paradigms decreased the need for students to attend to the scoring criteria and thus diluted the potential impact of the portfolio assessment.

The grading criteria were further compromised by the teacher's lack of time. Because I had that luxury, I noticed some details of Candice and Ramona's portfolio work that escaped the grading radar. For example, in the Evidence of Progress exhibition, Candice submitted as her early work a quiz on which she had trouble finding the nth term of a sequence of numbers. For her later work, she submitted something she failed to name on the accompanying reflection sheet. However, the later submission looked distinctly like class notes since they described three methods for solving these types of problems and included terms I had never heard Candice use ("Double the value then the [*sic*] factor the values"). Candice received 4 out of 4 possible points for "Student's work selection convincingly demonstrates progress." This score most likely reflected the "curving" of the grades, or it may have been an oversight because of the teacher's dearth of time.

The practices of helping and bluffing arose out of the participants' respective agendas. These practices and their associated strategies had a transformative effect on classroom assessments, mediating gaps in their official and unofficial meanings. At the same time, none of these practices were at odds with the participants' roles as students and teacher in the school setting. They were adapted to the larger practices of schooling and, for the most part, accommodated the respective agendas with little conflict or confrontation.

Conclusions

This study argues that assessment tools themselves do not sufficiently induce changes in classroom teaching and learning. Indeed, the portfolio assessment inhabited the same world as other assessments and was subjected to existing classroom practices. Its ambiguous demands for reflection and understanding were transformed in the classroom, accommo-dating the agendas of the participants in that setting. As this analysis illustrates, students and teachers have their own needs and sense of their roles, which must be addressed in considering any new reform tool or practice.

Looking closely at students' experiences with portfolio assessments in a geometry classroom highlights the need to consider the following when adopting this kind of reform:

Existing tasks and their accompanying practices

The students and teacher came to the performance tasks after years of experience with traditional academic work. Many traditional tasks still played a role in the curriculum, especially summative tests and quizzes, which comprised the majority of students' grades. Although performance tasks had been incorporated into the classroom, they did not have as great an influence on the grading system and seemed to have an add-on status. In this classroom, they had no obvious point of entry.

Performance assessments, to be effective, require a paradigmatic shift on the part of both students and teachers. This analysis focused on helping and bluffing and the ways they undo some of the cognitive demands of traditional assessments. "Helping" can be managed if teachers state explicitly what kinds of work sharing are truly helpful. Bluffing is trickier. Clearly, it goes against the kind of transparency in grading that a criteria-based assessment tries to establish, yet it is not obvious how else Marty could help students overcome the social stakes involved in engaging in their academic work. (See *The social world of students* below for one possibility.)

To be sure, the structure of the school and the myriad obligations competing for student and teacher time and energy almost preclude the spontaneous disengagement from these and other counterproductive practices. Marty, for example, was obliged to evaluate the portfolios in a form that could be plugged into the traditional letter-grading scale, a system that institutionalizes many of the assessment practices that portfolios are trying to move away from. It is not clear how portfolio assessments might be incorporated in such a scheme.

Crowded curriculum

The "mile-wide, inch-deep" description of the US mathematics curriculum has become a cliché because it so succinctly captures what we see. Teachers rush students from topic to topic, without providing many opportunities for them to think and understand. In this classroom, the performance tasks became one more thing to do and cover. They competed for precious time, precluding the kinds of in-depth explanations and conversations that would help students actually make sense of the mathematics. Recall Ramona's plea to Marty to "go over things more carefully." She recognized that she was not learning the mathematics deeply. If they are to be meaningful, portfolios require a depth of understanding that cannot be achieved in the context of a crowded curriculum. Teachers should work with big mathematical ideas and focus on cultivating mathematical meaning.

The social world of students

In this classroom, there was a strong distinction between the students' social and academic worlds. The academic world, for the most part, was something that students needed to "deal with" so that they could return to the more compelling social world of their peers. Portfolios, with their open-endedness, might have actually created more space for the "unofficial" classroom world. To address these competing demands on students' time, teachers might try to create classrooms in which those worlds are not so distinct so that participation in the academic does not entirely preclude the social. Imagine, for example, what could have been achieved if Candice had found a way to engage both her decorative explorations and her mathematical understanding, especially in the visually-rich subject of geometry. As long as social life and academics are placed in direct competition for students' time, the social will prevail for the majority of adolescents.

Acknowledgments

Thanks to Cathy Kessel, who collaborated with me on the data collection and preliminary analysis for this research. I am grateful for the financial support of the Mathematics Assessment Resource Services project, as well as UC Berkeley's Spencer Center for Integrated Studies of Teaching and Learning, both of whom sponsored this study. Beth Rubin and Elena Silva's thoughtful editorial guidance helped tremendously in my writing.

An earlier version of this chapter was presented at the 1998 Ethnography in Education Forum at the University of Pennsylvania, Philadelphia.

Notes

1 All names are pseudonyms. I refer to myself as "Lani" in the transcripts, since that is what the teachers and students called me.
2 Occasionally, when students have copied answers but know that they are also supposed to "show their work," they include nonsensical work to fulfill the requirements of the task. I distinguish pseudomathematical work from the sometimes rough, inchoate attempts to employ a new idea, concept or term that are characteristic of learning; the former is a kind of boundary work that helps students avoid cognitive work, while the latter indicates a preliminary attempt to engage with mathematical ideas.
3 Notice how the ambiguity and risk of the request decreased in response to the students' silence. Marty first asked for a student to "come up and explain," a highly ambiguous and risky endeavor. At the end of the excerpt, she solicited the definition of slope, thereby decreasing the cognitive and social demands of her original request. This transformation in her request concurs with Doyle's (1983) observation, quoted earlier.

Bibliography

Berman, P. and McLaughlin, M.W. (1978) *Federal Programs Supporting Educational Change, Vol. VII: Implementing and Sustaining Innovations.* Santa Monica, CA: Rand Corp.
Clarke, D. (1995) Using assessment to renegotiate the didactic contract. Paper presented at University of California, Berkeley, School of Education. April 24, 1995.
Doyle, W. (1983) Academic work. *Review of Educational Research*, 53(2): 159–99.

Gearhart, M. and Herman, J.L. (1998) Portfolio assessment: whose work is it? Issues in the use of classroom assignments for accountability. *Educational Assessment*, 5: 41–56.

Labaree, D.F. (1997) *How to Succeed in School Without Really Learning: The Credentials Race in American Education*. New Haven, CT: Yale University Press.

National Council of Teachers of Mathematics (1989) *Curriculum Standards for School Mathematics*. Reston, VA: National Council of Teachers of Mathematics.

National Council of Teachers of Mathematics (1995) *Assessment standards for school mathematics*. Reston, VA: National Council of Teachers of Mathematics.

National Council of Teachers of Mathematics (2000) *Principles and standards for school mathematics*. Reston, VA: National Council of Teachers of Mathematics.

Powell, A.G., Farrar, E. and Cohen, D.K. (1985) *The Shopping Mall High School: Winners and Losers in the Educational Market Place*. Boston: Houghton-Mifflin Company.

Resnick, L.B. and Resnick, D.P. (1992) Assessment for the thinking curriculum: new tools for educational reform. In: B.R. Gifford and M.C. O'Connor (Eds), *Changing Assessments: Alternative Views of Aptitude, Achievement and Instruction*. Boston: Kluwer Academic Publishers, 37–76.

Serra, M. (1993) *Discovering Geometry: An Inductive Approach*. Berkeley: Key Curriculum Press.

The Third International Mathematics and Science Study (TIMSS) (1997) *Attaining Excellence: TIMSS as a Starting Point to Examine Mathematics Assessments*. Chestnut Hill, MA: Boston College, Center for the Study of Testing, Evaluation, and Educational Policy.

PART II

Deliberate aims

Putting students at the center of reform

Chapter 6

Apprenticing urban youth as critical researchers

Implications for increasing equity and access in diverse urban schools

Anthony M. Collatos and Ernest Morrell

Introduction

> Jaime: Using the methodology of the sociology of education, political theory, and lived experience we are helping and making a difference in our lives and in the lives of others to come. Through the Futures program we had the opportunity to gain access to things that we normally would not have. Their goal was to help us achieve a higher education and with this in mind we visited colleges around California that we normally would not because of issues like transportation, money, or just not having the essential information, resources, and lack of access. Through this program I had many opportunities that I would never have had. I plan to major in sociology to create programs like these and help students of color have access to an equal and fair education ...
>
> (Conference Presentation, April 2001)

It is no secret that race, class, and ethnicity play a major role in determining access to college (McDonough, 1997; Wilds, 2000). Each year, countless intervention programs are created to equalize access to college with minimal results (Gandara and Bial, 2001; Perna and Swail, 1998; Swail, 1999). Often these programs begin with deficit assumptions about marginalized students, their families and communities, and seek to either transmit information or transform the habits of these students to increase access. Dissatisfied with deficit and subtractive (Valenzuela, 1999) approaches to college access, a team of university researchers and high school teachers looked toward critical sociology (Bourdieu, 1986; Bourdieu and Wacquant, 1992) to design a project that simultaneously increased college access for its participants and disrupted the system that perpetually provided unequal access to low-income students of color.

The James Madison Futures Project was created to apprentice urban teens as critical sociologists within a community of practice consisting of students, teachers, parents, university researchers, and community organizers. As investigators and educators, we intended to help students use critical research to develop the language needed to make sense of their experiences as urban teens attending a diverse bimodal school where the poor and students of color trailed far behind their White more affluent peers. Further, we aimed to facilitate the acquisition of tools that would enable these teens to forge alternative pathways leading to success at the high school level and access to competitive colleges and universities. Finally, we imagined that the critical research would be used in the struggle for social justice and access in urban schools.

This chapter examines the critical research and critical voices of the students of the James Madison Futures Project as they struggled to increase equity and access within a diverse urban high school. We begin by situating our work at the nexus of critical pedagogy and situated learning theory. We then introduce James Madison High School and the Futures project. Next, we describe our data-collecting strategies, which were influenced by our critical epistemology (Carspecken, 1996; Kincheloe and McLaren, 1998). From our data, we present three cases that we feel are illustrative of the ways that students were able to actively participate as agents of urban school reform at the local, district, and state levels. As critical researchers committed to urban school reform, the Futures students challenged unfair and exclusive testing practices, fought against tracking and ability grouping, and worked with American Civil Liberties Union (ACLU) attorneys in litigation against the state of California on behalf of students attending under-resourced schools. We conclude with a brief discussion of the implications of our work with urban teens for other educators and activists who wish to think of the possibilities of engaging urban teens as critical sociologists and agents of urban school reform.

Becoming agents of change within a community of practice

Situated learning theorists believe that learning as it normally occurs is a function of the activity, context and culture in which it occurs (Lave and Wenger, 1991). This contrasts with most classroom learning activities which transmit knowledge that is abstract and out of context. Social interaction is a critical component of situated learning – learners become involved in a "community of practice" which embodies certain beliefs and behaviors to be acquired (Wenger, 1998).

As the beginner or newcomer moves from the periphery of this community to its center, they become more active and engaged within the culture and hence assume the role of "expert" or "old-timer." These ideas are what Lave and Wenger (1991) call the process of legitimate peripheral participation. A community of practice is a site of learning and action in which people come together around a joint enterprise as they develop a whole repertoire of activities, common stories, and ways of speaking and acting (Wenger, 1998). Learning occurs constantly in these communities as people participate in activities that are more and more central to the core practice. This changing participation leads participants to take on new identities that are necessarily bound up with new knowledge and skills (Lave, 1996).

Critical pedagogists view schooling as a political and cultural enterprise and work with marginalized populations to transform existing social inequalities and injustices (Bartolome, 1994; McLaren, 1989). Critical pedagogists challenge the assumption that schools function as major sites of social and economic mobility and analyze schooling as a cultural and historical process in which select groups are positioned within asymmetrical relations of power on the basis of specific race, class, and gender groupings. Further, critical pedagogists, through problem-posing dialogue, generate categories or concepts for questioning student experiences, mandated texts and curricula, teacher ideologies, and oppressive school policies. Finally, critical pedagogists engage in revolutionary praxis, theoretically and empirically informed action that is then reflected upon to produce greater action (Freire, 1970).

The work of the James Madison Futures Project occurred at the nexus of critical pedagogy and situated learning theory, working to open up spaces for legitimate peripheral participation and authentic liberatory dialogue. In what follows, we describe James Madison High School and the Futures project in greater detail.

James Madison High: a tale of two schools

James Madison High and its 3,100 students are hailed as a school with a population that closely reflects the diversity of the state of California. James Madison has the following ethnic breakdown: 46.9 per cent White, 32.6 per cent Hispanic, 12.7 per cent African American, and 6.9 per cent Asian/ Asian American. Fifty per cent of the graduates are UC-CSU (University of California and California State University) eligible, compared to a 36.6 per cent statewide average. The average SAT score for James Madison High students is 1048 compared to a state average of 1011 and a national average of 1016.

Although these numbers seem to portray James Madison as a successful or at least above average school by traditional criteria, there exist huge disparities in achievement between students according to ethnic and socioeconomic background. The disparities are so great that James Madison High School is often referred to as two schools, one highly successful campus that services the affluent population (which is largely composed of White and Asian-American students who are residents of the northern portion of the city), and another, less successful urban school that services the low-income (African-American and Latino) students who live either in the poorest section of the community or commute on permit from a nearby city.

James Madison High School is often touted as an enclave of utopian diversity among California's troubled high schools. In an age of White flight from urban centers and resegregation in urban public schools (Anyon, 1997; Kozol, 1991), James Madison stands out as a rare and notable exception. It is a school where one still sees rich and poor, White and non-White roaming the halls together and, on the surface at least, still struggling with this experiment called democracy. All is not well, however, at James Madison. A foray into the classrooms and grade books of James Madison reveals a troubling tale of two schools, separate and unequal.

During the 1999–2000 school year only 6.8 per cent of African-American students at James Madison held above a 3.5 grade point average while 79.2 per cent held less than a 2.9, and 40.1 per cent held less than a 2.0. Only 9.1 per cent of the Latino student population held above a 3.5 grade point average while 74.1 per cent held less than a 3.0, and 43.9 per cent held less than a 2.0. A comparison of the grade point average distribution from the 1993–4 school year reveals that these numbers have held relatively consistent over a lengthy period of partnerships with local universities and an administrative climate of educational reform.

In addition, according to the most recent Family Report for James Madison High, African-American and Latino students remain largely underrepresented in the most rigorous, Advanced Placement courses. Without these advanced classes, these students are at a serious disadvantage in college admissions. Although nearly all of the students at James Madison take a college preparatory course load, those not enrolled in Advanced Placement classes are evaluated by college admissions based on a 5.0 scale because the school offers so many advanced courses. According to an admissions director at a local university, these students are evaluated more harshly than their counterparts who attend schools with fewer AP courses.

James Madison is a high school that boasts a high college acceptance rate to the most elite colleges in the state and across the country. When the data are disaggregated, however, they once again reveal that the wealth is not being shared equally. For example, while African Americans and Latinos comprise nearly 45 per cent of the school's population, they make up only slightly more than 12 per cent of the school's acceptances to the University of California system for the 1999–2000 school year.

Another traditional measure of academic achievement and college readiness is the SAT exam, offered several times annually to high school juniors and seniors and required by virtually every major university in the country. Once again, these aggregated data indicate that James Madison scores well above the state and national averages with a median score of 1048. The disaggregated data, however, show that African-American and

Latino students are approximately 200 points below the school mean and well below the state and national averages.

In 1999, the California State Senate passed Senate Bill 1503 which would give merit scholarships of $1,000 to high school students who scored either in the top 5 per cent of the state or the top 10 per cent of their high school on the Stanford 9 exam. Those students who met this criterion and also scored a 4 or 5 on a math or science Advanced Placement test would receive an additional $2,500 bonus. When James Madison High ran the numbers on their 600+ juniors who took the most recent Stanford 9 they found that 84 juniors would qualify for the scholarship. Of the 84, only three were African American or Latino despite the fact that they comprise 45 per cent of the school population.

To many progressives in the educational community, these numbers come as no surprise. For some time, researchers at nearby universities had collaborated with administrators, educators, and philanthropic foundations to address the issues of inequality in the district and to develop interventions that would break down some of the barriers to access for low-income students of color. Out of such collaborative dialogue emerged the James Madison Futures Project in 1997.

The James Madison Futures Project

The James Madison Futures Project intended to study and intervene in the pathways students of color follow through high school into higher education and the workplace. The project involved a group of Latino and African-American students just beginning high school in a five-year study of their pathways through and beyond high school. In addition to developing a body of information on the pathways that high school students commonly follow, the project investigators desired to create an alternative trajectory that would take underrepresented students through high school and into four-year universities. Alongside this work with students, the James Madison Futures Project planned to support the efforts of educators at James Madison High School to develop more powerful and equitable models of learning which offer students clear pathways to successful futures. It thus sought to reshape students' lives, the work of the school, and the understanding of the broader research and educational policy communities.

As investigators, we believed that such a study would alert students to the social inequality at the school while imparting the critical and academic skills needed to more effectively navigate James Madison High School. There were several core components of the project.

The James Madison Project Class was originally designed to provide project participants with new ways of understanding how to achieve success in school, new skills in writing and social science research, and new roles to play in school and beyond. Its aim was to make students more conscious of – and capable of asserting control over – their own trajectories by engaging them in a study of the trajectories of other young people. Mr Collatos taught the project class all four years.

The Summer Research Seminar component of the project provided students with internships as researchers with the project. These internships were designed to give the students a sense of ownership over the research project, promote important academic skills, and encourage them to take on significant new responsibilities. In addition to gathering information about university requirements that might be shared with classmates and younger students, the summer internships were also used to engage students in critical research and social action relating to the sociology of education and youth access to civic life, the media, public space, and a livable wage in urban cities.

As the students became more proficient at critical research, they were invited to give guest lectures to teacher educators, graduate students, practicing teachers, pre-service teachers, and educational researchers. The project students also interacted with politicians and educational policy makers who were interested in their research. During the final two years of the project, the students traveled all over the western United States giving talks, presenting the findings of their research, and making recommendations for changes in classroom practices and educational policy. Students' changing participation in the critical research community of practice necessitated an increased commitment to social action. Students participated in marches, rallies, and joined and created organizations that were struggling for equity and access for urban youth.

Finally, a major portion of the project was committed to college access. Students used class time to discuss the college admissions process and to fill out the necessary forms for standardized tests, financial aid, scholarships, and applications. A parent component, *Project Families,* was designed to help parents understand the college admissions process and how to advocate for their children at James Madison. The project also took the students on several field trips to colleges around the state of California, giving students the opportunity to sit in classes, and talk with university students, professors, and college counselors about the experience of attending a major university. During their senior year, several all-day college preparation workshops provided intensive support for writing essays, filling out applications, and searching for scholarships.

We both worked in this project for several years. Collatos was the lead teacher at James Madison and a graduate student at a nearby university. Morrell co-taught the project classes for the final two years of the project and coordinated the summer research seminars while employed as a researcher and instructor at the same university. We feel it important to be explicit about our roles as active and interested project participants as well as researchers. These multiple roles do not conflict, as is often touted in traditional research. Rather, we are inspired by the growing numbers of critical qualitative researchers that see both roles as integral to any researchers who are actively committed to social change and who seek to do work that is relevant to and inclusive of members of marginalized communities (Apple, 1990; Biklen and Bogdan, 1998; Carspecken, 1996; Kincheloe and McLaren, 1998).

During our multiple years of involvement with the Futures Project at James Madison High, we amassed the following data set, from which we will draw to study the trajectories that led urban teens to become agents of change within their bimodal school:

- *Comprehensive Field Notes*: Both Collatos and Morrell collected field notes about the students as they participated in the project class as well as non-project classes. Notes were also taken as students participated in summer research seminars, and other research and social-action related activities.
- *Formal and Informal Interviews*: Collatos, Morrell, and other members of the research team conducted annual interviews where students were asked to reflect on their growth as students and as researchers. In addition to these more formal interviews, many more informal interviews were conducted with students where they were asked to make sense of significant moments as participants in the project.
- *Audio and Video Tapes*: These audio and video data document students as participants in the project classes and the summer research seminar. They also document students' involvement in research and activism, as well (marches, protests, documentary film screenings, school board meetings, etc.).
- *Multiple Samples of Student Work*: These samples include essays and other written assignments for both project classes and non-project classes, research reports prepared during the summer seminars, essays written for an online journal, articles written for the school newspaper, and research conference papers.

From these data were constructed cases that illustrate how the students' legitimate peripheral participation in critical research facilitated greater equity and access at James Madison High. The first case references two students from the non-Advanced Placement track who used critical research to expose unfair testing practices at James Madison High. The second case describes students who challenged the school's efforts to increase ability grouping in classes. The final case explores different ways that project students maintained a commitment to urban school reform and social justice after graduating from James Madison High.

The "Golden" State Examination

The California Golden State Exams (GSE) are annual subject matter tests administered to ninth, tenth, and eleventh grade high school students examining them on subjects including mathematics, US history, laboratory sciences, literature, composition, foreign languages, health sciences, and visual or performing arts. Because the GSE are designed to encourage outstanding academic achievement in all public schools, the tests are administered at state expense for all public high school students.

Statewide recognition for high marks and participation in the Golden State Exams has grown steadily since 1987. The number of content area exams increased from two in 1987 to thirteen in 2001 and statewide participation during that time increased from 96,657 completed exams to over 1.2 million. In 1996, the California State Assembly created the Golden State Seal Merit Diploma to reward public school students who achieve high scores on the Golden State Exam. To be eligible for the Golden State Seal Merit Diploma, students must receive high honors, honors, or recognition on at least six Golden State Exams. Therefore, access to multiple tests is imperative for student eligibility for the Golden State Seal Merit Diploma (California Department of Education, 2001).

Besides the potential to receive the Golden State Diploma, the California Department of Education encourages student participation because "notice of success on the GSE becomes a part of a student's permanent transcript, signaling high achievement to colleges, universities, and employers" (California Department of Education, 2001).

In addition to recognition and an official diploma, students with qualifying scores on appropriate tests may receive $2,500 scholarships. While the benefits of participating in the Golden State Exam may be disputed, the California Department of Education believes high scoring participants receive greater opportunities for university enrollment and future employment.[1] The policies of James Madison High School support these benefits for a select few, rather than the vast majority of students.

> The students in Mrs Weiss' AP class are taking the Golden State Exam in Literature. Mrs Weiss addresses the class by saying, "You are competing with students throughout the state," and gives directions. The students comply by asking several procedural questions, but there is no critique of the test or even the "loss" of one class period for a state-sanctioned exam. The next day, Imani recounts a much different scenario of the GSE in her AP class.
>
> (Morrell Field Note, January 2000)

The day after the Golden State Exam was administered to Mrs Weiss' AP English class, Imani shares her experience with the GSE in a different section of AP English with the Futures class. Imani, a strikingly confident African-American female, explains how her class took the English Literature GSE a day late because a majority of her AP classmates threatened to boycott the exam. Because of student discontent, Vice-Principal Torres requested to speak with the students before the exam. As Imani reported her story, several Futures students added editorial comments about the administering of the test. Luz, a student in Mrs Weiss' AP English class, explained that, although her Spanish teacher allowed anyone to take the exam, she told the class the GSE was only for students with As or Bs. Another student in AP English, Roberto, added that his math teacher requested the top four students in his class to take the GSE last year. With shoulders shrinking as the conversation continued, a core group of non-AP Futures students in Mrs Weiss' "regular" English class listened intently. After a long discussion about the benefits of the Golden State Exam, two students in particular, Marianna and Wanda, were deeply offended. They asked critical questions about their exclusion from the exam and the inconsistencies across classes and subject areas. As the class period ended, we encouraged all the students to investigate the issue further.

Each semester the Futures students participated in a final exam centered upon their research, the social studies curriculum, and issues affecting student access. Concurrent with the GSE discussion, the Futures students and Futures adults were in the process of creating critical casestudies identifying impediments to college access for working class students of color. As a class we discussed the need to address the Golden State Exam policies and the exclusion of non-AP students. Marianna and Wanda expressed interest in researching the GSE, their exclusion from the test, and how this policy marginalized them as students. As a Futures team, we believed the creation of a final exam casestudy centered on the GSE would legitimize the efforts of the Futures students to gather information about the exam.

Although Marianna and Wanda struggled academically in school and found it difficult to envision themselves attending a four-year university, they were dynamic researchers. The only daughter and youngest of four, Marianna was strong-willed, critical, and a natural orator. With an infectious smile and personality, the project director once called Wanda, the "Futures Ambassador," for her ability to navigate effortlessly across diverse groups. Working on the GSE casestudy seemed to re-energize their desire to engage at school. For two weeks Marianna and Wanda researched the Golden State Exam at James Madison High School, gathered data and facts, and called upon resources at the local university. Most importantly, Marianna and Wanda interviewed students, teachers, the vice-principal in charge of testing, and the school principal. Incorporating her prior research experience, Marianna revisited her summer research notes dealing with resistance theory (Giroux, 1983; Solorzano and Delgado-Bernal, 2001) and

Wanda analyzed the GSE situation using the model of social reproduction (MacLeod, 1987) she developed several months earlier.

The day of the final exam, Wanda and Marianna presented on their research regarding the lack of access for non-AP students to the Golden State Exam at James Madison. Marianna explained students enrolled in an AP class were told it was mandatory to take the Golden State exam, even though the exam is voluntary. At the same time, students enrolled in non-AP classes were unaware the Golden State Exam existed. During their interview with Vice-Principal Torres, the students obtained a copy of a classified memo distributed to teachers. Wanda explained:

> We asked [VP Torres] whether she sent the memo out to all teachers or just the AP English teachers. She said that the memo went out to all teachers, but just to encourage the AP students to take the exam. She said that schools are ranked according to their scores on the Golden State Exam and, if the school scores well, it will bring in more students and give the school money. So, basically, what she was talking about was money, like this was all about money.

Marianna read the memo to the students. The memo clearly stated that all eleventh and twelfth grade students should have the opportunity to take the exam and the exams are voluntary. Based on her interview with the principal, Marianna explained that the administration is afraid of "White Flight" away from the school. The principal wanted to use the test to show wealthy parents that James Madison was still a high performing school. Marianna critiqued the actions and motives of both administrators.

Marianna noted that Mrs Weiss, her teacher, did not inform her regular English class about the exam. However, Mrs Weiss did strongly encourage all of her Advanced Placement students to take the exam and set aside an entire class period for the test. After learning of the "Golden" State Examination casestudy conducted by Marianna and Wanda, Mrs Weiss later apologized for not considering the GSE for all sections.

In preparation for her casestudy, Marianna printed out information about the GSE from the California Department of Education web site. According to the California Department of Education Golden State Exam Assistance Packet, procedures for administering the GSE are detailed in the coordinator and administrator manual. State Superintendent of Public Education, Delaine Eastin, eliminates any discrepancy:

> Although districts must offer the GSE examinations to all students, participation is voluntary. Therefore, comparisons of student achievement between school districts can lead to unfair evaluations, because not all students participate.
>
> (California Department of Education News Release, 2000)

While participation is voluntary, all eligible students must have access to the test. Furthermore, while the California Superintendent of Public Instruction clearly denounces comparisons of student achievement across schools and districts, the administration at James Madison High School felt pressure to attain high marks. Wanda and Marianna finished their presentation by saying that they felt oppressed by the school structures that prevented them having access to the exam.

The Futures Project created a space for marginalized students to learn about the inequities at their school site. It also provided an opportunity for these students to challenge unjust policies and practices that prevent equitable access. The efforts of Wanda and Marianna informed students and teachers of irregular testing practices and challenged the administration to reform testing policies.

Fighting challenges to detracking at James Madison

> Imani: When I walk into my school I see the way it provides access for some and inequity for others. In a school that prides itself on being diverse, this diversity is not reflected in the Advanced Placement classes. Affluent White and Asian students dominate these classes while in remedial, regional occupational programs and basic skill [classes] students of color are the norm. The James Madison Project provides a space where I am able to examine the role I play in my de facto segregated school.
>
> (Conference Presentation, April 2001)

From their inception, public schools in the United States have served various groups differentially (Tyack, 1974, 1993; Wollenberg, 1976). For example, in response to increasing immigration in the early twentieth century, schools developed a new two-tiered structure for mass compulsory schooling (Kliebard, 1987; Oakes, 1985). One tier was academic preparation for higher learning and the other was vocational preparation for skilled work. Students were sorted into these two tracks according to preconceived notions of intelligence as innate, intelligence test results, and perceptions of probable career paths of students from immigrant backgrounds (Oakes, 1985). Most immigrant students of lower socioeconomic status were tracked into vocational courses and prepared to be skilled laborers, while upper class and most White males were prepared for managerial and professional positions.

Secondary school tracking has persisted throughout the century, gaining strong support with James Conant's widely heralded argument for "common and comprehensive high schools." Conant's comprehensive high schools reinforced the practice of creating a fundamentally different curriculum for students based on their abilities and their projected role in the economy. He believed equal opportunity was a result of experiencing school placed within one's proper track placement. These century old ideas about how to prepare students best for a life beyond high school still drive the educational structures (Sorokin, 2000). Current disparities in education across class and race result, at least in part, from sorting students within comprehensive, public high schools (Welner, 2001). James Madison High School is no exception.

Influenced by their research and role as active change agents, several Futures students elected to serve on the associated student body government during twelfth grade.

By their senior year the Futures students had successfully conducted research at the local university for three consecutive summers. They had explored issues such as transformative resistance (Solorzano and Delgado-Bernal, 2001) and the negative impacts of ability grouping (Oakes, 1995). With overwhelming popularity, Jaime was elected student body vice-president, and Imani and Luz became at-large members of the associated student body (ASB).

During the late Fall of twelfth grade, Jaime and Imani walked into the Futures government class charged from a discussion that occurred earlier in their AP English class. Unlike their junior year, the Futures students were not clustered in their AP classes. Jaime and Imani recounted a lively discussion about tracking for Morrell earlier that morning. One of the star students in AP English Composition challenged Jaime and Imani to a debate on tracking. With the entire class against them, the two felt under the gun from the onset. It was no coincidence a similar argument raged amongst parents and educators earlier in the week.

Several key struggles over tracking existed within the school community and both the English and social studies departments at James Madison High School. An active movement existed in the community to create an additional "Honors" track between Advanced Placement and regular college prep English. A few days prior to the tracking debate in class, predominantly wealthy and affluent parents filled the school cafeteria at a PTSA meeting to challenge the English department to create an additional eleventh and twelfth grade track of "Honors" English classes. The parents argued a vast majority of their children were not eligible for Advanced Placement, but they believed the "regular" college prep classes did not challenge them. Parents publicly characterized "regular" college prep English students as "Students that don't care about learning," and "Some of them don't even know how to read." Their solution was to create a mid-range "Honors" track of English courses to exist between Advanced Placement and the regular college prep English courses. A similar struggle existed in the social studies department.

Due to declining enrollment and low retention rates of African-American and Latino students in Advanced Placement classes, the social studies department chair committed to serious reforms. During the 2000–1 academic year, not a single African-American student completed AP US History at James Madison High School. To increase diversity in upper level social studies courses, the department sought alternative support structures and admissions criteria for honors classes. However, the department also struggled with increasing pressure from the administration and the same affluent parents to create a tenth grade AP World History class. Tradition-ally, the social studies department believed in diverse classrooms and prided itself on teaching economically and racially diverse sections of world history. Several social studies teachers expressed concern; an AP World History course may become a European and Western Civilization course, rather than a history course that represented the diversity of the students in the classes. Similarly, new AP courses could cause segregation in World History classes. The tracking discussions around the English and social studies departments were not private dialogues, but rather public debates. With the assistance of active web sites, email list serves, and vocal presentations at public meetings, the predominantly White and affluent PTSA voiced its concerns. Consequently, students of color on campus were not immune from blatant justifications of tracking and meritocracy.

Jaime and Imani re-enacted the passionate argument for the project students who listened attentively and provided critical feedback when appropriate. Jaime pulled his copy of Oakes and Welner (1996) out of his backpack. The book, worn, highlighted, and heavily annotated, discusses detracking efforts. Jaime explained how he read certain passages from the book to his AP classmates, but they refused to "get it." Although he felt that he and Imani made a compelling argument, he also felt that the deck was stacked against them with only two against an entire class. This was the catalyst to a greater movement.

During the 1999 summer research seminar, Jaime and Luz studied student resistance, specifically Solorzano and Delgado-Bernal's concept of transformative resistance. Solorzano and Delgado-Bernal define trans-formative resistance as resistance in which a student has a high critique of oppressive structures and works towards social justice to change those structures. Collecting data for their summer research seminar, Jaime and Luz interviewed and collaborated with student defendants involved in a case challenging the state to rectify the inequitable number of AP courses across high schools in the state (*Daniel* v. *State of CA*, 1999). Similarly, Imani spent the 2000 summer research seminar researching youth access to democratic spaces. Based on their prior research and the timely public debates around AP courses, the ASB Futures students decided to initiate an informed and critical dialogue with the student body government.

Having experienced the wrath of meritocratic justifications for tracking from their Advanced Placement classmates, Jaime, Luz, and Imani sought advice on how to strategize their efforts. Upon request, Mr Collatos provided the first two chapters of Oakes' (1985) *Keeping Track: How Schools Structure Inequality* and the twelfth grade economics class incorporated the readings to analyze the role of schools in social reproduction. Issues of meritocracy and hegemony were also discussed. Following the critical read of the Oakes text, the ASB Futures students arranged dinner with university researchers (including Oakes) to discuss their struggles. After their meeting, the students arranged to speak with their ASB advisor to schedule time to discuss the issue of tracking on the James Madison High School campus.

For three weeks, Jaime, Luz, and Imani supplied the student body government with several articles about tracking and relevant research associated with differential tracks. A week after the articles were handed out, Mr Collatos inquired about the status of the tracking conversation. Imani responded,

> Every time we schedule a time to discuss the articles, the ASB president and the student school board representative always say we have something else to do today and we can discuss it later. They also keep asking for some articles in favor of tracking, before they have even read it.

Several days later, the Harvard-bound school board student representative arrived in class with an eight-page, self-authored paper documenting the legitimacy and positive benefits of tracking. In the end, the students never engaged in an open and sustained dialogue. The students with the most to lose by detracking classes successfully filibustered the dialogue with plans for the prom, Krispy Kreme Day, and the fashion show.

Whether or not Jaime, Luz, and Imani "won" the debate is immaterial to this analysis. Moving toward full participation required them to critically engage these wealthy classmates who were unwilling to admit or relinquish their privilege. Both Jaime and Imani cited evidence from empirical research and challenged their counterparts to provide data to back up their arguments. Jaime read from a relevant text and attempted to explain its importance to the debate. Imani tried to explain to her classmates why they held tightly to the myth of meritocracy.

While their efforts to inform and enlighten the student body government fell on deaf ears, the work of the Futures students deeply impacted the faculty of the social studies department. During their twelfth grade year, each Futures student created a legal brief documenting how inequity not only exists across schools, but within schools. Several students created written texts illustrating how AP classes, tracking, and the myth of meritocracy prevented all students from accessing admission to four-year universities. After hearing their experiences and their stories, the social studies department voted to postpone any decisions about creating an AP World History course until the following year.

Upon request from Jaime and Imani, the district Superintendent visited the Futures class as a critical friend on several occasions to discuss tracking, testing, and district policies. In his final year before retirement, the Superintendent repeatedly and publicly stated any student in James Madison High had the right to enroll in Advanced Placement or Honors courses. While it had been state law in California, few parents or teachers were aware that any student could elect into an Advanced Placement or Honors class. With a parent's signature, a counselor must enroll the student regardless of how that student fared on the Honors placement exam or assessment process. While intended to help increase minority enrollment in AP and Honors classes, the affluent parents viewed open enrollment as an opportunity and partial victory. Open enrollment changed policy, but it did not change practice. Since the implementation of the open enrollment policy, there has been no increase in the enrollment of African-American and Latino students in AP and Honors classes.

Becoming agents of school reform and social justice

Across most traditional indicators, the Futures students fared better academically than similar students at their school and across the state. Of the 30 students in the Futures project, 29 graduated high school and 25 gained acceptance to four-year universities. By Fall 2001, 17 had enrolled in four-year universities, six enrolled in two-year colleges, two enrolled in technical schools, four had entered the workplace, and one had joined the military. These figures contrast sharply with other African-American and Latino students at this same school. For example, of the 359 African-American and Latino students who enrolled as ninth graders in Fall 1996, only 260 (72 per cent) graduated; only 71 (20 per cent) were eligible for four-year colleges and only 28 (8 per cent) enrolled in California's four-year public colleges and universities.

Beyond the traditional assessments, the Futures students graduated high school with a strong sense of themselves as agents of school reform and social justice. Four years of participating in critical social science research enabled the Futures students as empowered intellectuals with tools to use in their struggles to promote greater equity and access for marginalized populations. Soon after graduation in late June, a handful of Futures students worked as critical ethnographers and mentors with the 2001 Summer Research Seminar. The summer seminar no longer served Futures students, but now served over 20 students from the greater metropolitan area engaging them around critical issues in education. The 2001 seminar focused on researching the conditions of public schools to inform the creation of a California Student Bill of Rights. The Futures students drew upon their experience and expertise both as critical researchers and students attending urban schools to assist the novice researchers, the new legitimate peripheral participants, in their endeavors. At the time of writing, the California State Assembly Committee on Education has amended the Student Bill of Rights (AB-2236) and it is currently under review by the Appropriations committee.

As they initiated their post-secondary school life pathways and moved toward more full participation as critical researchers and social activists, Futures students attending four-year universities actively recruited urban students for their colleges and hosted underrepresented students in official and unofficial capacities. Futures students on college campuses also selected jobs working with urban children, in migrant farm worker programs, and in minority outreach offices, and continued to engage in research around issues of educational access and inequity.

Conclusion

The legacy of the Futures students continues at James Madison High, as students, parents, educators, and administrators attempt to address the inequity the Futures students challenged and often overcame. The Futures Project and the work of the students continue to influence reform efforts at James Madison High School. Inspired by conversation with the Futures students, James Madison implemented a summer bridge program for underrepresented students challenging themselves with Advanced Placement classes for the first time. The Futures students attending colleges throughout California actively recruited, hosted, and informed 2002 Advancement Via Individual Determination (AVID) seniors from James Madison. Relying heavily on the social and cultural capital of the Futures students, 30 of 30 AVID seniors were accepted to four-year universities. With such positive results, James Madison High committed to doubling the size of AVID and the district office expanded the college access program to one middle school and another high school. Modeled after the summer research seminars, a college-credit research class was created around issues of education and power. Most recently, a student-led conference dedicated to increasing the equity and access for all students invited Mr Collatos to present data created by the Futures Project. The student-led conference coalition convinced the new Superintendent to create a district position dedicated to increasing access.

However, changes have not come without pains. After listening to painful stories recounting chronic negligent counseling of underrepresented students, the new Superintendent decided to restructure the entire counseling department and most of the high school administration. To reduce class size and overcrowding on campus, the Superintendent declared no new permits would be issued for students out of the district. This will disproportionately impact students of color negatively. In a backlash to the open support of equitable programs in a tight fiscal climate, parents with children "identified" as "gifted and talented" (GATE[2]) are demanding more funding from the district. Several programs originally created to increase minority student enrollment in Honors classes have been placed at risk because of race-blind ideologies and practices. In spite of the numerous efforts to increase equity and access at James Madison High, no systemic change has occurred.

It is also important to note that the Futures students' efforts toward increasing equity and access at a school-wide level also negatively impacted their individual prospects for college access. We noted several incidents where students were actually the targets of backlash pedagogy and unfavorable treatment because of their participation in school reform efforts. Also, certain students were denied access to advanced classes altogether or, once enrolled, were told by their teachers that they were unqualified to be there. The students who chose to remain faced opposition from other students as well as their teachers and their grades frequently suffered. Therefore, though most of the students did gain access to four-year colleges, their inability to successfully integrate into the most competitive classes at the school also prevented many of them from gaining access to the most competitive colleges in the region, including the most exclusive University of California campuses.

We are neither daunted nor dismayed by these challenges. Nor are we tempered in our optimism and passion for critical research in the name of college access, social justice, and urban school reform. Our experiences have taught us that not only can students be catalysts during such efforts, but they also have valuable expertise to contribute. When we begin to look at these urban school reform movements as communities of practice, we are better able to understand how the inclusion of marginalized voices contributes to critical learning and transformative action in school reform movements.

We urge other interested educators, researchers, reformers, and activists to consider the benefits of working with students and teachers on research and reform projects within a community of practice model that includes multiple apprentices, spaces for authentic and meaningful dialogue, and a commitment to social action. These critical and counter-hegemonic spaces facilitate students' movement from the periphery to the core as research experts and workers for social justice, but they also facilitate transformation and growth for adult participants as well.

Notes

1 According to the Golden State Exam Communication Assistance Packet (2002), the Golden State Exam program: (1) Challenges and motivates students to higher-level performances in key academic courses, (2) Recognizes and rewards students for their accomplishments, (3) Offers the opportunity to earn the Golden State Diploma, and (4) Increases the number of students who successfully complete course requirements for high school graduation and college or university admissions.
2 GATE stands for "Gifted And Talented Education" in the California public school system.

Bibliography

Anyon, J. (1997) *Ghetto Schooling: A Political Economy of Urban Educational Reform.* New York: Teachers College Press.
Apple, M. (1990) *Ideology and Curriculum,* second edition. New York: Routledge and Kegan Paul.
Bartolome, L. (1994) Beyond the methods fetish: toward a humanizing pedagogy. *Harvard Educational Review,* 64: 173–94.
Biklen, S.K. and Bogdan, R.C. (1998) *Qualitative Research in Education.* Needham Heights, MA: Allyn and Bacon.
Bourdieu, P. (1986) The forms of capital. In: J.G. Richardson (Ed.), *Handbook of Theory and Research for the Sociology of Education.* New York: Greenwood Press, 241–58.
Bourdieu, P. and Wacquant L.J.D. (1992) *An Invitation to Reflexive Sociology.* Chicago: Chicago University Press.
California Department of Education (2001) Golden State exam communication assistance package. Available on line: http://www.cde.ca.gov/statetests/gse/admin/eligibility2002/ (accessed March 12, 2002).
California Department of Education (2000, December) News Release, More than one million students take Golden State exam. Available on line: http://www.cde.ca.gov/statetests/gse/resources/newrelease.pdf (accessed March 12, 2002).
Carspecken, P.F. (1996) *Critical Ethnography in Educational Research: A Theoretical and Practical Guide.* New York: Routledge.
Freire, P. (1970) *Pedagogy of the Oppressed.* New York: Continuum.
Gandara, P. and Bial, D. (2001) *Paving the Way for Higher Education: K-12 Interventions for Underrepresented Students.* Washington, DC: NCES.
Giroux, H.A. (1983) *Theory and Resistance in Education: A Pedagogy of the Opposition.* South Hadley, MA: Bergin and Garvey.
Kincheloe, J.L. and McLaren, P.L. (1998) Rethinking critical theory and qualitative research. In: N.K Denzin and Y.S. Lincoln (Eds), *The Landscape of Qualitative Research.* Thousand Oaks, CA: Sage, 260–300.
Kliebard, H.M. (1987) *The Struggle for the American Curriculum 1893–1958.* New York: Routledge.
Kozol, J. (1991) *Savage Inequalities: Children in America's Schools.* New York: Harper Collins.

Lave, J. (1996) Teaching as learning in practice. *Mind, Culture, Activity*, 3(3): 149–64.

Lave, J. and Wenger, E. (1991) *Situated Learning: Legitimate Peripheral Participation*. Cambridge: Cambridge University Press.

MacLeod, J. (1987) *Ain't no Makin' it: Aspirations and Attainment in a Low-income Neighborhood*. San Francisco: Westview Press.

McDonough, P. (1997) *Choosing Colleges. How Social Class and Schools Structure Opportunity*. Albany, NY: State University of New York Press.

McLaren, P. (1989) *Life in Schools: An Introduction to Critical Pedagogy in the Foundations of Education*. New York: Longman.

Oakes, J. (1985) *Keeping Track*. New Haven, CT: Yale University Press.

Oakes, J. (1995) Two cities' tracking and within-school segregation. *Teachers College Record*, 96(4): 681–90.

Perna, L. and Swail, W.S. (1998) Early intervention programs: how effective are they at increasing access to college? Paper presented at the annual meeting of the Association for the Study of Higher Education, Miami, FL, November 7.

Solorzano, D. and Delgado-Bernal, D. (2001) Examining transformational resistance through a critical race and latcrit theory framework: Chicana and Chicano students in an urban context. *Urban Education*, 36(3): 308–42.

Sorokin, P. (2000) Social and cultural mobility. In: R. Arum and I. Beattie (Eds), *The Structure of Schooling: Readings in the Sociology of Education*. Mountain View, CA: Mayfield Publishing.

Swail, W.S. (1999) Do pre-college early intervention programs work? Paper presented at the West Coast College Board Forum, San Diego, CA, October 28.

Tyack, D.B. (1974) *The One Best System: A History of American Urban Education*. Cambridge, MA: Harvard University Press.

Tyack, D.B. (1993) School governance in the United States: historical puzzles and anomalies. In: J. Hannaway and M. Carnoy (Eds), *Decentralization and School Improvement*. San Francisco: Jossey-Bass Publishers.

Valenzuela, A. (1999) *Subtractive Schooling: U.S.-Mexican Youth and the Politics of Caring*. Albany: State University of New York Press.

Welner, K. (2001 *Legal Rights, Local Wrongs: When Community Control Collides with Educational Equity*. Albany, NY: SUNY Press.

Welner, K. and Oakes, J. (1996) Ability grouping: the new susceptibility of school tracking systems to legal challenges. *Harvard Educational Review*, 66(3): 451–70.

Wenger, E. (1998) *Communities of Practice: Learning, Meaning and Identity*. Cambridge: Cambridge University Press.

Wilds, D. (2000) *Minorities in Higher Education*. Seventeenth Annual Status Report. Washington, DC: American Council on Education.

Wollenberg, C. (1976) *All Deliberate Speed: Segregation and Exclusion in California Schools, 1855–1975*. Berkeley: University of California Press.

Chapter 7

"Here it's more like your house"

The proliferation of authentic caring as school reform at El Puente Academy for Peace and Justice

Anthony De Jesus

Introduction

> Here it's more like your house. You can call the teachers by their first name. Like I said, they all care about you and help you a lot.
>
> (Ramon, Junior El Puente Academy)

Based on interviews, participant observation and review of the literature written about El Puente Academy for Peace and Justice, this chapter presents and analyzes the voices of students as they discuss their educational experiences at this innovative community high school in Brooklyn, NY. The students (male and female; US born, immigrant-Latino/a, and African American) are all from working class and poor backgrounds and reflect a range of schooling experiences, academic performance and overall engagement in school and community activities.[1] Their voices offer insight into El Puente's structural and culturally responsive reforms as well as illustrate the importance of reciprocal relationships in engaging young people who have been traditionally marginalized in public schools. In an era where achievement is narrowly defined by the forces of standardization, these student voices provide compelling testimony that community-based school reform initiatives such as El Puente (whose name in Spanish means "the bridge") are not simply model alternative schools but meaningful alternatives to traditional schooling.

El Puente's reforms include its small size (150 students), relative autonomy, innovative curriculum and instructional practices, and identity as a community-based organization. As a school organized around issues of human rights and social justice, El Puente offers a culturally responsive counter-narrative to prevailing school reform approaches as it strives to privilege the cultures and histories of predominately Latino/a neighborhood residents and base their pedagogical philosophy on twelve principles of peace and justice.[2]

Themes of caring and safety are prevalent in student interviews and are linked herein to the body of literature on caring in education (Noddings, 1984; Rauner, 2000; Valenzuela, 1999). Students' descriptions of caring relationships and experiences of safety reveal significantly that a culture of engagement exists at El Puente, which powerfully contrasts the documented experiences of so many Latino/a students in US public schools (Anyon, 1997; Fine, 1991; Kozol, 1992; Nieto, 2000; Valenzuela, 1999) and may lead to improved academic outcomes (Katz, 1999).

Critical perspectives on school reform

The American Heritage Dictionary offers one definition of the term *reform* as "action to improve social or economic conditions without radical or revolutionary change."[3] This definition is indicative of much of the current discourse on school reform among policy-makers and educational elites in the US. Within this context, school reform tends to be understood as large-scale initiatives that seek to improve the outcomes of public schools through increased accountability and standardization (McNeil and Valenzuela, 2000). At the school and classroom level, school reform is often relegated to the alignment of curriculum and teaching with national and state standards (McNeil and Valenzuela, 2000) and seemingly democratic structural enhancements such as school-based management and shared decision-making. Unfortunately these "reforms," while espousing equality as a goal, do little to address fundamental inequalities in US schools and are viewed with great skepticism by critical educators.

Even in the progressive small schools movement, reform is focused on the organization of smaller schools and pedagogy and assessment approaches at the school level (Bensman, 2000; Meier, 1995). While important, these reforms fail to address inequalities in power relations between schools, educators and the constituencies they serve. They are essentially schools run by progressive professionals in the "best interest" of the communities served but which may inadvertently exclude these communities in school governance and curriculum design. Additionally, the question of who defines knowledge and in what ways cultural knowledge will be appropriated through curriculum, instruction and assessment is rarely addressed explicitly, tacitly devaluing the cultural resources of students from non-dominant cultures (Valenzuela, 1999).

This underscores the fact that what is most often neglected in this discourse on school reform is the participation in the creation and implementation of reforms by the communities most affected and impacted by "school reform" – that is students, their families and their geographic and ethno-cultural communities. Low-income communities of color rarely participate in defining the terms of school reform yet students from these communities are the most affected by its results. Moreover, as Nieto observes:

Students frequently have been overlooked as central players in school restructuring and reform efforts. If included at all, it is most often as recipients of particular policies and practices. Yet just as the redefinition of the role of teachers is critical in developing a critical pedagogy (Cummins, 1996), so too is the redefinition of students' roles.

(Nieto, 1999: 120)

As Nieto suggests, the exclusion of the voices and perspectives of school reform's consumers is the continued marginalization of low-income, Latino/a and African American students, their families and communities. This chapter seeks to contribute to a counter-narrative which privileges student voices in response to community-based, culturally responsive school reform efforts and interprets them within a critical yet transformative framework based on the work of El Puente Academy.

Historical background of El Puente Academy

El Puente Academy for Peace and Justice is a small, innovative high school in New York City that emerged from (and is part of) El Puente, a community-based organization in Brooklyn, NY. Founded in 1982 by Latino/a activists who sought to stem the tide of violence among young people in this predominately poor and working class Latino/a community, El Puente today is a vibrant institution that incorporates the Academy, three youth development centers (after-school programs) and a number of other community development initiatives. The organization was initially founded in response to a protracted period of youth violence during the late 1970s and early 1980s and the inability of existing social service agencies and schools to address these problems. Luis Garden Acosta, El Puente's principal founder and executive director, refers to the streets of north Brooklyn in 1981 as the "killing fields" where one Latino/a young person was killed every week that year as the result of gang violence (El Puente Calendar, 2000). In response to this crisis, the founders of El Puente Academy sought to create a holistic after-school learning community that affirmed the language, culture and identities of Latino/a students and linked the individual development of students to a broader vision of community development. According to Rivera and Pedraza the founders of El Puente:

rejected a service-provider ideology and instead sought to provide Williamsburg residents (who are mostly Latino/a) with opportunities, spaces and experiences so that they can determine what is best for them to live holistic, healthy, and productive lives. In essence, El Puente's founders embraced a belief in and practice of self-determination and community development.

(Rivera and Pedraza, 2000: 232)

In their efforts to develop effective youth development and culturally responsive after-school programming based on principles of peace, justice and human rights, El Puente's founders identified the need to address the schooling of the young people in their community, known as Los Sures – the south side of Williamsburg. In 1993, El Puente Academy for Peace and Justice opened as a New York City public high school under the auspices of New Visions for Education, a non-profit initiative founded "to create a critical mass of small, effective schools that equitably serve the full range of children in New York City" (Rivera and Pedraza, 2000: 227). Now in its ninth year, El Puente Academy serves 150 students in grades nine through twelve, 87 per cent of which are Latino/a and 11 per cent are African American. The majority of students are residents of North Brooklyn and come from low-income backgrounds. While a New York City Public School, the fact that El Puente was founded by Latino/a community activists, who explicitly sought to create a school whose purpose is linked to community development (for the community, by the community), creates organizational conditions that are more reflective of the interests and values of local Latino/a residents than those of professional school district administrators or school planners. In this context, educational caring emerges from more profound origins and takes on additional meaning.

"Here it's more like your house." Authentic caring, closure and *confianza*

The students interviewed consistently reported that they appreciated not only El Puente's small size, but also its emphasis on relationships and creating community. This manifests in many ways – including the limited physical space (El Puente Academy and the offices of the community-based organization are housed in a former church building) obliging close interaction among the 175 or so people who use the building every day. More importantly, students experience this closeness on an interpersonal basis – primarily with their facilitators (as teachers are called at El Puente) with whom they develop close personal ties. Trina, an African-American freshman believes that the emphasis on relationships and small size of the school distinguishes it from other schools. She described El Puente this way:

> It's nice, it's different, and very unique. It's a loving school. When you come into that school. Everybody accepts you. Everybody kind of embraces you. Takes you in. It's a lot smaller than the average high school. And I think we are closer, we get along more because everybody gets to know each other – everybody gets familiar with the teachers, the staff. They [facilitators] take their time with you, and they ask you if anything is bothering you. They're caring.

Trina's experience of acceptance and her observation that "we get along more because everybody gets to know each other" suggests that interactions among students are shaped not just by the size of the school but also by the nature of relationships between facilitators and students. To be sure, interpersonal conflict occurs at the Academy yet students indicate that the staff's commitment to developing reciprocal relationships creates conditions that students experience as similar to the care and protection they (ideally) experience in their families.

Emphasis on the quality of interpersonal relationships between adults and students is a salient characteristic of Academy practice that students consistently reported as a significant component of their academic experiences. Ricardo, a Dominican born sophomore stated:

> El Puente's a very good school because the teachers really treat you like a family. In some other schools you gotta call the teacher Mr Rodriguez or Mr This, Ms That. At El Puente, you call your teacher by their first name – like one of your friends. If you got a problem [in other schools] they tell you – "you can do anything you want, after my class." At El Puente they don't do that. If you do something bad, they all sit with you and have a meeting with the principal and they try to help you in whatever you need. They sit with you and talk to you like if it was a parent to a son.

By abandoning the use of formal surnames, El Puente's facilitators communicate their interest in redefining the traditional "power over" model of teacher/student relations for a "power with" model (Kreisberg, 1992). Because he feels cared for by his facilitators, Ricardo does not see school as a place where adults focus narrowly on academic content and routines or where he must be guarded and distrustful of authority figures that will punish or suspend him. He went on to say:

> I never had that experience in any other school. Cause they never do that – like in other schools they talk about "Oh, you've been behaving bad – suspension!" That's all they do right away – suspension – bring your parents – that's all they do. Here at El Puente they treat you differently.

Students suggested that facilitators are not preoccupied with controlling students and managing conflicts at El Puente like faculty in larger schools often are (Noguera, 1995). Rather, they are interested in understanding and addressing the root causes of a student's problem through a pedagogy of caring.

Ramon, a Brooklyn born, Puerto Rican student, echoed Ricardo's comments as he remarked:

> The teachers care about you. If you're doing bad they won't just leave you alone. Everybody cares about you in this school. It's safe; I like it, it's small so you know everybody. It's a nice school. Here it's more like your house. You can call the teachers by their first name. Like I said they all care about you and help you a lot. They do a lot of one on ones. The way they do classes is different too.

Trina, Ricardo and Ramon all describe powerful experiences of being cared for by facilitators at El Puente. These experiences of authentic caring resonate with Valenzuela's (1999) observation that "Latino/a students' precondition to caring about school is that they be engaged in a caring relationship with an adult at school" (p. 79). The students described El Puente as different from other schools they have attended or heard about through friends and relatives and they value the nature of the relationships that they have developed with adult facilitators at the Academy. These statements illustrate the way that authentic caring manifests in the teacher–student relationships at El Puente and reveals that the teacher–student relationship is central to the work of El Puente Academy.

Students strongly suggest that such reciprocal relations are occurring for them at El Puente in ways that at the very minimum meaningfully engage them in the schooling enterprise and generate important social and cultural resources or social capital.[4] According to Coleman (1988), community and organizational structures that foster social capital are characterized by social closure, a cohesive set of shared norms and sanctions "that allows the proliferation of obligations and expectations" (p. 107). Greenberg and Moll (1990) refer to these "reciprocal exchange relations that form social networks" as *confianza* (mutual trust) (p. 321) and argue that they are critical in the engagement of Latino/a youth in schooling. These social conditions lead to the analogy that Ramon made that El Puente is "more like your house," and Ricardo's statement that facilitators "sit with you and talk to you like if it was a parent to a son." These statements illustrate a student experience of *confianza* and indicate that students perceive alignment between their families' orientations toward their education and their experiences with facilitators within the Academy. Further, Valenzuela (1999) asserts that what Latino/as expect from schools in addition to academic preparation is an emphasis on self-awareness and respect, which she articulates by using the Spanish term *educación*.

> Educación is a conceptually broader term than its English language cognate. It refers to the family's role of inculcating in children a sense of moral, social and personal responsibility and serves as the foundation for all other learning. Though inclusive of formal academic training, educación additionally refers to competence in the social world, wherein one respects the dignity and individuality of others.
>
> (Valenzuela, 1999: 23)

Based on Valenzuela's definition – the notion of *educación* or *ser bien educado/a*[5] (to be a well-educated person) is deeply rooted in relationships and social ties characterized by *confianza* and representing the cultural values that El Puente operationalizes through the twelve principles.

Creating a culture of caring

El Puente Academy's emphasis on relationships stems from its history and institutional identity and is organized symbolically around the broader organization's mission: *To Inspire and Nurture leadership for Peace and Justice* and its twelve principles for peace and justice. El Puente's principles (and the four cornerstone principles: love and caring, collective self-help, peace and justice, and mastery) are embedded in their organizational culture, are prominently displayed throughout the facility and publications and are evoked on a day-to-day basis by students and staff. Great emphasis is placed on how the principles are lived by members of El Puente's learning community. In my interviews with them, students discussed at length how these principles were central in their experiences as members of the El Puente learning community. Carmen, a Puerto Rican freshman student, reflected on how the visual representation and community practice of the twelve principles (particularly the principle of "love and caring") impacted her during her first day as a student at El Puente:

> When you first go into the school you see a big round circle and it says all the stuff the school is about [the twelve principles]. When I first saw it, I thought it was like a [night] club or something. I saw loving and caring and didn't really understand at first. Then, I saw people giving each other hugs, just saying welcome.

Carmen's introduction to the El Puente community stands in sharp contrast to the often-intimidating experience of entering a new school as a freshman. As Carmen suggests, the principle of loving and caring symbolizes the nature of relationships that El Puente's members aspire to and often achieve. When I asked her what the school and principles meant to her she replied:

> It's about loving and caring, support, community, like we're all one – united. The way people interact with each other, you know? They give you support when you need it. The facilitators are good. They care about the students. Basically, they treat you like friends. You can call them by their first name, just like they call you by your first name. It mainly has to do with respect. They're caring.

She connects her understanding of the twelve principles to the respect and support she received from facilitators and students. In our discussion, using the language of caring Carmen described how she felt about her facilitators at El Puente in contrast to her prior experience with teachers in junior high school.

C: In other schools, the teachers don't care if they even teach, as long as they're getting paid. They gotta give enough credit to the teachers in this school. If you compare these ones to in other schools ... I don't know, they really don't care – as long as I'm getting paid, "go ahead, talk." That's how it was at my old school.

AD: So these facilitators care more about teaching?

C: Yeah and they care about their students.

AD: Would you say that's a big difference?

C: Yeah, to come from another school to this.

Carmen's observation relates well to Valenzuela's (1999) educational caring framework. Building on a framework developed by Noddings (1984, 1992), she analyzed competing notions of caring among predominately Anglo teachers[6] and Latino/a students that are rooted in fundamentally different cultural and class-based expectations about the nature of schooling. In the traditional high school which Valenzuela studied these expectations inevitably clash and when they do, they fuel conflict and power struggles between teachers and students who see each other as *not caring*:

The predominately non-Latino/a teaching staff sees students as not sufficiently *caring about* school, while students see teachers as not sufficiently *caring for* them. Teachers expect students to demonstrate caring about schooling with an abstract, or *aesthetic* commitment to ideas or practices that purportedly lead to achievement. Immigrant and U.S.-born Latino/a youth, on the other hand, are committed to an *authentic* form of caring that emphasizes relations of reciprocity between teachers and students.

(Valenzuela, 1999: 61)

El Puente's teaching staff is more diverse than most NYC public schools and alignment between parental expectations and facilitator identity and orientation is high. During the period of this study (2000/1) the full-time teaching staff at El Puente Academy were 41.7 per cent Latino/a (5), 41.7 per cent White (5) and 16.7 per cent African American (2) (El Puente Academy Organizational Chart, 2001). Regardless of the race of individual facilitators, it is clear from student responses that the practice of authentic caring is rooted in El Puente's epistemology – the opportunities for El

Puente's students to engage in authentically caring relationships with a diverse group of facilitators abound.

Teresa, an African-American senior, also spoke of the importance of the twelve principles in operationalizing the school's mission and practice. As a student who transferred to El Puente after a difficult first year at a large traditional school, she illustrates the significance of the twelve principles in contrast to her experience in her previous school.

> This whole thing of basically having twelve principles is different right there – you can't ask no other school like "what's your mission" cause I don't really think they have none (*laughs*). I think it's just to get those students out – cause they also push a lot of students ahead without them making their grades. And I haven't seen that done in this school.

Teresa's critique of the lack of a mission in her former school and the practice of "pushing students ahead" suggests that educational engagement at El Puente is related to both high expectations and a high level of support placed on her by facilitators and is operationalized by an espoused commitment to the twelve principles. Teresa went on to discuss her experiences with facilitators:

> They're caring; they take their time out with the students. Make sure they're passing their classes. If you're not passing they stay after school knowing they could be doing other things. Cause most of the teachers take out their time and stay here with you and make sure you got the work down.

Critics might express concern that such highly personalized and informal relationships valued at El Puente diminish boundaries and authority relationships between youth and adults. Teresa, however, believes that facilitators at El Puente negotiate relationships that are indeed bounded, respectful and conducive to student development.

> I think they come down to our level in a mature way. Like they can hang out with us and talk to us on our same level – but it's like they're not really with us. They know how to have a good time with us – how to talk to us – how to find out what we're thinking but at the same time not really act childish. They still know their place – have a good time and let the student know that they are older and they do have a certain respect – so if you're sitting down with a facilitator you don't cuss or anything.

Teresa recounted to me how her experience at El Puente transformed her outlook on learning. She suggests that El Puente's limited physical space may actually provide one advantage in that it assists facilitators in engaging students in their classrooms.

> I get along with people better. I get along with more people. I'm not always fussing, arguing or fighting. I'm not always getting into trouble. And I learn a lot more and go to more classes – cause there's nowhere to hang out! There's nowhere to cut classes in this school. In my old school – I had a big school so you could go on the bridge, out in the west wing, or hang out in the lunchroom, in the gym. There's a lot of cutting spots. You could just chill in the bathroom, on different floors. But now there's like just one bathroom – everywhere you look there's a facilitator sending you to class making sure you got permission to be out of class, so you have no choice. And it makes no sense just to go in the class and not do any work.

Teresa's comments, particularly her statement that "it makes no sense just to go in the class and not do any work" provide evidence of a form of social closure. In addition to the Academy's constrained physical space limiting the number of places where students might wander or cut class, the Academy's emphasis on caring personal relationships creates a sense of obligation that students be engaged in academic pursuits.

Most of the students interviewed reported that at first, El Puente was a very different place and they couldn't quite understand the Academy's emphasis on interpersonal relationships and caring. Teresa's experience reveals, however, that over time students also come to participate in the school's culture of engagement by helping socialize newer students into the "ways of the school."

> My grades improved, my personality – I get along with a lot of people better cause they're like – friendly. When I first came here – a lot of students were trying to get to know me and I was like – "why are you asking me all these questions?" And they were like "I'm just tryin' to get to know you." And I was like "all right!" Cause, I didn't like that at first – but now I understand why they do it.

Like Teresa, students over time come to embrace a community-based approach to learning based on *confianza* or what Rauner calls an *ethic of care*:

> Organizations can be caring by consciously arranging their practices, programs and policies along an ethic of care. Individuals in their professional capacity perform caring actions, but the organization, by virtue of its structure and functioning, also can facilitate and promote effective caring behavior.
>
> (Rauner, 2000: 3)

El Puente's ethic of care is organized around the twelve principles, curriculum and support mechanisms that facilitate the transformative experiences of caring described by students. These include the Holistic Individualized (and Group) Process (HIP) and the *Sankofa* curriculum.

The HIP process: "It would mean a lot to see your eyes when you speak to me"

With the preponderance of violence experienced in schools throughout the United States in recent years, and El Puente's institutional origins (as a response to the "killing fields") the physical and emotional safety of students is a high priority. Metal detectors, increased security, elaborate forms of surveillance and coercive control, however, are not hallmarks of El Puente's commitment to the principle of safety. While the Academy provides a form of cultural protection by fostering a small tightly knit learning community based on *educación* as articulated by Valenzuela (1999), HIP (Holistic Individualized [and Group] Process), as it is known, avoids a reliance on unilateral discipline policies and seeks to understand more broadly and flexibly the needs of individual students and the origins of conflicts among members of the learning community. Through assessment and reflection, young people develop goals with adult mentors and create individualized action plans. Consistent with the school's commitment to holism, through a weekly HIP seminar students focus their goals and action plans in the areas of body, mind, spirit and community within the following four major components: individual and collective self-help, group development, wellness, and community action and development.

The HIP process is tied to El Puente's twelve principles and manifests formally and informally in ways that are quite distinct from mental health and intervention models (or lack thereof) in traditional schools – and is characterized by resisting the deficit orientations that proliferate within and outside of schools. HIP is a manifestation of El Puente's attempt to create its own language for what traditionally is known as student support services or simply, counseling. Julie, one of El Puente Academy's HIP co-ordinators, described the process to me:

Instead of like looking at all young people as what their deficiencies are or that they have these problems and we have to fix them, we look at them as a whole person and see what [experiences] they bring to the table. And a lot of it is positive and a lot of it has to do with environmental factors and a lot of it has to do with some strengths that they have but they have put in other areas in their life that need to be refocused. If we look at them as an individual instead of looking at their deficit we can see what's really going on and we can work from there. It's a much more empowering model, it's much more youth-focused, it's positive and it allows you to go more places than if you look at them through all of the things that they have wrong.

Importantly, HIP is not the exclusive domain of the "counseling" staff and while trained counselors and health professionals are key resources and coordinators, all staff (and some trained students) participate. A compelling example of HIP is found in the following excerpt of dialogue I observed during an intervention between two students (one male and one female) who were threatening to assault each other during class. Julie was asked to mediate.

JULIE: What happened?

SERGIO: Just suspend me! I don't want to fuckin' talk about it! Just suspend me!

JULIE: Relax. You are really angry and hurting inside, tell me what happened.

SERGIO: I don't want to talk about it – just suspend me! I want to go home! Why don't you just send me home? That's what they would do at my old school.

JULIE: I know you haven't been here [at El Puente] long but we don't do that at this school. You're very angry, why don't you take a deep breath and relax.

(*Sergio sarcastically takes a deep breath.*)

JULIE: Can you look at me and tell me what happened?

SERGIO: (*With head tilted and eyes looking down, he avoids eye contact.*) She was yelling at me loud and pissed me off – so I threatened to hit her.

JULIE: Can you look at me when you speak? It would mean a lot to see your eyes when you speak to me. They're the window to the soul.

(*Sergio repeats himself while nervously attempting eye contact.*)

JULIE: Thank you Sergio. Lissette, can you tell me your side?

LISSETTE: Yeah, like he said – he was talking bad about my mother and I have a very close relationship with my mother who is sick with cancer, so it really hurt me to hear that so I yelled at him and he told me to shut up.

SERGIO: Yeah, but I was joking, I didn't know that your mother was sick. I don't have a good relationship with my mother – so it's easy for me to talk about mothers, that's my bad. I didn't mean nothing bad.

JULIE: Do you think transferring your negative feelings toward your mother to other people is going to make your situation better?

SERGIO: No, but sometimes I don't think about how other people feel about it cause I don't know what it's like to have a mother who's there for you.

JULIE: That's a really sad situation, Sergio, and I don't think that there is much that I can do to make it better but I do know that expressing that

anger toward other people like you did is not going to help your situation. Do you agree?

SERGIO: Yeah – you have a point.

LISSETTE: I can't imagine what it would be like to have a bad relationship
with my mother. I kinda overreacted too – sometimes I'm like that –
you know. It gets me into trouble. I'm sorry.

SERGIO: I'm sorry for talking bad about your mother.

(Author field notes)

Sergio, as a newer student to the Academy was unfamiliar with the HIP
process and El Puente's approach to discipline and at his previous schools
apparently had developed a pattern of escalating his behavior with the
expectation that it would lead to a suspension. Alternatively, Julie's
response was to explore the underlying causes of the particular conflict
and lead the students through a discovery of these causes and toward a
resolution.

This vignette illustrates a compelling alternative to the punitive disciplin-
ing element in schools (Noguera, 1995). Mediations such as this are common
at El Puente where efforts are made to address the underlying emotional
needs of students that may lead to conflict. HIP constitutes a strong example
of a structural reform designed to avoid unilaterally punitive or "zero
tolerance" approaches in addressing school conflict. To be sure, there are
situations that require more serious disciplinary action and while the
Academy adheres to the Board of Education's discipline policies, their
commitment to the principle of safety facilitates greater trust among
students and adults. These conditions allow students to receive support
from staff rather than constantly expect punitive and coercive adult power.
HIP coordinators and facilitators strive to support students in confronting
feelings and issues that are uncomfortable and often left unaddressed in
schools in a way that communicates that they are valued as individuals
and members of the community. Like Sergio, so many students (and adults
too) are conditioned to unilateral discipline policies and models of
punishment. The HIP process attempts to prevent conflict by strengthening
students' interpersonal capacity to function as contributing and healthy
members of a community. HIP reveals a strong commitment to the best
interest of students in the context of what's best for the community.

Julie observed:

When somebody gets in trouble at El Puente, they never want to get in
trouble again because it's painstaking, it's like every level they go
through is a whole process unto itself. If it's two people that are fighting,
the process goes like this. Two people are fighting, they are brought
up, the crisis intervention team comes together and they focus on okay,

who is available, who's close to these people and we set up a plan of action.

As challenging as this process is for many students (and adults), HIP provides insights into how El Puente confronts the problem of violence on the local level through the principle of safety.

A student who struggled academically and behaviorally earlier in his high school career, Reggie now clearly articulates his goal of attending a state university in the South. An African-American junior who through his friends is aware of the practices utilized in other schools to curtail violence and conflict, he explained to me why he believes El Puente is a safer place to learn:

> It's not worth it to fight or to get in conflicts you know, cause this school right here, there's something special about it, you know. They treat you with a lot of respect. They give you a lot of freedom here. They don't hassle you. They don't check you when you come to school. They don't have metal detectors. They trust you. You know? This is a good school. Most schools now – they got metal detectors – they pat you down. I don't be wantin' that! My friends tell me: "Yo! I don't want to go to school. They're not teaching me nothing. They [the teachers in their schools] don't care!" This school [El Puente], if you cut school or don't come to school – they call your house and ask why. Other schools – they don't care – they just mark you absent. If you don't come – absent, late, cut. They don't care!

Reggie's statement suggests that his sense of feeling respected and trusted by facilitators solidifies *confianza* and informs a school cultural norm of safety rather than the preoccupation with control and punishment that is so prevalent in urban schools (Noguera, 1995). Reggie's experience at El Puente has been so positive that he credits the school with the fact that he is currently in school:

> Yeah, if I was at another school, I think I would be out playing basketball right now or sitting at home asleep – while my mom's at work. Only once I cut school – and they called my house. I don't cut school no more.

While no single strategy can inoculate schools against the barrage of violence and conflict so present in the lives of young people and our broader society, the HIP process attempts to protect students from punitive discipline policies which reinforce violence (in the form of coercive and rigidly applied codes of conduct) rather than prevent it (Noguera, 1995). Additionally, HIP models reflective problem-solving strategies for students as an alternative to violence.

Sankofa: a culturally responsive and caring curriculum

El Puente's approach to curriculum values and incorporates students' cultural capital or funds of knowledge[7] (Greenberg and Moll, 1990). For example, the *Sankofa* curriculum is a ninth and tenth grade English, Global Studies and Fine Arts curriculum and is organized around the essential questions, "Who am I?" and "Who are we?" Students explore poetry, art and cultural histories which address personal identity and the diasporic history of communities of color. Students present individual portfolios of art projects, writings, and research about themselves and their families. The following description of the *Sankofa* curriculum provides an example of how it is designed to provide students with an academic foundation rooted in their cultural and linguistic identities:

> *Sankofa* is an African word that means, "going back to the source." By going back to explore their roots, students have a better understanding of the cultural influences and historical events that have shaped who they are today. *Sankofa*, however, is not just a two-year integrated humanities curriculum, but really a state of mind, a way of life. It attempts to answer two existential questions that have captured the imagination since the first pulsations of life were felt on this earth: Who am I? And who are we? Using these two fundamental questions as a framework, history, language, culture and identity are presented as key lenses through which to explore those questions.[8]

Additionally, the Academy organizes annual integrated curricular projects across disciplines and seeks to link them to students' cultural and historical journeys as well as the history and geopolitics of the local Williamsburg community. The Sugar Project, for example, was inspired by a local Williamsburg landmark – the Domino Sugar factory – and linked English, Global Studies, Biology, Dance and Visual Arts.

> Young people studied the history of sugar and its effects (i.e. slavery dependent cultivation in the Caribbean and Latin America) as well as the patterns of consumption in the United States. Students in biology conducted a school-wide survey of the amount of sugar and sugar-based products consumed daily by young people in Williamsburg. The English and Global Studies classes investigated the histories of people who worked on sugar plantations and studied the cultures of resistance which grew out of their struggles. Video, dance and visual arts classes studied the cultural and spiritual expressions that emerged from struggles and oppression related to sugar in Africa, Latin America and the Caribbean.[9]

As these descriptions emphasize, curriculum is not merely "delivered" but is practiced and lived by facilitators and students at El Puente – it is for them "a state of mind, and a way of life." Students described the ways in which the *Sankofa* curriculum and El Puente Academy's culturally affirmative approach to curriculum and pedagogy are relevant to their lives and provide them with important historical knowledge grounded in their identities. Carmen described the significance of the "who am I book," an element of the *Sankofa* curriculum, and how she is engaged through lessons on the Taino indigenous people of the Caribbean:

> We are exploring ourselves. In Global Studies we're learning about Tainos – the indigenous people of Cuba, Dominican Republic and Puerto Rico. We're learning about our roots. My facilitator brought in some Taino artifacts and showed us all the weaponry and stuff and it was cool. El Puente finds a way to teach you and you have fun at the same time. In all the classes we are learning about who we are because we write this book, the "who am I book." That's stuff I never really thought about before.

Similarly, Julio, a US born sophomore of Salvadoran and Ecuadorian parents described how the *Sankofa* curriculum helped him clarify confusion about his Latino/a identity:

> This year, one important thing that I really learned was what the difference was between Latino/a and Hispano/a. I used to be confused before, I didn't know the difference. Like when you say that you're Spanish or something like that – it's like you're saying you belong to Spain but they're the ones that conquered us and gave us our language. But [saying] Latino/a, is recognizing your whole group and your background – like we're part African and Indian, and there are other parts too, it's not just one thing. Now I say that I'm Latino/a, 'cause I know where I come from.

By basing its curriculum and pedagogy on students' community and cultural resources, El Puente Academy seeks to remedy culturally subtractive and marginalizing schooling experiences for Latino/a students and provide them with an academic and cultural foundation for acquiring the academic and social knowledge and skills for success in the US (e.g. New York State learning standards). Stanton-Salazar describes this foundation as a bicultural network orientation:

> a consciousness that facilitates the crossing of cultural borders and the overcoming of institutional barriers, and thereby facilitates entree into multiple community and institutional settings where diversified social capital can be generated and converted by way of instrumental actions

(i.e. where instrumental social relationships can be formed, and social support and funds of knowledge can be obtained).

(Stanton-Salazar, 1997: 25)

By appropriating both student funds of knowledge and the codes of power (Delpit, 1995) of the dominant society, El Puente makes great strides toward providing Latino/a and African-American students with the kinds of educational experiences necessary, not only for their educational/ occupational success in the US but also with the orientation to apply these skills toward the development of their community. Indeed, El Puente serves as a cultural bridge for Latino/a and African-American students to the forms of knowledge and skills valued by the dominant society, while privileging their own cultural funds of knowledge as a foundation for learning. Nieto discusses the relevance of the bridge metaphor:

> A bridge provides access to a different shore without closing off the possibility of returning home; a bridge is built on solid ground but soars toward the heavens; a bridge connects two places that otherwise might not be able to meet. The best thing about bridges is that they do not need to be burned once they are used; on the contrary they become more valuable with use because they help visitors from *both* sides become adjusted to different contexts ... You can have two homes, and the bridge can help you cross the difficult, conflict-laden spaces between them.

(Nieto, 1999: 115)

While the "conflict-laden" spaces Nieto mentions serve as a constant challenge to marginalized students in the US, El Puente Academy provides students with the rare spaces to understand the cultural tensions inherent within being a Latino/a in the US and to experience educational success.

Conclusion

In an era where educational policy makers are preoccupied with increased standardization, testing and accountability as markers for school reform, the voices of El Puente's students as presented in this chapter supply important evidence that the elements of educational success for Latino/a students are related to conditions and experiences which they described above.

In addition, the student perspectives on El Puente in this chapter have important implications for policy makers, educators and community practitioners. Individuals, organizations and institutions that are interested in fostering the conditions that engage Latino/a and other marginalized students can learn from both the structural and cultural reforms revealed by students in this chapter. Structural reforms include small school size, innovative curriculum such as *Sankofa* and integral partnerships with community-based organizations and communities. Cultural reforms or organizational practices that foster these conditions include an emphasis on reciprocal student/teacher relationships and social experiences that occur within a close-knit learning community. Additionally, the mission and principles of El Puente offer students and staff important symbols and conceptual frameworks upon which to base their practice.

Of course, the conditions that facilitate caring relations between adult and students are not easily created and, as in the case of El Puente, often emerge out of dire circumstances that lead communities to seek control over their educational futures. These conditions cannot be standardized but rather emerge when communities have or create the opportunity to define and implement schooling and knowledge production in ways that privilege their cultural values and histories as a foundation for incorporating the forms of knowledge required for success in the dominant society. Policy makers, school leaders, practitioners and other would-be school reformers would do well to heed their voices and work toward creating school structures that meaningfully engage culturally marginalized students in learning.

Notes

1 Eight students participated in a casestudy project a collaborative study, during the 2000/1 academic year. The study was sponsored by the Center for Puerto Rican Studies at Hunter College (CUNY) and El Puente Academy for Peace and Justice. The project included a participatory design whereby a group of El Puente staff (Alfa Anderson, Rossy Matos and Hector Calderón) collaborated with a university-based researcher (myself) in developing research questions and protocols, and interviewing students and parents. While the research design process was a collaborative one and I am indebted to the individuals mentioned above, the bulk of data collection and all of the analysis herein is provided by this author.
2 El Puente's twelve principles were developed by youth participants in conjunction with the organization's principal founder Luis Garden Acosta and Frances Lucerna, the academy's founding principal. They are love and caring, collective self-help, peace and justice, mastery, holism, development, mentoring, creating community, unity through diversity, respect, creativity and safety. El Puente lists its four cornerstone principles as love and caring, collective self-help, peace and justice, and mastery.
3 *American Heritage Dictionary of the English Language*, third edition, The Houghton Mifflin Co.
4 Putnam (2000) defines social capital as connections among individuals – social networks and the norms of reciprocity and trustworthiness that arise from them (p. 19).
5 In Latin America (as within US-based Latino/a communities) use of the terms *educación* and *ser educado/a* can relate to social class and race-based differences and strongly imply racial inferiority toward persons of African and indigenous

descent. Notwithstanding this limitation, I argue that within the US schooling context, Valenzuela's usage of the term provides a useful distinction in understanding Latino/a communities' orientations toward education and expectations from public schools.

6   By Anglo I refer to individuals from Anglo American or European American extraction – also popularly known as "White."

7   Greenberg and Moll (1990) refer to *funds of knowledge* as "an operations manual of essential information and strategies (Latino) households need to maintain their well-being" (p. 323).

8   New York Network for School Reform Final Report (2001) p. 17.

9   Ibid. p. 19.

Bibliography

Anyon, J. (1997) *Ghetto Schooling: A Political Economy of Urban Educational Reform.* New York: Teachers College Press, Teachers College Columbia University.

Bensman, D. (2000) *Central Park East and its Graduates: "Learning by Heart."* New York: Teachers College Press.

Coleman, J. (1988) Social capital in the creation of human capital. *American Journal of Sociology*, 94, Supplement: 95–120.

Delpit, L. (1995) *Other People's Children: Cultural Conflict in the Classroom.* New York: The New Press.

Fine, M. (1991) *Framing Dropouts: Notes on the Politics of an Urban Public High School.* Albany, NY: State University of New York Press.

Katz, S.R. (1999) Teaching in tensions: Latino immigrant youth, their teachers, and the structures of schooling. *Teachers College Record*, 100(4): 809–40.

Kozol, J. (1992) *Savage Inequalities: Children in America's Schools*, first Harper Perennial edition. New York: Harper Perennial.

Kreisberg, S. (1992) *Transforming Power: Domination, Empowerment, and Education.* Albany, NY: State University of New York Press.

McNeil, L. and Valenzuela, A. (2000) *The Harmful Impact of the TAAS System of Testing in Texas: Beneath the Accountability Rhetoric.* Harvard Civil Rights Project. Available on line: http://www.law.harvard.edu/groups/civilrights/conferences/testing98/drafts/mc neil_valenzuela.html [August 12, 2000].

Meier, D. (1995) *The Power of Their Ideas: Lessons for America from a Small School in Harlem.* Boston: Beacon Press.

Moll, L.C. (1990) *Vygotsky and Education: Instructional Implications and Applications of Sociohistorical Psychology.* Cambridge and New York: Cambridge University Press.

Moll, L.C. and Greenberg, J.B. (1990) Creating zones of possibilities: combining social contexts for instruction. In: L.C. Moll (Ed.), *Vygotsky and Education: Instructional Implications and Applications of Sociohistorical Psychology.* Cambridge and New York: Cambridge University Press, 319–48.

Nieto, S. (1999) *The Light in Their Eyes: Creating Multicultural Learning Communities.* New York: Teachers College Press.

Nieto, S. (2000) *Puerto Rican students in U.S. schools.* Mahwah, NJ: Lawrence Erlbaum.

Noddings, N. (1984) *Caring: A Feminine Approach to Ethics and Moral Education.* Berkeley: University of California Press.

Noddings, N. (1992) *The Challenge to Care in Schools: An Alternative Approach to Education*. New York: Teachers College Press.

Noguera, P. (1995) Preventing and producing violence: a critical analysis of responses to school violence. *Harvard Educational Review*, 65(2): 189–212.

Putnam, R.D. (2000) *Bowling Alone: The Collapse and Revival of American Community*. New York: Simon and Schuster.

Rauner, D.M. (2000) *They Still Pick Me up When I Fall: The Role of Caring in Youth Development and Community Life*. New York: Columbia University Press.

Rivera, M. and Pedraza, P. (2000) The spirit of transformation: an education reform movement in a New York City Latino/a community. In: S. Nieto (Ed.), *Puerto Rican Students in U.S. Schools*. Mahwah, NJ: Lawrence Erlbaum.

Stanton-Salazar, R.D. (1997) A social capital framework for understanding the socialization of racial minority children and youths. *Harvard Educational Review*, 67(Spring): 1–40.

Valenzuela, A. (1999) *Subtractive Schooling: U.S.-Mexican Youth and the Politics of Caring*. Albany: State University of New York Press.

Chapter 8

The color line in student achievement

How can small learning communities make a difference?

Jean Yonemura Wing

If I wouldn't have joined the Technology Academy[1] when I did, I probably would have dropped out by now. Yeah, the way I was headed, I would have probably dropped out in my tenth grade year.[2] Yeah, I just didn't want to come. The classes were, like, oversized. I had, like, one class had 35 kids in it and I had – most of them were sitting on top of things like this [a ledge]. There weren't that many desks or chairs.

… It [Technology Academy] has helped me with future plans, because now I understand why I like computers so much, because I like to work on them, or around them, use them, stuff like that. And this will help me in my future, because most of the things that are going on now are going to be done by computers… .

(Robert, interview, 05/26/99)

Robert is an African American student who graduated in the Class of 2000 at Berkeley High School – a large, racially diverse high school[3] plagued by a persistent achievement gap that breaks down along racial and socio-economic class lines. So glaring is this gap that Berkeley High has been described as "two schools under one roof" – one school whose SAT scores consistently exceed state and national averages[4] and whose predominantly white, middle-class graduates attend the nation's top universities,[5] and another school in which African American and Latino students are disproportionately represented among those receiving Ds and Fs or listed on the suspension rolls,[6] or are at risk of not graduating. Meanwhile, most teachers in this school of 3,200 see 150–175 students a day, with a typical class size of 32+, and each academic counselor serves a caseload of more than 550 students. Thus, Robert's reflections on the Technology Academy, one of several small learning communities[7] within Berkeley High School, illustrate the potential of such small schools programs[8] to support better academic outcomes and corresponding life chances for those students least well served by the traditional, factory-model or "shopping mall" high school[9] (Powell *et al.*, 1985).

The color line[10] in student achievement is not unique to Berkeley High, and in recent years, the problem has drawn national attention (The College Board, 1999; Ferguson, 2001; Jencks and Phillips, 1998). Although some see this achievement gap primarily as the result of income disparities (MacLeod, 1987), others have found that middle-class students of color also perform significantly below their white, middle-class peers (Singham, 1998), including those from the same communities and schools (The College Board, 1999).

Breaking up large, urban high schools – whether by creating small, autonomous schools such as New York City's Julia Richman High School (Ancess, 1995) and Central Park East Secondary Schools (Meier, 1995; Wiseman, 1994), or by forming small learning communities like the Technology Academy within larger high schools (Oxley, 1990; Little, 1998) – is widely viewed as the most promising reform to address student engagement and achievement at the high school level (Raywid, 1997/8; Lee and Smith, 1995). Proponents of small schools argue that their human scale allows for other positive changes, such as a sense of belonging, collaborative, student-centered teaching, or increased parent involvement (BayCES, 2001). Small schools are also widely touted as a way to reduce violence and truancy (Alexander, 2001; Bailey, 1999) without resorting to the lock-down, metal-detector, prison-like approach of many urban high schools (Devine, 1996). Small schools are seen as safer schools, so it is no coincidence that federal funding became available for school restructuring into smaller learning communities in the aftermath of the 1999 Columbine High School massacre.

While many studies focus on smallness and personalization of education, few examine whether small size contributes to closing the achievement gap, or whether and how smallness promotes student achievement. Moreover, only a handful of studies (Bensman, 2000) capture student voices and reflections in trying to determine what about smallness matters most to students. According to the students, it is not just smallness that makes the difference, but particular aspects of good schooling that smallness affords. It is these aspects that need to be understood in order to answer the question: How can small learning communities help erase the color line in student achievement?

This chapter foregrounds the perspectives of Class of 2000 students in Berkeley High School's Technology Academy, a small school program that represents one approach to boosting academic achievement and outcomes for students of color, particularly African Americans, Latinos, and Southeast Asians. The student voices are drawn from a larger, four-year study – the Berkeley High School Diversity Project's[11] longitudinal study of the Class of 2000. This Class of 2000 research includes analyses of school records data and annual student survey responses for the whole Class of 2000. It also includes 33 individual casestudies of racially diverse students,[12] who were interviewed as well as shadowed for an entire school day once each semester during their junior and senior years. This study has provided baseline data on the racial achievement gap, and has helped to identify the strengths and shortcomings of various reforms aimed at reducing disparities in student academic performance at Berkeley High. I led the Diversity Project's Class of 2000 Committee from September 1996 to June 2000, working with a team of teachers, classified staff, administrators, parents, high school students, and University of California graduate and undergraduate students.

The data for this chapter are drawn from the casestudy interviews of five Class of 2000 students enrolled in the Technology Academy. These five students initially caught my attention because they represented a disproportionate number of students of color who were still regularly coming to school in their junior year, and who in many cases were doing better academically than their peers in the mainstream high school. This chapter focuses on what students have to say about the practices, characteristics, and features that they identify as making a difference. The student voices belong to Robert, Raul, Will, James, and Candace.[13]

Introducing the students

Robert describes himself as "a mixture of different races ... Jamaican, African American, Puerto Rican." As a young child, he frequently moved to faraway ports in East Asia, Jamaica, and Hawaii while living with his father, who was in the military. He has 13 brothers and sisters, and during high school he lived with a younger sister, an older brother, and his mother. He took care of his mother, who was in and out of the hospital with advanced diabetes, and he held an after-school job. Of the casestudy students in the Technology Academy, Robert's grades were the lowest and his overall engagement with schooling the most tenuous, though he expressed an interest in history, computers, football, and photography. He was once suspended in his freshman year, following a fight. Robert graduated with a 1.5 GPA (grade point average),[14] but did not go on to college.

Raul is a Chicano student, and an avid soccer player and coach. He was born in Oakland, California, but spent his first two years living with his family in Mexico before they moved back to Berkeley. While in high school, he lived with his parents, both of whom grew up in Mexico and neither of whom has a college education, and with his younger sister and brother. Raul was fluent in Spanish and English. His father was an industrial mechanic in a steel mill, and a former professional soccer player from Mexico. After graduating high school with a 2.9 GPA, Raul enrolled in community college and also worked in a science-related job.

Will's father is ethnic Chinese from Vietnam, and his mother is Vietnamese. He was born in Vietnam, but left at age eight, with his parents and younger brother, as they made their way on foot across Southeast Asia. He lived in a Hong Kong refugee camp for four years, and entered the United States at age thirteen, having never attended school and having never learned to read or write in any language. His father worked as a restaurant cook and his mother worked in a computer hardware factory. By the time he graduated high school, Will, with a 3.4 GPA, was eligible for admission to the University of California system, but chose to enroll in community college with future plans for medical school.

James is an African American student and an exceptional basketball player. He grew up in poverty, and went to live with his grandmother after his mother could no longer take care of him. James' grades took a nosedive in the ninth grade, but he was determined to become a top student. He says his grandmother did not provide much academic support at home because she had been a sharecropper, and "never understood why I put my school work ahead of my chores." At age eighteen, he became an "independent" student, leaving his grandmother's home and working his way through high school, with support from his mentor and her husband. He consistently kept his sights on college, hoping to major in communications. After graduating with a 3.1 GPA, he chose to attend a historically Black college in the South.

Candace is an African American/Filipino student and an accomplished dancer. Her father is a disabled veteran with whom she has had little contact. During high school, she lived with her grandmother because her mother had lost her job and they subsequently lost their apartment. Candace worked after school at the same place as Robert, and maintained a high 3.5 GPA after a downturn in ninth grade. She was admitted to the University of California, Berkeley, on a full scholarship designated for students who have surmounted major challenges along the road to college.

Before proceeding to the student perspectives, here is a brief background on the Technology Academy.

What is the Technology Academy?

The Technology Academy began in Fall 1990, and serves about 180 students in grades 10 through 12. This small school-within-a-school program recruits students primarily from a pool of ninth graders whose GPA is 2.5 or below, and who are viewed by teachers, parents, or other adults as achieving below their potential. The students are predominantly African American, with a few white students and small but significant numbers of Latino and Asian (Southeast Asian and Chinese) students,[15] almost all living in Berkeley flatlands[16] zip codes or outside the Berkeley school district in neighboring urban communities. For the Class of 2000, Technology Academy students were 58 per cent male and 81 per cent African American. The gender and racial/ethnic make-up of the students is significant in measuring the positive impact of the Academy. This is because in the high school as a whole, African American male students are the most at risk of not graduating, and they were disproportionately represented in the Academy's Class of 2000 cohort.

Students and their parents or guardians go through an interview process before admission, and upon enrolling, the student signs a contract signifying commitment to the program. Student turnover is extremely low, with almost all remaining in the program through senior year. Students typically take their English and history classes and one computer technology class within the Academy, while taking other courses in the mainstream high school with non-Academy teachers.

This small learning community focuses on technology as providing the knowledge and skills required for many different jobs and careers, or for fields of higher education. Its main goals are to provide the extra support needed for every Technology Academy student to graduate and continue their education beyond high school,[17] and, according to program director Ms Pearl,[18] "to build a community of learners so that the kids do not feel as isolated on the Berkeley High campus, and that they have advocates there for them" (Interview transcript, 05/18/00).

Ms Pearl sets the standard within her staff for supporting and counseling students. This includes helping students to overcome difficult life circumstances that affect their school performance, following up on their self-defined academic priorities and learning contracts, and providing access to jobs and real-world internships in areas of student interest.

Teachers volunteer for the Academy,[19] though Ms Pearl seeks out those that she calls "child-oriented teachers."[20] Reflective of the high school teaching staff as a whole, most Academy teachers are white. However, given the racial and socio-economic composition of the students, the teachers are generally interested in working with students of color. Technology Academy class size is kept to 23 students or less, compared to an average of 32+ in the mainstream high school.

Ms Pearl says that the program is "not working on the achievement gap," but rather is putting a floor under students who are most likely to fall through the cracks. She sees the Academy contributing toward "closing the gap not so much in high school, but in life beyond high school." Nearly every student graduates, and most go on to college or community college, or enter well-paying jobs in the region's booming biomedical industry.[21] The Technology Academy has proven effective in terms of retaining and graduating students whose previous academic record would have predicted a non-graduation rate of over 30 per cent, and in terms of preparing students for work and post-secondary education. For the Class of 2000, 97 per cent of Academy students graduated, while one non-graduate went directly to adult school to obtain his high school equivalency. The median cumulative GPA for Class of 2000 seniors in the Technology Academy was 2.4, with a low of 1.4 and a high of 3.7.

What besides smallness makes a difference?

Interestingly, the five casestudy students rarely, if ever, mentioned the small class size or the characteristic of smallness. However, the scale of the program was an implicit precondition for other features they described as improving school achievement and outcomes, particularly for those facing challenges in life and in school. These student-identified features fell into several categories: the feeling of choosing and being chosen; the importance of caring teachers; and connections to jobs and real-world internships that relate to the students' interests and enhance their economic prospects, both during and after high school.

The feeling of choosing and being chosen

When asked why they joined the Technology Academy, almost all of the casestudy students mentioned choice – a feeling of choosing and/or being chosen for the program at the end of their ninth grade year. Students painted a picture of being noticed for their potential, of being picked from the shadowy margins of the larger high school and placed in the spotlight of a small school program. It made them feel somewhat special.

Raul expressed a sense of being chosen because of his Latino heritage. He said:

> Well, the Technology Academy, I found out because Ms Pearl, I mean, just saw me in the hallway once and it was like, hey, you're ... going to be a tenth grader, right? And I was like, "Yep," because they needed more Latinos in the program – Chicanos, Latinos, and I was one of them out of, I think, two were chosen. Just me and some other guy.

Raul added that his father only completed high school in Mexico, and here in the US, he works in heavy industry, sometimes putting in a 16-hour day. Seeing the toll his father's work has taken on his life, Raul declared, "That's why I would like to stay in high school, continue, go on to college and get a good education, to get a good job, work in a good place... ." Being invited into a program that actually wanted more Chicano/Latino students and that promised extra support was enough to convince Raul to join.

Will also chose the Technology Academy after a personal invitation from Ms Pearl. "I took a computer class when I was a freshman and she talked about it, and I said, 'Okay.' " Since his very first experience with school in the seventh grade, Will searched for programs that offered extra skills and support. He saw the Technology Academy as offering guidance toward fulfilling the high school graduation requirements and state university eligibility, enabling him to complete his entire K-12 education in just six years.

Candace chose the Technology Academy out of her determination to raise her achievement and go to college – something neither of her parents had been able to do. Enrolling in the Academy became part of her academically oriented high school identity, alongside her identity as a dancer. She explained,

> Like freshman year I started off really bad. Sophomore year I had a 4.0, still messing around with my friends. I didn't let my friends get involved with, like, bringing me down, you know. Just keeping a good grade point average, with all the stress that I'm going through at home and school.

Candace was also drawn to the Technology Academy "because they had all that advising and because it was computer-based, and I like computers." She added, "I want to travel. I want to design web pages, and act, and dance."

James, who had already experienced academic ups and downs in middle school, joined the Technology Academy as a sophomore because, like Candace, he was looking for an environment that could help him turn his grades around from a D average in his ninth grade year. He was determined to go to college and to become a broadcast journalist, and he was aware of the Academy's reputation for academic support for students like himself who felt motivated to do better. In James' case, he willingly gave up playing varsity basketball in order to concentrate on school. He commented,

> I think a lot of teachers doubt me because of my academic ability, not only to study but just do well in school, from my K [kindergarten] through ninth grade years. So, a lot of teachers, I think, had doubt in me.

But in the Academy, he sought and found teachers who "know what I'm about." Asked what these teachers would say about him, he stated, "Very ambitious, intelligent. He's a climber, like a person who overcomes just a lot of challenges, a climber who climbs a high mountain. A believer. A helpful person."

The students knew that enrolling in the Technology Academy meant joining a grade-level cohort of 60+ students who would take many classes together with a certain set of teachers. They would have a group identity and a feeling of belonging. However, the sense of being seen not only as a group but also as individuals with potential, and the sense of personally choosing and being chosen, are things that these students still recalled as seniors.

The importance of caring teachers who "make sure you're on top of things"

Much of what seems to work in the Technology Academy can only be understood in comparison and contrast with the larger high school. At Berkeley High, as in many large US high schools, Valenzuela's concept of "subtractive schooling" is operative, and contributes to high rates of failure for students of color who enter high school in the regular, grade-level track. Valenzuela, in describing conditions at Seguín High, could be talking about Berkeley High in her observation that,

> ... [T]he feeling that "no one cares" is pervasive – and corrosive. Real learning is difficult to sustain in an atmosphere rife with mistrust. Over even comparatively short periods of time, the divisions and misunderstandings that characterize daily life at the school exact high costs in academic, social, and motivational currency.
>
> (Valenzuela, 1999: 5–6)

This feeling that "no one cares" is linked to the anonymity of a typical big high school, where conditions are ill-suited to getting to know students well or for caring about them as individuals. For students of color, this feeling is more pronounced, as they find themselves relegated to the lower track classes and racially segregated academic spaces (Oakes, 1985).

In contrast, the hallmark of a small school program is its human scale, offering the opportunity for teachers to know each student well. Thus it was not surprising to hear each and every casestudy student talk about "teachers who care" when citing factors that make the Technology Academy different from the mainstream Berkeley High. What stood out, however, were the ways in which students linked this sense of caring to some form of personalized academic follow-up. According to these students, one major way through which teachers show that they care is by caring about how students are doing in school, such as whether they are on track to graduate. Moreover, teachers demonstrate their caring through deeds, and not just through caring words.

Candace described the way students relate to their Technology Academy teachers this way:

> The teachers, like, having a relationship with a teacher, having one-on-one talks and stuff about my academic records, just having the teachers be on top of things with myself. You know, most teachers at Berkeley High School don't even have time to check your school records and see how you're doing, so they [Technology Academy teachers] do that. They make sure you stay on top of things, and that's a good thing.

James introduced the notion of family, and used the same phrase as Candace – making sure the students are "on top of things," meaning their school-work.

> The Technology Academy is a sense of – it's family-oriented. I think Ms Pearl is the mother of them all, like "The Don,"[22] you know, who makes sure you're on top of things … It's small. It is. Everyone knows everyone. The teachers are very smart and helpful.

Consistent with the literature, the program's small size and the "everyone knows everyone" atmosphere, as James put it, allows teachers to get to know a cohort of students over time, and allows for a closer, more positive teacher–student relationship.

Other students affirmed the role of the director in setting a model and standard for caring through academic follow-up. Will said that Ms Pearl is "basically my counselor for four years. Yeah, she's better than that [i.e. the school counselors]. She helps out students. Like if there's a certain class that I want to get, she would try and get it to me."

In addition, Ms Pearl routinely obtains individual report cards for every Academy student on the day the grades are reported, so that students need not wait until another grading period is almost over to receive their report cards by mail.[23] She occasionally calls individual students out of class to discuss an unexplained drop in grades or unexcused absences from class. She stops at a student's after-school, fast-food job and buys a hamburger that she does not plan to eat, in order to spend a couple of minutes checking in with the student without arousing the attention of his manager. These are the kinds of practices that students describe as "making sure you're on top of things," and that inspired James to affectionately call Ms Pearl "the Don." She goes out of her way to build trusting relationships and connect with students across racial and class differences – something too few teachers are willing to do.

Robert added that the students often seek out Ms Pearl and other Academy teachers, underscoring the role of student agency in response to teachers who are perceived as caring. As Robert put it,

> The reason why Ms Pearl knows me is because … I've worked with her a lot, and she's the reason that I had the job, and she knows me because I'm always in her office trying to see what I could do to do better in classes and stuff like that.

Raul spoke of the amount of attention that students received from Academy teachers, and, again, linked this attention to academic follow-up. He said,

They, they go to you. They, they spend time with you. For example, Mr Jenkins, he helps me out a lot. He helped me out a lot with my college essay. He comes up to me and he'll say, "Hey, is it alright? Do you feel that it's how it's supposed to be?" Yeah, and I mean, they pay a lot of attention to you – a *lot*.

Finally, James explained the importance of teachers going the extra mile by making themselves available to students outside of class. He said, "You know, be here in your prep periods to help that student." He defined caring as integral to good teaching. "You really need to care for your student. And that's what teaching's about – not only to educate, but care for a student, also." James found this kind of caring in his Academy teachers, and in some other teachers in the mainstream high school.

Robert agreed with this definition of caring. Speaking of one Academy history teacher, he said,

She's the greatest teacher I've had because she's there to help. ... Most teachers will give you a certain time to come in and help – be helpful. She'll be here. She says she'll be [here] fifth period, seventh period, eighth period, after school, and she won't leave until you're done, you have what you need.

This statement is significant because Robert's GPA was the lowest of the casestudy students, and he had once considered dropping out of high school. Robert's statement testifies that even students with low grades and weak academic skills can be eager to learn, and they may be willing, on their own time, to seek the help of teachers who demonstrate this type of caring.

These characteristics of Technology Academy teachers – of deliberate, individual academic follow-up, of counseling and helping students to navigate their way to graduation and beyond, of encouraging questions and one-on-one work outside regular class time – are not accidental, but are built-in. Academy staff meet every two weeks after school to discuss interdisciplinary curricula, special projects and field trips, and student and family events. Some time is always reserved to discuss individual students who need immediate or coordinated teacher follow-up. Such students include those who have missed classes, taken a plunge in grades, or were facing particular difficulties at home or outside of school. After discussing the possible source of the problem, the teachers plan ways to provide extra support, or to intervene in closing the loop between home and school by enlisting the help of parents or guardians. Small class size and teacher collaboration make this degree of follow-up a possibility, but program staff must take conscious steps to make it happen.

Real-world internships and connections to jobs

The Technology Academy attracts students from working-class, flatlands neighborhoods, and many already have an interest in computer technology. The Academy provides real-world learning experiences and avenues to employment in related fields, both during and after high school. The students are coming of age in a world and a nation where the gap between rich and poor is growing ever wider (Wilson, 1997), and where jobs that pay a living wage require computer and mathematical literacy (Castells, 1996; Moses and Cobb, 2001). As Raul put it,

> ... [C]omputers are going to be the future. So I think that I have to learn as much as I can from computers as possible. They're going to be real essential in like the future, I think. I mean ... computers are going to become the base of everything.

In this context, the Academy plays a role in potentially improving students' economic standing in the job market and the quality of their lives in the future.

Indeed, jobs were a necessity, not just an experience, for most of the casestudy students. All five worked during high school – over the summer or year-round – to help pay for their own clothes and entertainment, to contribute to their households, or to support themselves entirely. Four found their jobs through Technology Academy connections. In these cases, the jobs were related to computer hardware, software, or training. Students cited opportunities for immediate and future employment as a practical benefit.

Raul explained,

> If you're into computers, then the Technology Academy is a great thing. It's a great thing for you because Ms Pearl, she has so many connections with computers, with people that know computers. She, like, got this one guy a job at a computer center where he could learn how to fix computers. He just loved it. ... Yeah, he's going to get a job there, I think, I'm pretty sure. He's learning so many things about computers.

Similarly, through Academy connections, both Robert and Candace secured after-school jobs at a computer-related agency. Robert also learned about a free computer class at a community non-profit agency and enrolled, saying, "It's just a place where they teach you how to do your own web site design from scratch and stuff like that."

Will remarked that he did not have to work during the school year, though he wanted to. After his junior year, he completed a paid summer internship at a biotechnical company, where he conducted lab tests on metals. His plan after graduation was to work full-time in a biotechnical lab while attending community college and majoring in biochemistry. He said,

> I'm not sure [about working in biotechnology long-term], because my main goal is to be a surgeon ... a heart surgeon. But that will take too long, so I want to major in biochem first, and decide whether I want to be a surgeon or not.

The connections Will made during high school provided him with a job that pays a living wage, should he decide not to pursue medical school. He added, "The thing is, I can gain a lot of experience when I work there, and I'm going to write it on my résumé when I apply for a job. It's a good thing."

Candace commented,

> That was the main thing I liked about the Technology Academy, because they try to get you opportunities out in the working areas and stuff like that. For college, they let you know about things ahead of time before the other high school students. ... So they have helped me.

She worked year-round, but she also took full advantage of special academic programs that she heard about through the Academy, including the University of California's Early Academic Outreach Program. In the summer before senior year, Candace says her job plus academic pursuits kept her very busy.

> ... I went to Stanford for two weeks, and it was a computer camp for all girls. And I spent the pre-college academy at Cal [University of California, Berkeley] during the first, I think, six weeks. That was fun. I took pre-college classes of biomedical science, SAT prep, and a geometry class.

Long-term impact

Of the five casestudy students, Candace and James went directly to prominent universities after graduation. Will and Raul went to community college, leaving open the option of transferring to a four-year institution or pursuing graduate or professional degrees. In many respects, the casestudy students reflected their cohort. The Technology Academy had 63 graduates in June 2000. Of those, over 70 per cent went on to college.[24] Most stayed in California, although a few went to private colleges in other states, primarily historically Black institutions in the South, such as Fisk, Howard, and Clark Atlanta. Several went to other post-secondary institutions including career colleges and a musical recording school, while a handful joined the military, AmeriCorps, and the Job Corps. The where-abouts of two remained unknown.

The program's long-term impact can be seen not only through GPA gains or graduation and college-bound rates, but also through witnessing students' social growth, and their acquisition of social and cultural capital (Bourdieu, 1997). Social capital – or the non-material resources and benefits available as a result of belonging to certain social networks – is valuable in helping a student to gain access to institutional resources. Valenzuela states,

> Positive social relations at school are highly productive because they allow for the accumulation of social capital that can be converted into socially valued resources or opportunities (e.g. good grades, a high school diploma, access to privileged information, etc.). Beyond helping individuals attain such human capital as education and skills, social capital fosters the development of trust, norms, and expectations among youth who come to share a similar goal-orientation toward schooling.
>
> (Valenzuela, 1999: 28)

A good example of student conversion of social capital into "socially valued resources or opportunities" is the way students worked with Ms Pearl to get the classes they needed, and the way Academy staff connected students with technology-related jobs and opened doors for Candace's college-preparatory summer. The Academy also provided cultural capital – knowledge and information, and ways of speaking and acting within the dominant culture – which helped students to successfully navigate the larger high school and the world of work.

In his story of Central Park East Elementary School (CPE) and its graduates, Bensman underscores the value of such non-material benefits provided by one small school in Harlem.

> In effect, students told me that if I want to explain their high rates of academic achievement, I must look at the school as more than an academic environment. Rather, I should examine it as a learning community where adults structured the relationships between adults and children, and among the students, in order to foster the students' academic, emotional, *and* social growth.
>
> (Bensman, 2000: 6)

On any given week, one Technology Academy graduate or another may stop by to see Ms Pearl and let her know about college life or a new job, and sometimes a new baby. Former students have gone on after high school to become successful in many walks of life. One, two, even ten years down the road, students still feel a warm, positive connection to their school-within-a-school and its beloved director, and she sees them as living examples of "closing the achievement gap in life."

Conclusion

Small learning communities like the Technology Academy are not the only reform with track record of reducing racial achievement disparities at the high school level. Moreover, not all small schools programs focus on equity in educational outcomes for students. This is one reason why, in the literature, there are more studies about the effect of small schools on school violence or on student engagement than about evaluating their impact on student achievement, especially for marginalized students of color and poor students. In other words, while small schools and programs may create favorable conditions for other reforms that foster greater equity in student outcomes, they do not automatically lead to such equity reforms. It comes down to a question of purpose and priority, and ultimately, the political will to educate all children.

Also, there are many models of small high schools that have succeeded in raising student achievement, but few at large, integrated high schools like Berkeley High (The College Board, 1999). The best-known small high schools – located in major cities like New York and Chicago – were created to replace or provide an alternative to failing inner-city schools whose student populations were predominantly students of color living in poverty. These are mostly small, autonomous high schools of 500 or fewer students. However, the Technology Academy exists within a large, integrated high school in a medium-sized, university city, where predominantly white students from affluent and middle-class backgrounds successfully navigate the complex high school, and gain the knowledge and credentials to secure a bright future. These students "succeed in the shadow of failure," according to a former student School Board member, Niles Xi'an Lichtenstein, who added, "Can a school be called 'good' when a third of its students are failing?"[25] In this context, the Technology Academy's ability to graduate all or almost all of its seniors each year is a true accomplishment, with consequences that go well beyond walking the stage in cap and gown.

What conclusions might be drawn, then, from the perspectives of the Technology Academy students in the Class of 2000, in terms of how to raise academic achievement for those students who are least well served by the mainstream high school?

In the mainstream Berkeley High, marginalized students in the bottom two GPA quartiles generally experience the least choice in classes and teachers, the fewest supportive relationships with adults, and the least access to interesting and challenging curricula. For the Technology Academy to have an impact on student achievement, it was not enough to be small. It needed to incorporate choice and agency, caring and supportive relationships with adults, a curriculum that students saw as interesting and useful, a demonstrated belief in each student's potential, and relevance to students' jobs and futures.

Small scale did make other things possible, however, and was integral to the design of the Academy. Small cohorts encouraged a student academic identity as a community of learners who are making their way through high school together. Small classes within a coherent program enabled Academy teachers and students to get to know each other well, over more than one or two semesters. Smaller caseload, in turn, gave teachers more time for collaboration, curriculum development, and for systematic follow-up with students.

Students, especially those achieving below their potential, responded positively to teachers who saw them as promising, and who cared about how they were doing in school and where they were headed after high school. Program leadership also appears to be crucial in setting a tone and example for other teachers, as students repeatedly called attention to Ms Pearl's role. According to the five casestudy students, there is simply no substitute for deliberate and consistent academic follow-up, and for advising and coaching and sometimes prodding, both inside and outside of class time. This type of caring implies a belief that *all* students are capable of learning and achieving, thus quietly challenging widely held beliefs regarding race and academic ability.

Like many other students from working-class and poor family backgrounds, the five casestudy students led complex lives and often carried adult responsibilities outside of school, including caring for family members and holding jobs. A small school's ability to assist students in finding paid internships and jobs that coincide with their interests, and that provide learning opportunities, can be of practical importance and can actually help students to stay in school.

An overarching theme regarding the Technology Academy also emerged from the lives and experiences of Robert and James. It has to do with second chances. Although the disparities in achievement started long before high school, and were exacerbated by factors outside the domain of school, it is never too late to transform the educational experience for students who have fallen behind or experienced failure.

Finally, I end with some thoughts for the broader small schools movement. With the federal government, Bill Gates, and others pouring millions into small schools restructuring efforts, many schools and districts across the country are moving in this direction. Small schools are in fashion. However, more research is needed to determine what kinds of small schools work in raising student achievement and closing the achievement gap, and if they work, how? More thought is needed to determine how best to measure success. While a small school may celebrate the growth and accomplishments of all of its students, perhaps the true measure of its success lies in the distance traveled by students who started at the bottom of the class. In pursuing this research, student voices and experiences – especially those least well served by existing large schools – can play a vital role in understanding what about smallness, or besides smallness, matters most to them.

Notes

1 Technology Academy is a pseudonym for an existing program.
2 National statistics indicate that more students drop of high school in their tenth grade year than in any other single year.
3 Berkeley High School is the only public high school in Berkeley, California, and has been called the most integrated school in the US (Noguera, 1995). From 1996–2001, Berkeley High School's enrollment rose from 2,800 students to more than 3,200 students. During that time, the racial/ethnic make-up of the student body fluctuated somewhat, but was approximately 38 per cent white, 35 per cent African American, 10 per cent Latino, 11 per cent Asian, 5 per cent multi-racial, and less than 1 per cent Native American and Filipino.
4 1999 average SAT scores for Berkeley High illustrate this point. BHS: 551 verbal, 563 math; State: 492 verbal, 517 math (California Department of Education, Educational Demographics Unit, 2002).
5 The Class of 2000 sent 4 graduates to MIT, 2 to Harvard, 3 to Stanford, 5 to Columbia, 4 to Brown, 39 to UC Berkeley, 16 to UCLA, and 27 to UC Santa Cruz, to name just a few.
6 During the 1999–2000 school year, African American students represented about 80 per cent of the students sent to On Campus Suspension (OCS), yet they made up only 38 per cent of the student body. Meanwhile, white students, who also made up about 37 per cent of the student body, represented only 9 per cent of OCS referrals (Gregory et al., 2001).
7 Small learning communities at Berkeley High School are also called "small schools programs" or "schools-within-a-school." They are part-day, theme-based, academic programs of choice, with students taking the balance of their classes in the mainstream high school. They are not autonomous small schools sharing a campus, as is the case of Julia Richman High School in New York City.
8 Berkeley High School is home to more than 15 formal and informal small learning communities. The Technology Academy is one of several formal pro-grams. An example of an informal small learning community is the Advanced Placement program. By junior and senior years, students who take multiple Advanced Placement offerings (in science, math, foreign language, and English) find themselves in the same classes with the same group of pre-dominantly white, middle-class students, and are taught by the same pool of highly qualified teachers. Although the AP program is not a structured small learning community with a formally established cohort of students and team of teachers, in reality it is all of these things.
9 Powell, Farrar and Cohen likened the large US high school to a shopping mall, and called secondary education "another consumption experience in an abundant society" (Powell et al., 1985: 8). According to this analogy, in an institution such as Berkeley High, students "have wide discretion not only about what to buy, but also about whether to buy" or simply to browse or to stay away from the mall altogether (p. 8). The best-served students tend to be

those who already know what brand and style they want, and have the currency to purchase it.

10 This phrase is taken from W.E.B. DuBois, who said, "The problem of the twentieth century is the problem of the color line, the question is how far differences of a race ... will hereafter be made the basis of denying over half the world the right of sharing to their utmost ability the opportunities and privileges of modern civilization." This quote first appeared in DuBois' article "Of the training of Black men," which appeared in *Atlantic Monthly* in September 1902, and can be found in Dorothy Winbush Riley's (1995) book *My Soul Looks Back*, 'less I Forget, p. 64. DuBois' most famous use of the phrase "The color line" appears in his 1903 book *The Souls of Black Folk*.

11 The Berkeley High School Diversity Project (1996–2002) is a school-university partnership that engaged in school-wide action research and organizing efforts to catalyze school reform aimed at reducing the achievement gap and addressing patterns of racial segregation at the high school.

12 The casestudy students for the overall Class of 2000 study represent a stratified random sample of high-, middle-, and low-achieving students from each major racial/ethnic group.

13 All casestudy student names are pseudonyms.

14 GPA, or grade point average, is based on a four-point scale. A grade of A = 4 points, B = 3 points, C = 2 points, D = 1 point. Course grade points are added up and averaged, resulting in the student's GPA. A GPA of 2.5 is equivalent to an average grade of B–/C+.

15 Latino and Asian students make up just 10 per cent and 11 per cent, respectively, of the total student body. Thus, even a few Latinos and Asians per grade level is significant. As this book goes to press, Latino students now make up 20 per cent of the Technology Academy.

16 Geographically, the Berkeley hills zip codes in the north and east areas of the city are generally home to the most affluent families, who are predominantly white. Meanwhile, working-class and poor families generally reside in the south and west Berkeley flatlands neighborhoods.

17 Program director Ms Pearl defines post-secondary education as any formal education beyond high school, ranging from career college to graduate school.

18 All teacher names are pseudonyms.

19 Most Academy teachers are also assigned to teach in the mainstream high school.

20 The only adult speaker at the Class of 2000 graduation ceremony was a teacher elected by the Class of 2000 students. He happened to be a Technology Academy history teacher.

21 These are students concurrently enrolled in Berkeley High School's Biotech Academy, which provides specialized science classes to prepare students to enter the biotechnical industry as skilled laboratory technicians, after one year in community college.

22 "The Don," as in *The Godfather*.

23 Teachers in the mainstream high school often refer to Ms Pearl as a "saint" for going so far beyond the norm to help her students succeed. Although meant as a compliment, calling her a "saint" also serves as an excuse for some teachers who would rather not have to teach this population of students, many of whom have low academic skills and hard lives.

24 National studies show that 76 per cent of African American students in the Class of 1998 received a high school diploma (excluding General Education Developments/high school equivalency certificates), while less than 40 per cent attended college (Greene, 2002). The Technology Academy's Class of 2000

graduation rate of 97 per cent and college-going rate of over 70 per cent greatly exceed the national averages for African Americans, who made up 85 per cent of the Class of 2000 cohort.

25   Statement at Berkeley School Board meeting, January 2001.

Bibliography

Alexander, M. (2001) A small solution to the large problem of school violence. *San Francisco Chronicle*, January 15.

Ancess, J. (1995) Coming down the home stretch: transforming a comprehensive high school into an educational campus. Paper presented at the annual meeting of the American Educational Research Association, San Francisco, CA.

Bailey, J. (1999) The case for small schools. Center for Rural Affairs monthly newsletter, January.

Bay Area Coalition of Equitable Schools (2001) *Why Small Schools?* Oakland, CA: BayCES.

Bensman, D. (2000) *Central Park East and Its Graduates: "Learning by Heart."* New York: Teachers College Press.

Bourdieu, P. (1973) Cultural reproduction and social reproduction. In J. Karabel and A.H. Halsey (Eds), *Power and Ideology in Education* (1997) New York: Oxford University Press.

California Department of Education, Educational Demographics Unit (2002) *Dataquest.* Available: http://data1.cde.ca.gov/dataquest.

Castells, M. (1996) *The Rise of the Network Society.* Malden, MA: Blackwell.

College Board (1999) *Reaching the Top: A Report of the National Task Force on Minority High Achievement.* New York: The College Board.

Devine, J. (1996) *Maximum Security: The Culture of Violence in Inner City Schools.* Chicago: University of Chicago Press.

DuBois, W.E.B. (1902) Of the training of Black men. *Atlantic Monthly*, September.

Ferguson, R.F. (2001) A diagnostic analysis of black–white GPA disparities in Shaker Heights, Ohio. In: D. Ravitch (Ed.), *Brookings Papers on Educational Policy*. Washington, DC: Brookings.

Greene, J.P. (2002) *High School Graduation Rates in the United States*. A Manhattan Institute for Policy Research report prepared for the Black Alliance for Educational Options. Available on line: http://www.manhattan-institute.org/html/cr_baeo.htm.

Gregory, A., Moran, D. and Mosely, P. (2001) The discipline gap: teachers and the overrepresentation of African American students in the discipline system. Paper presented at the annual meeting of the American Educational Research Association, Seattle, WA, April.

Jencks, C. and Phillips, M. (1998) *The Black–White Test Score Gap.* Washington, DC: Brookings.

Lee, V.E. and Smith, J.B. (1995) Effects of high school restructuring and size on gains in achievement and engagement for early secondary school students. Research Report 143, ED370210, ERIC Document Reproduction Service.

Little, J.W. (1998) The student experience of restructuring high schools. Paper presented at the annual meeting of the American Educational Research Association, San Diego, CA, April.

MacLeod, J. (1987) *Ain't No Makin' It: Leveled Aspirations in a Low-income Neighborhood*. Boulder: Westview.

Meier, D. (1995) *The Power of Their Ideas: Lessons for America from a Small School in Harlem*. Boston: Beacon Press.

Moses, B. and Cobb, C.E., Jr (2001) *Radical Equations: Math Literacy and Civil Rights*. Boston: Beacon Press.

Noguera, P. (1995) Ties that bind, forces that divide: Berkeley High School and the challenge of integration. *University of San Francisco Law Review*, 29(Spring): 719–40.

Oakes, J. (1985) *Keeping Track: How Schools Structure Inequality*. New Haven: Yale.

Oxley, D. (1990) *An Analysis of House Systems in New York City Neighborhood High Schools*. Philadelphia: Temple University Center for Research in Human Development and Education.

Powell, A.G., Farrar, E. and Cohen, D.K. (1985) *The Shopping Mall High School: Winners and Losers in the Educational Marketplace*. Boston: Houghton-Mifflin.

Raywid, M.A. (1997/8) Small schools: a reform that works (synthesis of research). *Educational Leadership*, December/January: 34–9.

Singham, M. (1998) The canary in the mine: the achievement gap between Black and White students. *Phi Delta Kappan*, September: 9–15.

Valenzuela, A. (1999) *Subtractive Schooling: U.S.-Mexican Youth and the Politics of Caring*. Albany, NY: SUNY Press.

Wilson, W.J. (1997) *When Work Disappears: The World of the New Urban Poor*. New York: Vintage.

Wiseman, F. (Filmmaker) (1994) *High School II* (Film). Available from Zipporah Films, 1 Richdale Avenue, Unit 4, Cambridge, MA 02140, USA.

Chapter 9

"We have a motion on the floor"

Montclair High School and the Civics and Government Institute

David Lee Keiser and Shana Stein

> To become an integrated person is not only to understand the worlds in which we live and work, but to become the kind of person who will take part in shaping those worlds. This emphasis on critique of current realities, and on participating in the re-creation of our worlds, is a central part of democratic life.
>
> (Beyer, 1996: 17)

The need for students to engage in the democratic critique and participation to which Beyer (1996) refers has lately become acute. Due both to the contested 2000 Presidential Election, and the terrorist attacks on September 11, 2001, students in this country's schools have had the opportunity to examine what it means to live in the social and political democracy of the United States. Of course, most debates about democracy are less momentous than those precipitated by the two events mentioned above, and yet, one function of debate and critique – about any subject – is both to strengthen and challenge the democratic process. In this time of heightened student civic engagement in school – brought on in recent years by school shootings as well as national crises – many topics generate heated debate and constructive critique. Much as the Columbine shootings galvanized movements towards educating for compassion, the recent challenges to working democracy have renewed many educators' commitment to enculturating students into a democratic society (Aronson, 2000; Goodlad *et al.*, 1990). Some whole school reforms, such as the Coalition of Essential Schools, operate under democratic principles of participation, consensus building, and equity (Sizer and Sizer, 1999). Schools unaffiliated with whole school reform and renewal organizations can also create democratic spaces for students to learn about and enact democratic principles.

At Montclair High School in northern New Jersey, a small, democratically run student congress meets regularly to enact and review legislation. On one recent Friday, the congress needed to raise money for a trip to Washington, DC. A representative brought a motion to sell lollipops and use the profits for the trip. After much debate, the issue was tabled. One student described the process,

> I remember it was like, we spent, God knows how long it was, an obscene amount of time debating about one brand of lollipop versus another and how everyone always thought, "well no, that brand was nasty, I don't want to eat that, no one will ever buy it." This went on for a really long time and everyone got really bitter with the entire process and we all sounded like a bunch of bureaucrats arguing over the simple flavors of lollipops for a sale. It was kind of a weird thing to me, so much fierce debate over a trivial thing.

Although this student dismissed the debate as "trivial," a visiting professor who witnessed the congress noted his impressions of the democratic process:

> I had no idea that lollipops were so complicated. To their credit, the students thought through the issues with this seemingly simple and innocuous candy, and carefully analyzed tangential concerns such as: What kind of lollipop should be sold? What will happen to the wrappers? Is one type of lollipop stickier than another? Where will the sticks end up? Each of these concerns has implications, and each was addressed in turn, through parliamentary procedure. At the end of the legislative session, no decision had been reached. Talk about an accurate model!

Their congress mirrors some of the struggles facing adults in leadership roles within a democratic process. For example, the discussion about lollipop sticks touches issues of environmentalism, school safety, and cleanliness, as well as due process. As in actual governmental congresses, individuals raised different issues important to their constituencies, and argued for their relevance within the legislative session. Although the lollipop decision was indeed tabled, it was the process itself that both exemplified and illustrated the tediousness of parliamentary procedure and due process. The event also provided a lens into the workings of this small learning community, and raised some key questions about the impact of this particular school reform:

- How does the Civics and Government Institute (CGI) help students gain the knowledge, experience, and tools needed to be more active and participating citizens in our democracy?
- By enacting their own "mini" democratic government, to what extent do the students feel more equipped to take action to create change?
- How are issues of race and class addressed within this community?

These questions frame this chapter, which provides a brief examination of this small learning community as an example of school reform and examines the extent to which the Civics and Government Institute provides spaces for students to learn to raise questions, to critically and democratically engage issues under the mentorship of teachers, and for the exchange of free and honest dialogue about issues of race and class. It probes the views of diverse students attending CGI on their experiences of being part of a small learning community focused on fostering democratic participation. Interviews with students revealed that the students felt challenged, cared for, and, eventually, well prepared both for college and for civic participation in a democratic society. Explicit instruction in, modeling of and practice in the daily workings of a democratic environment allowed students to participate in difficult and fruitful discussions on thorny issues, such as the school's racial achievement gap. It also fostered in students valuable skills of self-expression, listening, and negotiation among various perspectives. After a brief introduction to the school and the Institute, the voices of students will be examined with attention to the above questions.

Montclair High and the Civics and Government Institute

Due to the township's cosmopolitan culture and the school district's diverse student body, Montclair High School is well positioned to address issues of diversity, equity, and access to knowledge for all students (Goodlad and Oakes, 1988). During the 2000–1 school year, the Montclair High School student body was approximately 50 per cent Black, 40 per cent White, and 10 per cent "other," including Asian and Latino. Within CGI the students discuss and debate issues such as the racial demographics of the high school and the implications thereof. In the words of one (White male) student,

> In CGI people have the chance to voice their opinion about the achievement gap and they are able to give possible solutions, whereas in the regular school, without a smaller learning community, it is hard to get your voice out and be heard.

Students debate and openly address current and critical events such as the War on Terror, the 2000 Election, and, more locally, the racial achievement gap within the school district. The Institute is seen by many students, teachers, and parents as a rigorous intellectual environment attending to government studies and internships, within a rigorous small learning community. When we asked a student how the Institute dealt with difficult issues that arise, he spoke to the diverse academic elitism present within CGI.

I think that CGI definitely fosters open discussion on the issues. It's an elite microcosm of the school. Generally speaking it's the best and brightest African American students paired with the best and brightest Caucasian students and the best and brightest "other" students, Latin American, Asian, etc., discussing the issues openly, so it's a real intellectual environment where the achievement gap can really be discussed, ideally openly.

This statement speaks both to the high level of discourse within CGI, and to the maturity of the discussion itself, as many students welcome the opportunity to address issues salient to their lives. In focus group interviews, CGI students cited issues of diversity, leadership, and access to knowledge as salient to their success in and contentment with the Institute.

The town of Montclair, New Jersey, and its high school have long struggled with issues of diversity, integration and equity. Researcher Michelle Fine writes,

Montclair, New Jersey, is one of the few communities nationwide that has worked to keep the dream of integration alive, not without troubles, not without disappointments, not without a court order. But the town has struggled to provide both excellent and equitable education to all its students – poor, working class, middle class, and rich; White, African American, biracial, Latino, Asian American.

(Anand *et al.*, 2000: 162–3)

In the town, as well as the high school, issues of race, privilege, and access to education are neither simple nor hidden, and CGI has been a pivotal lens through which to examine these issues, both theoretically and practically. Students apply to participate in CGI, then once in the Institute students enact as well as debate issues. Even within a small learning community, however, not all voices always get heard. In discussions with students, they focused on issues of power, access to knowledge, the development of leaders and leadership, and the role and impact teachers have. When asked about how power is distributed among the students and the teachers, one student suggested that school rules trumped parliamentary procedure.

To be honest I don't think that any one student in CGI has that much power. I mean obviously, we're all capable of writing legislation, we can all put ideas forward and write bills and everything but then, everything gets so bogged down, we have to vote for it in both the House and the Senate and a lot of the times things will get failed or never even get on the floor and so it's difficult for much to get done at all. And of course, the teachers have final say, regardless of how self-governed we are they are the final check.

(White female)

Much like the student critic of the lollipop debate, this student speaks to the slow nature of bureaucracy, and the frustration of due process. The Civics and Government Institute, founded in 1997, is a small learning community that focuses on the study of government and social issues. The mission of the Institute is to create a more informed participatory citizenry, with a student-run Congress, executive branch, and Supreme Court, all of which operate under the student-written CGI Constitution. It provides an educational environment through which students can develop an understanding of their roles as functioning, socially responsible members of the community, state, country and world.

In this small learning community, students enact and embody a working government with bills, debates, and visiting dignitaries. Recently in Washington, DC, they met with Justice Clarence Thomas; previously they also visited with such dignitaries as then-Attorney General Janet Reno and with Senator Jon Corzine, ex-Senator Bill Bradley, and many local legislators. Such trips concretize for students the enormity of what they study, and provide them with valuable experiences, memories, and indeed, social capital. Students participate in drafting bills and lobbying for them, chairing committees, abiding by and occasionally amending the constitution, and protesting perceived injustices. A teacher/mentor is assigned to advise and assist each student.

CGI is open to all students who complete the application process, including teacher recommendations and parental consent. However, the issue of parental consent, or, indeed, parental lobbying is not simple, as teachers must accede not only to district and school administrative requirements, but to parents pressuring them; because CGI is high status and has a successful reputation, competition is steep, and how to ensure diversity with excellence presents a similar challenge to the one public universities have when poring over undergraduate applications.

All sophomores and juniors serve as members of the House of Representatives and are considered for positions in the executive branch and on the Supreme Court, and all students serve on at least one committee. Seniors commit two periods each day to CGI and must complete twenty hours of community service and a senior internship. In addition to standard and advanced academic tests, CGI utilizes alternative assessment in that students must submit an exit exhibit/portfolio to be assessed by a panel of teachers, parents, peers, and other community members. Seniors serve in the Senate, in the executive branch or on the Supreme Court.

CGI has struggled, successfully at times, to maintain the diversity of the high school, but that too was a process. When CGI began in 1997, it was seen by many teachers, students, and parents as an elite program intended only for students in high honors and Advanced Placement classes. Approximately forty students enrolled during the first year. By the 2001–2 school year, however, enrollment had increased from 40 students to 172, due both to the popularity of the Institute and to an aggressive campaign to diversify it.

Making diversity a part of the conversation: struggling with thorny issues

Since its inception, CGI has struggled to both maintain diversity among its students and faculty and also provide a space for students to engage difficult discussions and concerns about diversity within the Institute. CGI offers a place where students can talk about issues of great importance to them, and gives students an acceptable way of dealing with these issues because it legitimizes and encourages debate.

> When I first came into the program, it was a time when it actually was a small learning community. Being that in my class of 2002, there were only maybe five minorities, we couldn't gravitate towards the people who looked like us because there were virtually no people who did look like us. So, we just naturally inserted into the rest of the population and we also helped in giving the deception, I should say, that CGI was diverse, because we basically rotated the ethnic minorities in the Institute when we were sending people out to recruit and I was one of those people. The same five minorities got recycled every time we went somewhere, but I think that in the bigger class, people just naturally gravitated towards people that looked like them because that is the first thing that you see.

This student, a Black girl, supports the idea that in a smaller educational environment, minority students have less choice to self-segregate. At the same time, the statement is rich with word play (give the "deception" not "perception") and speaks to the eloquence the Institute tries to instill in its students. The comment also recalls Tatum's (1997) analysis of the stigma and self-consciousness that students of color endure to fit in to high tracked classes and spaces. Smaller classes force students to interact more closely and perhaps learn more from each other. Still, when students of color represent a significant minority, thorny issues arise. For example, this student also mentions that the minority students are used to promote diversity within the program, and are perhaps used as overproportional representatives.

Some students feel that diversity is not necessary, that race is not an issue and that the program should be only for students who are already interested in government issues and have significant leadership skills. Other students experience CGI in a different manner. Among the students with whom we spoke, unsurprisingly, White and Black students differed in their perceptions of racial issues within CGI. In this chapter, the general race and gender of the student is given to illuminate these different perceptions. Some White male students did not see race as a factor in the creation and development of leadership opportunities. One saw leaders as being the students who cared about, personally connected with, and promoted the well-being of the Institute.

> I don't think that race can or ever will be a big issue just because in the past it never has been and the leaders that have been born in our Institute, it's not because of race. I guess it's just because they have the time to actually think of ideas and ways to promote the well-being of the Institute whereas people with not as much spare time can't do it.

Although this student expressed a need for the open dialogue and forum for discussion, at the same time he coded his language in terms of effort and dedication to the Institute – individual variables – rather than in terms of social capital, networks, or entitlement – group variables. That is, his comment underscores the difficulty many White people have in addressing race, or acknowledging racism as he doesn't "think that race can or ever will be a big issue." Other students questioned the attention the Institute and school give to diversity, citing both a perceived liberal bias among the teachers, and the difficulty of institutionalizing issues. One student felt that CGI did not represent a diverse political spectrum.

> One thing I notice is that all the teachers are Democrats and very liberal. The fact that we always have Democratic speakers, Senators, and it's troubling because we are in a community where we are supposed to learn about politics and we are only getting one side of the world. It would be nice to have different perspectives on things and [to give] kids more opportunity to get them more knowledgeable.
>
> (White male)

In response to the perceived need for students – in particular, though not exclusively, students of color – to talk about issues of diversity, students formed the Minority Achievement Committee (MAC) within the Civics and Government Institute. One Black female student we spoke with summarized the intentions of the committee,

> The purpose of [the Minority Achievement Committee] was in response to a general feeling of alienation among the CGI students, mainly among the students who could be considered to be minorities. Basically

what we do on the Committee is working towards achieving our goal. What we recently did is created a bill, it hasn't been passed yet because it hasn't been presented in Congress, the bill focuses on respect and specific disciplinary actions against people who intend to make people feel alienated through disrespectful comments and actions. We fully intend in the future to gather statistics on specifically our school and nationwide and see how we feel we can tackle [the achievement gap] not only within the Institute, but hopefully school-wide and district-wide.

To help the committee gather data, students created and distributed a survey intended to elicit student input and make decisions about what issues to prioritize. When we asked this same student about the results of the survey, however, she hesitated.

I haven't seen the results but, basically, what I did see was that it tended to be the minorities that felt excluded, felt as if they didn't have that sense of belonging that CGI is intent on getting for people. It seemed as if the non-minorities didn't see a problem.

Like other popular school activities, students find out about CGI in part by word of mouth as siblings and friends describe the Institute to peers. To address the issue of access to the Institute, there is also a committee within CGI that is responsible for recruiting new students into the program. When we asked students about how they came to be in CGI, their responses ranged from parental or peer pressure to curiosity. Two of our Black female focal students spoke about how they found out about the Institute. One told us that "A teacher in CGI that had been teaching me in my freshman year thought that it would be a good idea," which speaks to the faculty commitment to diversify the institute. The second student proudly proclaimed that "I was interested in politics and doing something unique while I was in high school. I found out through my friends."

These responses defy common assumptions about Black and White student networks in school (Ferguson, 2001): that is, one perennial challenge to equitable academic spaces is the importance of a powerful social network, often linked in the literature to predominantly White spaces (Fine et al., 1997; Oakes et al., 1997). In this case, two Black girls used their social and academic networks to insert themselves into CGI and, by doing so, insured both a "unique experience" and access to a high-powered academic community. Of the twenty-eight students in the 2001 graduating class, twenty-five went either to Ivy League schools or small competitive colleges.

In terms of student access to knowledge, some White students felt that the opportunities in CGI were open to everyone equally, but others seemed cognizant that they might be blind to the perception of their peers in terms of access and opportunity. A White female student summed it up succinctly:

I think that there are the same opportunities for everybody. I have never seen anyone actually being excluded for whatever reason, but maybe that's because I am White, and so I am not coming from the same perspective. But I understand that it can be hard because there are so many people with similar interests and similar backgrounds and everything, but it's not impossible and it's not totally exclusive.

While the student is clear in her analysis of access, she also understands that her views are shaped to some extent by her race. Her final point, "it's not totally exclusive," illustrates the difficulty of maintaining diversity at all echelons of the Institute. Indeed it recalls the fact that as of this writing there are no Black governors or senators in the United States government.

A White male student spoke about opportunities being open to anyone who wanted to seize them in CGI. He felt that anyone in CGI could choose to be more involved at any time. His comment, however, raises issues about how students know what "choice" they "have to make."

On a recent college tour I went to Boston College. When I got there it was very apparent to me that it was a Catholic school, and during the tour, a question came up from one of the students, "How Catholic is this school?" And the guy said, "it's as Catholic as you want it to be." And I almost feel the same way about CGI. Your level of involvement is decided by you. You can be as involved as you want to be, you can do activities outside of the school, you can do activities during school, and they can all revolve around CGI, but it's a choice you have to make.

Students' levels of involvement were shaped by many factors, including interest in government (does the material itself interest them?), social networks (are their friends in the Institute?), and academic ability (can they handle the workload?). These factors did not preclude the inclusion of other students in the Institute, however, as approximately 15 per cent of CGI students are currently classified with special needs, including one student who became the first sophomore of the year to pass a bill. Notwithstanding its attention to diversity and special education, however, CGI still struggles with disparate levels of involvement among its students. And, as previously stated, students differ in their explanations for why this occurs. One student, a White male, acknowledged the different levels of involvement:

I think that CGI definitely offers opportunities for all students and even encourages all students to participate and speak their minds but at the same time, there is really just a group of about twenty that are really actively involved, who take it upon themselves to find out what's going on and be active in the community of CGI. One of the problems of CGI, there is nobody there saying, "well, hey we have thirty people who are doing excellent, are complete leaders, they are great kids, but then there's a hundred or so who are just sitting quietly and just getting completely passed over."

One way the Institute tries to dilute the concentration of students at the top is through the dispersion of responsibility. In a program like CGI, when students have an important responsibility, they are required to work closely with their teachers and their peers, and sometimes with administrative or district authority, thus developing important life skills as well as academic skills. For example, students on a committee to organize a Fall retreat for three days have to plan agendas and activities, make phone calls to bus companies and camping facilities, and write fliers and letters to parents, administrators, etc. These logistical details give them invaluable real life experiences and foreshadow for them what it means to organize and to lead.

Not all students rise to the challenge, however, and within CGI there are also students who dominate. Some students do not share responsibilities and powers with others, and hoard their privileges. While students differ in how they explain this, certainly those most involved see it as less of an issue, perhaps assuming that all students feel as entitled as they do. A White male student acknowledged the competitive nature of some students:

> There are more like two groups in CGI: people that want to be here and people who are simply here. Those that are simply here sometimes never make the transition to wanting to be here because those that want to be here take all the power, take all the responsibility, don't ever share.

There are many opportunities for students to engage in a large setting open dialogue in CGI, and many students participate. Within the bureaucracy of trying to "get things done," they are able to engage in student-led discussions. Like most school activities, high-interest discussions elicit greater student input. For example, one student describes the negotiation of judges for a talent show.

> I think every once in a while, at least last year, not so much this year yet, we have a really good Congress session. There was one last year when there was a talent show proposed and there were some discrepancies over who would judge the talent show. Everyone said you had to define who the judges would be and then the kid who wrote the bill defined who the judges were and the decision was very rigid and there was some great debate and it was one of the only times that I have seen people really passionate about what they were saying on the floor

of the CGI Congress and it was very heartening. Originally, there were no guidelines for who the judges would be, the kid who was writing the bill was going to decide who the judges were, everybody said, you are African American, your general taste is rap music and you are going to choose your friends because naturally you are going to choose your friends. So, he defined the characteristics for a judge as one White male, one White female, one Black male, one Black female and one male teacher and one female teacher. There was a lot of really good debate and a lot of disagreement and there is not usually that much. Bake sales do not usually bring as good debate as, "Do White people listen to rap music?"

The above excerpt, spoken by a White male student, is steeped in normal adolescent angst about cliques as well as issues specific to CGI. It touches upon the ways by which CGI allows a space for students to grapple with issues of equity (who gets to judge?) and popular culture (do White people listen to rap music?). These issues serve as examples of negotiation, constituency, and committee appointment within the Institute, but as with actual governments, some issues, such as the lollipop debate, elicit less student interest.

Voicing your opinion and being heard: mentoring students who question

The stated goals of CGI speak to the importance they place on student voice. Of course, students and teachers do not explain this in the same way; that is, while they learn parliamentary procedure, they also learn the social skills associated with a civically educated person. CGI develops students who question, and this purpose is made clear in both written descriptions and anecdotal evidence. The students come to embody that from which they learn, and see modeled by their teachers, including the behavior of a civically engaged citizen. Below find a brochure description of the program, followed by two brief student quotations.

The Civics and Government Institute seeks to promote an active, informed, and responsible citizenry by allowing students to experience education within and beyond the traditional classroom. This program focuses on an inquiry-based model in order to create problem-solving citizens in the community. Through community service, public internships (some of which are within organizations dedicated to social action), research, administrative responsibilities and intense academic work, students seek to understand what it means to be an informed and participatory citizen.

> You gain perspective on many different issues, you learn public speaking and argument development. You can also boss people around in committees.

> You should be loud in voicing your opinion.

Both student opinions address the issue of empowerment within CGI, which is itself an empowered place. CGI is a unique academic community within Montclair High School. It combines the rigor of AP academics with the excitement of an elective. Many students in CGI express that they are well aware that the program is special: class size is lower, classes are blocked – two periods twice a week rather than daily – students travel to Washington DC each year to meet with judges and senators, they make the township newspaper regularly, etc. And engendered in this unique academic space are the growing pains of a burgeoning student constituency; students now not only study United States government and monitor and develop the CGI constitution, but (want to) lobby the administration about issues related to CGI. A White male student addresses the power that the students feel they possess to effect change within the school:

> Sometimes teachers can do a better job of getting everyone involved. There are certain students that are really ambitious and there is no trouble getting them to do things, but other students need more prodding and [increased involvement] is not available to them especially if they are stubborn and refuse to listen. We have been having a lot of trouble fighting the administration to keep the class size smaller but I think if they open that up to us, we might be able to argue that more effectively for ourselves and present the problems to the administration. I think that it might be more effective if the students were allowed to argue to the administration along with teachers.

The above excerpt speaks to both academic and procedural leadership development in the Institute. During the course of their CGI curriculum, students develop argumentation, parliamentary procedure, critical writing, and related skills. Also, they develop the agency needed to address the issues in front of them in the Institute. That is, the students in the Institute manifest parliamentary praxis in applying the democratic skills they learn to immediate issues.

The faculty in CGI encourages and models for the students the behaviors of an involved populace. Students connect with their teachers, and ally with them to create forums to address problems. In that sense, teachers try to insure that all students are prepared to lead within CGI, to pass on what they learn to the next entering class. One Black girl in the Institute sums up the procedure:

You can always just go and talk to your teachers and your concerns will be addressed, no matter how personal or impersonal. We'll always find a forum for them to be addressed. For example, there was a problem with communication and we (the seniors and the teachers) were under the assumption that the underclassmen knew parliamentary procedure and of course, they didn't, and now that we know that, there is going to be a forum held during the lunch period to fix that.

The final sentence underscores the confidence many CGI students embody: "… we (the seniors and the teachers) assumed … of course they didn't." The student's identification with her teacher, coupled with her dismissal of the younger students' ignorance of parliamentary procedure, bespeaks a mature, successful, representative of the small learning community. Other students spoke to the opportunities for unique leadership within the Institute, the diversity of roles and responsibilities afforded the students. One called the Institute a "different place to feel empowerment and leadership," and, after the student-led dialogue meeting, felt like "a leader here, if not [within the larger] Montclair High School."

Several elements, then, contribute to students' sense of belonging and agency within CGI: the process of learning democratic governance within an academically challenging and nurturing academic setting and the opportunity to lead younger students, to pass on, in a sense, the mantle of structure and procedure. It is through that critical engagement that students emulate the passion their teachers model for them. CGI students consistently spoke about the importance of and the appreciation for teachers' commitment to the Institute:

A lot of what the teachers do is become our friends and mentors and that helps us a lot. I have had one teacher for three years, and he was my student teacher and my history teacher for two years. He's also the advisor to the Model United Nations Club, which I am a pretty big part of and I just go to him and talk about really random things, like, "hey, I just visited a college this weekend and I really hated it." And he'll say why and I explain it. In that way – and I can do that with pretty much any of the teachers – of just listening to you and knowing a little bit about you which helps you feel comfortable with them. But then that expands to the Institute and you feel comfortable within the Institute because you know that the teachers respect you so you kind of assume that students will also, just for that. And it really helps to have teachers as friends I guess.

(White male)

It does help to have teachers as friends. In many ways, students develop social capital within this nurturing relationship. First, it never hurts to be on good terms with those grading you; second, close access to teachers allows students greater input into CGI itself; and third, the skills developed within this relationship transfer outside the Institute and may lead to important references and connections for the future. Teachers not only serve as stewards of schools, then, but as mentors to students within a small learning community (Goodlad *et al.*, 1990; Wenger, 1998). White and Black students alike spoke to the receptivity of the teachers, and the ways in which they felt heard. For example, one Black girl spoke of the willingness of teachers to engage students as active learners:

> One of the best qualities about CGI is its wide variety of teachers. I like that they are always willing to help me and always willing to listen to me. And they are always interested in my opinion and they actually think that what I have to say matters.

Students feel validated when they are listened to, particularly by important and powerful figures like parents and teachers. This validation can strengthen the symbiotic communicative relationship, and increase students' openness to learning.

> I think that one of the things that is really good about the teachers is that they constantly reinforce the fact that they are there for us, not just on an academic level, but also on a personal level. It's almost like positive brainwashing, they say it so much that kids actually start to believe it and eventually when they feel comfortable they will come to those teachers.

The same student who felt heard by the teachers identified another, key component of successful learning communities, which she terms "positive brainwashing." Within CGI, the party line is to thrive, to do well, to speak and write well and clearly, to read critically, and to question and develop arguments, the "brainwashing" it takes to develop an informed citizenry. In addition, the close connection between teachers and students cements the strength of the community. A senior Black female hinted at the calling of teaching, the energetic selflessness that many teachers emit. She spoke of the possibility of cross-cultural connection, of the fact that a teacher need not be Black to connect with and inspire her:

> I think that it is their passion more than anything else, that engrosses me because with so many other teachers they just honestly don't care, all they're here for is a check, fulfilling the curriculum that is set up for them by the state, and then leaving and going home and taking care of their own issues but these teachers are actually concerned about our issues also. I like the fact that there are some teachers within CGI that

I share commonalities with, not just the fact that the teacher is Black and I'm Black. I personally like having a teacher who feels strongly, who not only teaches about different people, but who actually is involved in issues in the country, who goes to seminars and meetings and is involved in organizations that help women and people of minority races.

Thus, in addition to modeling constitutional law and parliamentary procedure, some teachers model social activism as well. Although questions remain as to whether smaller learning communities such as CGI prepare and enculturate all students equally, there is some evidence of this in CGI. In this student's opinion, her teacher attends to issues of diversity and social justice. The teacher mentioned – also one of the authors – embodies the concern for social justice she instills in her students, and the agency that is developed from that relationship fuels the success of the community, as students feel compelled not only to do well themselves, but to leave the Institute viable and strong for the next Congress.

Leadership, access, and diversity concerns: implications for the future of CGI

> In an effort to maintain hope alive, since it is indispensable for happiness in school life, educators should always analyze the comings and goings of social reality. These are the movements that make a higher reason for hope possible.
>
> (Freire, 1990: 107).

The United States government convinced the populace of its civic and democratic resilience both in November 2000 and on September 11, 2001. This was done to keep order and to maintain hope for the future. For its part, CGI wrote and voted on a resolution against immediate military intervention in Afghanistan. This vote, which narrowly defeated the measure, aired on the local NBC affiliate. Thus, the Institute continues to innovate and engage students. The Institute is at its highest capacity, and recent elective courses include the Poetry and Prose of the Vietnam War. Still, in addition to student legislation, academic innovation, travel, and debate, CGI still deals with normal adolescent pressures, cliques, and clubs, as well as with constitutional amendments. Also, students learn the mechanics of getting things done, the hidden curriculum of connections and chutzpah.

"If you have a loud enough voice or an intelligent enough opinion or if you speak to the right people, you can do anything in this Institute, but if you don't, you are never going to get anywhere." With this summation, a White male student articulates what it means to lead: to speak well and to "the right people." CGI offers a place where students, with the help of their teachers, can at least try out their own form of a working democracy, which, like American democracy, embodies both promises and challenges in its attempt to prepare educated, informed citizens.

A note on method

One of the complicating challenges of working in a dynamic school is that detached research is nearly impossible for those who work there. This chapter derives from unbridled teacher enthusiasm, opportunity, access, academic work, and, especially, from the many people involved in making happen the issues and events briefly described here. Ms Shana Stein works in CGI and has in two years made significant contributions to the high school; Dr David Lee Keiser is the Montclair State University liaison to Montclair High School, a nationally known Professional Development School.

After an invitation to publish and after requesting consent from the superintendent, principal, the Institute faculty and the students who agreed to focus groups, we met with students several times, first to introduce the project, then to generate interview data, and lastly to debrief. The students we interviewed described themselves as cohesive, never satisfied, oddly retentive, curious, attentive, reflective, eclectic, and skittish. One of us (Stein) teaches in the Institute, while the other (Keiser) prepares and super-vises student teachers, some who work within the Institute. The work behind this chapter fits well into the school's current school reform: the establishment of small learning communities, of which CGI was the first. In the 2002–3 school year, four additional small learning communities will exist, as well as CGI. All school research is complicated by issues and lenses of race, class, and culture, and within a desegregated school district the challenges are perhaps more nuanced, but no less steep.

Bibliography

Anand, B., Fine, M., Surrey, D. and Perkins, T. (2000) *Keeping the Struggle Alive: Studying Desegregation in our Town.* New York: Teachers College.
Aronson, E. (2000) *Nobody Left to Hate: Teaching Compassion After Columbine.* New York: Freeman and Co.
Beyer, L. (1996) *Creating Democratic Classrooms: The Struggle to Integrate Theory and Practice.* New York: Teachers College.
College Board (1999) *Reaching the Top: A Report of the National Task Force on Minority High Achievement.* New York: The College Board.
Delpit, L. (1988) The silenced dialogue: power and pedagogy in educating other people's children. *Harvard Educational Review,* 58(3): 280–98.
Ferguson, R. (2001) A diagnostic analysis of Black–White GPA disparities in Shaker Heights, Ohio. In: D. Ravitch (Ed.), *Brookings Papers of Education Policy.* Washington, DC: Brookings.

Fine, M. and Weis, L. and Powell, L. (1997) Communities of difference: a critical look at desegregated spaces for and by youth. *Harvard Educational Review*, 67(2).

Freire, P. (1990) *Pedagogy of Hope*. Seabury, MA: Continuum Press.

Fullan, M. (1999) *Change Forces: The Sequel*. London: Falmer Press.

Funderburg, L. (2000) Race in class, after integration. *The Nation*, 270(22), 26–9.

Goodlad, J. and Oakes, J. (1988) We must offer equal access to knowledge. *Educational Leadership*. February: 16–22.

Goodlad, J., Soder, R. and Sirotnik, K. (1990) *The Moral Dimensions of Schooling*. San Francisco: Jossey-Bass.

Karp, S. (1994) Detracking Montclair High. In: Rethinking Schools (Ed.), *Rethinking our Classrooms: Teaching for Equity and Justice*. Milwaukee, WI: Rethinking Schools, 176–8.

Lee, V. (2001) *Restructuring High Schools for Equity and Excellence: What Works*. New York: Teachers College Press.

Lightfoot, S. (1983) *The Good High School: Portraits of Character and Culture*. New York: Basic Books.

Manners, J. (1998) Repackaging segregation? A history of the magnet school system in Montclair, New Jersey. *Race Traitor*, 8: 51–99.

Meier, D. (1995) *The Power of Their Ideas: Lessons for America from a Small School in Harlem*. Boston: Beacon Press.

Oakes, J. (1985) *Keeping Track*. New Haven: Yale University Press.

Oakes, et al. (1997) Detracking: The social construction of ability, cultural politics, and resistance to reform. *Teachers College Record*, 98(3): 482–510.

Sizer, T. and Sizer, N. (1999) *The Students are Watching*. Boston: Beacon Press.

Tatum, B. (1997) *Why are all the Black Kids Sitting Together in the Cafeteria?* New York: Basic Books.

Villegas, A.M. and Lucas, T. (2002) *Preparing Culturally Responsive Teachers: A Coherent Approach*. Albany: State University of New York Press.

Wagner, T. (1994) *How Schools Change: Lessons from Three Communities*. Boston: Beacon Press.

Wasley, P.A., Hampel, R.L. and Clark, R.W. (1997) *Kids and School Reform*. San Francisco: Jossey-Bass.

Weis, L. and Fine, M. (Eds) (1993) *Beyond Silenced Voices: Class, Race and Gender in United States Schools*. Albany: State University of New York Press.

Wenger, E. (1998) *Communities of Practice: Learning Meaning and Identity*. Cambridge: Cambridge University Press.

Williams, B. (1996) *Closing the Achievement Gap: A Vision for Changing Beliefs and Practices*. Alexandria, VA: ASCD Press.

Chapter 10

"I'm not getting any F's"

What "at risk" students say about the support they need

Beth C. Rubin

Introduction

> My first semester report card was almost all F's, but now that I am in MOST getting my work done I'm not getting any F's.
>
> (Missy,[1] tenth grade MOST student)

When one enters teacher Steven Hesperian's room during fourth period the overwhelming impression is that everyone is very busy. The room is large and sunny, with many windows, a bank of computers, and individual student desks arranged in casual groupings. On a typical day, some students are sitting by themselves and others are sitting in small groups. A few students are at the computers, others are working with Janelle Barry, the Chapter I instructional aide, and some have left for the library, the computer center, or other teachers' classrooms. Almost without exception students are engaged in school-related tasks.

The students themselves confirm this understanding of what goes on in Making Our Success Today (MOST), a support class for ninth and tenth grade students at Mountain High School. "In MOST you do your work," Tommy, a student struggling in his academic classes, told me. "The teachers help you so you can do your work." Missy, quoted above, attributed her academic reversal to "getting my work done" in the MOST class. These students are telling us, in plain language, about the type of support that is meaningful and necessary to them.

Some educational researchers call for whole school reform and structural changes in order to meet the needs of "at risk" students. Others advocate deep-seated changes in curriculum and pedagogy. Proponents of high stakes testing believe that this approach will raise achievement for all children by holding schools accountable for student scores. This chapter supplements these more sweeping reform prescriptions with what the students themselves say they need – an inventory of supports, strikingly concrete and immediate in nature, which allow them to surmount the daily challenges of life in an academically rigorous public school. This casestudy provides evidence that many of the changes needed to support struggling students are surprisingly simple, although they may require schools to redirect resources in order to implement them.

Approaches to supporting "at risk" students

The use and meaning of the term "at risk" has shifted over the past several decades from a deficit model attaching the quality of "risk" to individual students, families, and even whole racial and/or ethnic groups to an approach situating risk in school and societal environments (Land and Legters, 2002; Jagers and Carroll, 2002; Padron *et al.*, 2002). As it is commonly couched today, an "at risk school environment" alienates students through its poor pedagogical practices (Haberman, 1991), badly maintained physical plant, and systemic dysfunction. Such schools are marked by,

> ... low standards and low quality of education, low expectations for students, high non-completion rates for students, classroom practices that are unresponsive to students, high truancy and disciplinary problems, and inadequate preparation of students for the future.
> (Padron *et al.*, 2002: 71)

While serving to highlight the shortcomings of the school environment rather than the individual student, this alternative conception of "at risk" does little to help us to understand the plight of students who struggle academically in otherwise excellent schools. Schools such as Mountain that exhibit a "bimodal" pattern of achievement, with a strong association between students' race and class backgrounds and their school performance, serve some of their students quite well and serve others poorly.[2]

Responses to improving the education of "at risk" students in bimodal schools have included a wide variety of structural, whole school approaches, including detracking, the creation of small learning communities, career academies, reforming the roles of school boards and school superintendents, class size reduction, and even the implementation of standardized testing (Oakes, 1992; Stringfield and Datnow, 2002; Slavin, 2002). Others have suggested a complete overhaul of school curriculum and teaching practices, recommending, for example, the implementation of multicultural education, culturally responsive pedagogy, and critical pedagogy (Banks, 1994; Giroux and Simon, 1992; Ladson-Billings, 1995; Sleeter, 1991; Wink, 1997), as well as "back to basics" initiatives. Students' experiences with some of these approaches are presented in other chapters in this volume (e.g. Rodriguez, Woody, Rubin, Horn, Keiser and Stein, Wing).

These large-scale approaches have many merits, particularly in challenging deeply rooted and long-accepted inequalities in school practices and outcomes. Still, in many of today's large bimodal schools, attempts to support "at risk" students are often undermined or swallowed by approaches aimed at raising the bar for "all" students. Studies which suggest that one-on-one tutoring by qualified teachers, extra time for core subjects, structured "catch-up" time for students below grade level, and instruction in study skills make a big difference for struggling students corroborate findings from this study and point to the need for a careful examination of what "at risk" students need to be successful in school (Slavin, 2002; McPartland *et al.*, 2002).

A "risky" context: supporting marginalized students at Mountain High School

Mountain and MOST

Mountain High School is located in affluent, suburban Pine Valley in Northern California. The majority of the school's students live in Pine Valley itself, with significant minorities coming from neighboring rural towns with predominantly white, middle and working class residents, and a neighboring small city, Cedar City, with predominantly African American, working class residents. Twenty-five per cent of the students at the school are of color, with African American students the largest group among the students of color and smaller numbers of Asian American, Latino, and mixed ethnicity students. The school is highly ranked among California high schools, with a low drop-out rate and a high rate of students going on to attend four-year colleges.

MOST was a support program for students deemed "at risk" by the school. Students enrolled in the program were scheduled into a MOST class as one period of their regular seven period day. Almost all of the students coming to Mountain from Cedar City were placed in a MOST class. While this placement might strike an observer as an example of prejudging students based on race and class, Janelle, a long-time Cedar City resident who had worked for over twenty years to support Cedar City students attending Mountain, felt that the placement was a matter of survival. As she told me,

> We're particularly talking about students who came here from Cedar City school district, mainly because they came in four, five or six years behind the rest of the students. So when they came in they were, you know, way back, stepped way back from the rest of the students. They definitely would need the attention that we're trying to give them ... [they're coming from a place] where they've been beat up and stepped on and not given, not educated at all ... they're passed on. Regardless of how far behind they are they're still passed on. And when they get

here ... they get slapped in the face. And I've seen it happen with too many kids so that's where, because of that, that's where the focus, that's why the focus is on them. Because of their lack of skills.

As Janelle observed, entering Mountain's challenging academic environment after nine years of inadequate K-8 instruction presented Cedar City students with serious difficulties, particularly in their detracked English, social studies and science classes. These difficulties contributed to a bimodal pattern of achievement at the school. While 53 per cent of the school's white graduates, all hailing from Pine Valley and surrounding rural communities, had completed the entrance requirements for the state's public universities by the time they graduated, only 12 per cent of the school's African American graduates, almost all from Cedar City, had completed those same requirements. Increased support services had reduced the drop-out rate of African American students at Mountain to zero per cent, a significant change from past years, but achievement across race and class lines remained uneven. Mountain, while lauded as a private school education with a public school price tag by many residents of Pine Valley, was a "risky" environment for its working class students of color.

Troubled by this disparity, English teacher Steven Hesperian, a spry, white man in his late forties with a devastatingly sarcastic sense of humor, founded MOST. Working with him from the program's inception was Janelle Barry, an African American woman in her mid-forties who, when asked, would share her incisive and blunt opinions about the school. While the initial impetus for the program was to support Cedar City students, students of all backgrounds who were struggling in their academic classes gravitated toward the class, and it was quickly expanded to serve a broader constituency of students experiencing difficulty at Mountain. The mixture of students found in MOST had educational implications, as will be discussed later in the chapter.

Researching MOST

The MOST class described in this chapter, taught by Steven and Janelle, was one of the most diverse classes to be found at Mountain. Of the nineteen students in the class (eight boys and eleven girls), there were five African American students, one Asian American student, one Latina student, three mixed ethnicity students, and nine white students. Seven of the students were in tenth grade and twelve were ninth graders.

To conduct this study I observed the class twice weekly for three months, creating a set of fieldnotes for each visit. I followed the voluntary grouping patterns of students, their work habits, and the conversation trends of the majority of the class, took detailed notes of conversations between students and teachers in which school progress was explicitly discussed, and observed and wrote fieldnotes on the general movements and interactions of the teacher and the aide with the students as well as interactions explicitly regarding academic identity. I surveyed all nineteen of the students and interviewed five of them. I also interviewed Steven and Janelle, the school counselor Kyle Demerest, and Sally Peoples, the assistant principal with counseling and administrative responsibilities for the MOST program.

As a teacher at Mountain at the time of the study, I was not a stranger to the students or the teachers in MOST. Four of the study participants were students of mine at the time of the study, and three were former students. This both deepened and made more difficult my work. I had to remain constantly aware of the impact of my relationship with the students on the research process. I was surprised, however, by how little the students seemed to notice or question my presence during the course of the study. Although at times it was difficult to "make the familiar strange" (Erickson, 1986: 121), in the end I think that my work was made more honest and more complex by this constant interplay of near and far perspectives. Through these perspectives, I gained a rich sense of student experience and opinion and discovered that the students with the most need at Mountain were asking for and responding to very basic definitions and forms of support, which are described below.

The meaning of support

This section describes the forms of assistance that MOST students found to be valuable to them as they navigated the challenging academic environment of Mountain High School.

Students need time

> The most important part of MOST would be the time ...
> (Kelly, ninth grade MOST student)

Time and access to resources, while not glamorous, were of fundamental importance to the students in MOST. When asked in a survey about the most important part of MOST, the student respondents all emphasized "time to get their work done" as a key benefit of MOST class. Students needed extra time for various reasons. Veronica felt it took her longer than her peers to complete her work. She told me,

> I guess you could say that the time is very important to me. Because it takes me a longer period of time than other kids to finish my work. And the extra period of time helps me very much.

Other students expressed the need for more time to complete difficult work. Jason wrote that the extra time in MOST "helps me to get my work done that is difficult or takes a long time to finish, such as projects, or math." Brenna responded, "MOST helps me to do my hard work ... I get extra time and extra help in difficult subjects."

Not having enough time to get work done was a reality of Mountain High School, particularly for students having difficulty in their academic subjects. Janelle reflected that the students she worked with,

> ... definitely need the time. Because in a lot of classes they don't get any time. Or in some they get a little time, but it's not enough time. So when you have a class like MOST they need to go here, there and do [take care of things they do not have time to take care of during regular class time].

Some students valued the time to begin or even complete homework during the school day, "so," as Mary told me, "that I can rest, relax and be with my friends after school." Or, as Ginger said, "it helps me to have more time to do my homework, and to have more time for things after school." Some students felt that because of their lack of motivation they just wouldn't get work done if not for the time in MOST. As Penelope said, "It gives me extra time to get homework done. I'm a slacker and would probably never get it done at home, so personally I benefit a lot from it." Students' desire to utilize MOST for time to do work on homework and projects was so strong that they resented any time directed towards other activities. Kyle Demerest, counselor and former MOST teacher, told me that "... they resented time being taken away from their homework when it was spent on skill-building or some clinical activity. They wanted to be able to just get in there and have some time to do some work."

Students need help to meet raised expectations

Many MOST students appreciated the challenging work they encountered at Mountain, but needed time and assistance to catch up with their peers who came from different "feeder" districts and learn what they had missed. Many students found the move between middle school and high school to be a difficult transition. This was particularly acute for students coming from Cedar City, whose previous schooling, as noted earlier, had been less than rigorous. Veronica, reflecting on the differences between high school and middle school, was shocked by:

> ... the amount of homework. And more strict about getting it in. Because this year I've been doing my work a lot more because it's so much stricter and it's like it actually matters a little bit more than it did

last year ... [last year] you have to do *something*, but not as much, if they *think* that you were trying ... The teachers were really gullible.

Other students noticed this difference between middle school and high school as well. Isaac reflected that,

It's like, when I was in middle school a book report wouldn't be nothing for me to do. We'd read it [the book] in class, and then time for the book report you'd just go back and look and like do it. It wouldn't be hard. And then I got here and it's like a whole different story. It's like read this section on your own, and do this and that ...

The higher accountability and complexity of work for students noted by Veronica and Isaac was something which Veronica, at least, ultimately appreciated. She reflected, "I didn't really like that [being able to get away without doing much work] last year because I don't think I learned much ... then you get like this year and you don't know anything." Veronica felt the low expectations of her middle school both cheated her out of a good education and left her unprepared to face the challenges of high school.

Over the previous few years Mountain had implemented a variety of reforms, including detracking English and social studies, moving to a block scheduling system, and creating a more integrated, project-based curriculum in all subject areas. In English, social studies and science classes, for example, students were assigned demanding long-term projects requiring research and in-depth writing assignments that had to be word-processed and go through multiple drafts. These educationally valuable innovations increased all students' needs for time and resources, and were particularly challenging for MOST students. Group projects and longer essays called for different thinking skills than many MOST ninth graders were required to use in middle school, and students noticed the difference. Danny told me that, "they ask you more harder questions. It's mostly like longer. They go into more detail ... There's way more reading ... over here it's like mostly your own opinion [as opposed to factual questions]."

Janelle felt that some of Mountain's innovations, particularly block scheduling, intensified the time pressure on the struggling students with whom she worked closely. The time crunch, she told me, was

... part of the structure of their whole schedule ... especially with this hour and a half system, teachers really feel like "well, I only have you three times a week, two days of an hour and a half [the third class period was 45 minutes long], so you've got plenty of time to get what I said done." Now all the teachers are feeling this way, when are they going to get time? They get overwhelmed, you know, there's no time. And I go through a lot of that – no time. They're constantly going,

going, going. Trying to figure out how I'm going to get this done, and this is due at the same time. It's a lot of work. They start getting overwhelmed.

Block scheduling resulted in a greater volume of homework at one time than many students were used to, and students often needed help figuring out how to manage their time effectively in order to complete these larger assignments.

In this more challenging context, then, access to time and resources through MOST helped the program's students, many of whom did not have access to computers at home. Veronica, for example, reported, "most teachers ask [you] to type papers. I don't have a computer, and in this class I can type my papers because there is a computer available." Library time was also at a premium among Mountain students, who were frequently asked to research and write papers in math, science, English and social studies classes. Melissa told me, "I usually go to the library to do research since I almost always have some type of research project to be working on." Several students went to the library each day from the MOST class, and the room's computers were always fully occupied.

Assistant Principal Sally Peoples saw this time factor as the key to MOST's ability to support Mountain's detracking effort. "We go on the assumption that everybody can do the same thing in the same amount of time," she told me. "And some of the kids just cannot. So I think in terms of a strategy to support heterogeneous grouping it's essential. And I believe in the heterogeneous grouping." Sally resisted school district office pressures to "curricularize" MOST in order to maintain this aspect of the program.

Students need qualified adults to assist them

> If I didn't have MOST I'd still do my work but if I needed help I'd have to go to the library.[3] Since I have MOST I don't have to take all that time out and go over there ... I'd have to go home and do it, and I don't have any help because my dad is working until like ten o'clock at night. On certain days until 12:30 in the morning. I have an older brother, but he doesn't live with me. He's twenty-one, he lives with a friend ... My grandmother, she's like Janelle. Actually she's a teacher at Eastridge school in Cedar City ... Sometimes I go to her house, but she's always busy. She takes care of like four of my cousins. She has four little kids now.
>
> (Tommy, tenth grade MOST student)

When surveyed about how MOST helped them, almost all of the students explicitly mentioned the teacher's help as important to them. The most important part of MOST, according to Eric, was "the working part and the help I receive from the teacher." Mark agreed that "teacher's help" was the most important facet of MOST for him. Not all students regularly had adults at home to help them with their homework and in MOST both Steven and Janelle provided constant academic support to students. As one of the consequences of "not being taught" in middle school was lowered academic skills, this extra assistance from trained adults familiar with the Mountain curriculum was vital.

Students received direct academic support from Steven, almost always at their request. Students asked Steven to explain essay assignments, proofread papers, respond to thesis statements, or simply to clarify confusing concepts in any subject area. Steven's academic sessions with students tend to be extended rather than brief. On March 11, for example, Steven worked with five students, Tommy, Melissa, Isaac, Veronica and Danny, sitting with each of them for prolonged periods of time, and was asked for follow-up by several. His encounters with each student asking for help were multiple and extended over the course of the period.

For some MOST students, the academic support provided by both Steven and Janelle was key to their academic survival, particularly in their detracked English and social studies classes. Tommy, for example, was assigned to write an essay on the play *Romeo and Juliet*. It was a complex assignment, as is the language of the play itself, and he was struggling. If Tommy were a student in a school that tracked its students in English it is likely that he would have been assigned to a lower track, and would never have encountered either the text or such an assignment. Over the course of a ninety minute block period in MOST, Steven was able to help Tommy work his way through understanding the play, grasping the concept of a thesis statement, and generating his own thesis about the play. The workshop atmosphere of MOST allowed Tommy to ask for expert, individualized assistance when he needed it, and to work independently in a supervised situation. This assistance was distinct from the type of help usually available to students while an academic class is in progress, or that which might be obtained with a quick question between classes, and made possible his success in his detracked English class.

Janelle Barry provided academic support to students as well, including access to the treasure trove of supplemental materials she had accumulated over twenty-eight years of making the Mountain curriculum accessible to struggling students. These materials included audiotapes, videos, "Cliffs Notes," and annotated versions of books. She used these materials to help students keep up with their peers in the detracked English and social studies classes, as in the following example from my fieldnotes:

Tommy ... tells Janelle that he doesn't understand the book the English class is reading (*Romeo and Juliet*). He says, "This book is confusing to me," telling Janelle that he's never read a book where people talk like they do in this one. Janelle tells Tommy "I'll get you an edited version that lays it all out for you," and asks him to remind her about this tomorrow.

This type of tailored support was critical, making the difference between a student such as Tommy being able to satisfactorily complete a difficult assignment and receiving a failing grade for that assignment.

Janelle was willing to go far beyond what is traditionally seen as the teacher's role to support the students in her charge. "If I can't help them in a particular subject, if the teacher can't, if there is a way I find a way to get the student help," she told me. She reflected that she was constantly:

> ... running to get the materials, tracking down students, seeing that they done this, that and the other to keep their grades up ... I even found myself working at home and in the library on my own. On Mondays and Tuesdays sometimes I'm in the library [Cedar City library] until seven or eight o'clock at night. Right after school with the students. And I find that kids might need my help, and sometimes they just want me there. It's like "I know I'll do it if Janelle comes down." Sometimes I go, they don't want my help, they just want me there. So I go down there and sit with them and work with them. And sometimes they need my help, and just ... somebody has to be there with them. It's like they can't go out on their own – just go down and do it and get it over with.

Struggling students often wait until the last minute to complete difficult assignments, frustrating the adults attempting to assist them. Janelle would step in to help even when students acted irresponsibly, knowing that her assistance often meant the difference between success and failure.

> On vacation I spent Monday, Tuesday *and* Saturday, Saturday wasn't supposed to be because that was my vacation, and I still met two students that said they had done this project that was due the Monday coming back and, you know, told me in my face that they had, and that everything is fine, and the parent called me Saturday and said that it turned out her daughter had been lying, and on and on and on and could I help. So I went down to the library and another one joined. The one who insisted she had done everything. My last day of vacation I spent four hours in the library. But, you know, I was kind of angry at her in a sense ... but you know, they just need someone with them. Keep them on track, and they know they won't stay on track unless some adult is there that knows what they have to do. I enjoy it.

Many students seemed to need a great deal of support, both academic and emotional as they completed their work, and Janelle was willing to spend hours of her free time helping them in this way. Both Steven and Janelle, by committing themselves to assisting their students in whatever way was necessary, smoothed the way for Mountain's "at risk" students.

Students need a caring adult at the school to push them through the tough times

Many MOST students commented that they had trouble getting motivated to complete their assignments. Steven, they noted, was able to give them the extra push they needed to complete their assignments. "Mr H. usually makes me do work even when I don't want to," Eric told me. "It is great to have someone like that. In the long run it is worth it." Melissa described Steven as "a motivator who knows your name and doesn't let you get away with slipping grades as easily as other teachers might," and Mary dubbed the MOST class "a great kick in the butt."

Whether it be through a quiet inquiry about grades and homework or a questioning of a student's basic approach to an entire school year, this pushing of students, the "kick in the butt" referred to by Mary, distinguished the MOST class. Steven described this as being "a thorn in their side ... a pain in the ass." This blunt, almost confrontational approach with students was at times embarrassing and difficult for them.

Talk with the students about work, grades, and behavior was not sugarcoated, as in the following example from my fieldnotes:

ISAAC: Can I read Tommy a poem?
STEVEN: He's got so much to do he doesn't know which end is up.
TOMMY: I've got three pages written.
STEVEN: Keep writing. That won't be three pages typed.
TOMMY: Four pages?
STEVEN: Tommy, the point is to get something said.
TOMMY: OK, no need for a lecture. I asked you a question. No need for a lecture.

For students who resisted school and who might have given up entirely, this "pushing" forced them to carry on with tasks that were unpleasant, difficult or overwhelming.

Students need to be known

Students in MOST expressed the desire to have a teacher know them and their school progress well enough to personalize support. Melissa told me that she liked "knowing I can turn to Mr Hesperian if I'm stressed out about school; [I get one-and-a-half] hours to do what I need to do, including sleeping in the nurse's office some days when I feel very bad." When it came to her school work, she told me, "… [he] usually knows how I'm doing in school, or he will ask me. I'm not obligated to ask for help, something I really have a hard time doing." This familiarity with both the students and the school's curriculum allowed Steven to provide support, both academic and personal, when and how it was most needed. "I've developed a pretty familiar relationship with most of these kids," Steven told me, "and I know a lot about them, not only their school life, but their personal lives. So I relate to them more on a personal level than I think most teachers would with most students."

Other adults involved with the program concurred that this familiarity was an important aspect of MOST. Sally Peoples reflected that Steven had "a wonderful connection with kids, a good solid connection. I think that there are kids still at Mountain that wouldn't have been here necessarily without some sort of connection to an adult." Kyle Demerest, school counselor, commented that he did not

> believe that students only listen to kids their age and that they shut off all adults. I think students listen and talk to those they think hear them. So if you let a student know that their voice matters and I hear it, then you've developed a relationship, and it's the relationship that allows you to get the work done.

This personal connection helped the teacher make decisions about when to give a student "time to breathe" and when to be a "thorn in their side." It also provided students with a touchstone at the school, "somebody who," as Steven said, "you need anything, this is one person you can go to."

Both Steven and Janelle formed relationships with students that seemed to help students feel safe and connected as they functioned within a larger school environment that constantly challenged their self-worth. Being placed in a class explicitly because of their academic difficulties could potentially put students in a vulnerable position. Frederick Erickson (1994: 383) writes, "in pedagogy it is essential that the teacher and students establish trust in each other at the edge of risk." This trust, developed in MOST, seemed to allow students to utilize the day-to-day support offered by the program.

The meaning of intelligence

While the daily support described above was essential for the success of "at risk" students at Mountain, equally important was how MOST fostered in students a more "fluid" understanding of their own academic competence and helped individuals to reconstruct (or to construct, in some cases) identities as academically competent students. Unlike students in lower academic tracks (e.g. Oakes, 1985; MacLeod, 1987; Page, 1987), many MOST students saw themselves as just as smart as their peers who were not in the program, just in need of additional assistance. These beliefs were affirmed and sustained in the face of Mountain's competitive academic environment through the program's diverse make-up and Steven and Janelle's fostering of a sense of community and encouragement of peer-to-peer assistance within the class.

Students need a way to positively define their academic struggles

The students I spoke with in MOST did not feel that they were in the program because of an intellectual deficit. They saw themselves and their peers as a varied group, brought to MOST by a diverse assortment of needs. In describing MOST Veronica told me, there were "all different kinds [of students] ... Yes there is students that need work on behavior, but not all of them. Then there are other students like myself that need more time on homework or extra help in a certain class." Eric reported,

> There is a variety of students in MOST class. There are good students who do all of their work and use their time wisely. There are students who don't do work and sit around and do nothing – their schedule usually gets changed. There are students who are trying to bring their grade up and do most of their work.

Both Veronica and Eric defined themselves as students attempting to do better in their academic work, rather than as deficient in some way. They also described a support class serving a variety of student needs, allowing them to move more fluidly between categories.

This characterization of MOST students as needing more time, some help with organizing their workload, or extra motivation was a dominant theme, and superseded any talk of them not being smart. Jason told me, "Most of the kids in here have academic trouble. It's not because they're not smart enough. It's usually because they have trouble concentrating or need just a little more time to do work." MOST students were "students that can do work, but need more support," said Isaac. They were "all kinds of students who need more time to study or do homework other than at home," according to Ginger.

Some lacked motivation, said Mary, and were "kids who need an extra little kick in the butt to help them get started and realize that you can't just breeze by in school."

These students did not characterize themselves as fundamentally distinct from their peers, hopelessly behind in school, or alienated from their identity as students, but rather defined themselves as students who were working hard to do better, and just in need of a little extra assistance.

Students need to not feel stigmatized when receiving assistance

MOST students did not feel that being in the class stigmatized them within the high school. Veronica told me that her friends who were not in MOST

> think it's just mostly like a study hall, and they wish they had it because it is mostly just like a study hall, some extra time to do your work. But it's … just a little more personal. Most of them would like to have a class like that.

Tommy echoed this idea, telling me,

> When I tell them [friends outside of MOST] that I have MOST they'll be like "What class is that?" "A class you get to do your homework in." They'll be like "I wish I had that class." Because they have [lots of work from] other classes too.

The multi-faceted diversity of the class contributed to this sense of MOST as an open environment rather than a stigmatizing setting. The class contained students who were from both Pine Valley and Cedar City, from various middle schools, from various racial/ethnic backgrounds, and who were taking a variety of courses. There were students in the MOST class taking all levels of math, different types of science (the school offered both the innovative Integrated Science sequence and the more traditional science courses), and varied levels of foreign language.

The partially detracked nature of the school also provided students with a more permeable vision of ability. As mentioned earlier, all of Mountain's ninth and tenth grade students were in the same English and social studies classes. Students in MOST did the same academic work as their non-MOST peers, and thus were not differentiated from their peers through a distinct curriculum. MOST students were able to widen their vision of themselves as learners through the diversity of their class.

Adding to this fluidity was the easy flow of non-MOST students in and out of the classroom. Steven was a popular teacher with connections to a wide variety of student groups through his work as MOST teacher, Summer transition program teacher, track coach, peer resource teacher, and English teacher. During the course of my observations many students, mainly from Steven's ninth grade core classes, entered the room – Ian and Carol, students who had their "resource period" at the same time, and Rebecca, Eddie, and Holly, high achieving students who were able to escape whatever other class they had during that period. These students came in to ask Steven questions about assignments, and often chose to stay in the room and work on their assignments after they had conferenced with the teacher. This added to the sense that MOST students had that their presence in the class was nothing to be ashamed of.

Students need to find community in their struggles

Students in MOST seemed reassured by the realization that they were not the only ones who were struggling in school. Veronica told me that she did not mind having Steven ask her about her progress in her other classes while they were in the MOST classroom because "in MOST you *know* that other kids have problems. In English it's like different because you know a lot of people are getting straight A's and you don't want them to know you're getting a lower grade than them." Tommy felt that MOST was a place where it is all right to let your vulnerabilities show, a place where "I don't really need to get embarrassed because everyone else is doing it [struggling in school] too." Steven felt that the MOST class was a place where struggling students could find community, reflecting that,

> ... in some ways I think kids get in the class and rather than being stigmatized there's a tacit acknowledgment of, oh yeah, we know who we are, and there's a commonality that brings a lot of kids together who otherwise wouldn't [be together] ... They get into the classroom and they have a commonality.

Ninth grade school counselor Kyle Demerest echoed these beliefs, saying that MOST,

> ... takes away any thinking that "I'm in this alone," or that "I'm the only one person having this same experience." It takes away the shame component of it, takes away the feeling that "I'm broken, and nobody understands it, and nobody is just as broken as I am." So once we can remove that, then you can start seeing hope that it can be fixed or made better in some way ... [It] opens up other options [in terms of] ways they see themselves as students.

Thus an important part of students being able to define their struggles positively was to form a community with others experiencing similar difficulties. This transformed students from being individuals with deficits to a community of peers brought together with the explicit goal of overcoming shared challenges in an atmosphere encouraging mutual support, as will be discussed below.

Students need a chance to be experts

> ... I've noticed how they're really helping each other now, the students in the class. They get in groups and work on science or math, and they're really leaning on each other, which is good. They don't even call the teacher sometimes – "oh, I know how to do that," and they go over and help the person, which is really good, you know, helping each other.
>
> (Janelle Barry, Chapter I Instructional Aide)

Students in MOST did not only receive academic support from teachers, they often turned to each other to clarify assignments, study for tests, review concepts, share strategies, or even just to check spelling. This student-to-student interaction allowed students to demonstrate competence to one another, bond over common work, and receive assistance from an insider's perspective. Student collaboration came in many forms. It could be as quick as a brief question to a neighbor about an assignment:

VERONICA: (to Danny sitting behind her) Are you almost done with your science – I was going to ask what this says.

or how to spell a word:

KEISHA: (to Isaac) You can spell it M-A-R-Y or M-E-R-R-Y.

It also could take the form of a regular friendship/study group, as with Kelly, Brenna and Mary who were in the same math class and often worked together on math assignments. It could be a test-oriented study group formed to prepare for a specific test, such as the one formed by Jim, Veronica, Missy, Danny, and Angie on March 4 to study for a science test. Some students, like Veronica and Sandra, moved in and out of groups, while others had more constant groupings.

Peers in MOST shared student-centered strategies for coping with difficult school work – strategies that would not necessarily be presented in a class or even be understood by the teacher giving the assignment. In the following example, Danny was going about an assignment in a very time consuming manner, using a strategy which was modeled by the teacher for a previous assignment, but which was inappropriate for the new assignment in question. Veronica, intimately involved with the same assignment, was able to help him out. The following excerpt from fieldnotes shows this interaction:

DANNY: [translating Shakespearean language into modern language] "Oh my god, that makes me mad."
VERONICA: We don't have to go line by line.

DANNY: I know, but …
VERONICA: You're writing it different than I am.
DANNY: How are you writing it?
VERONICA: OK … you do it your way, I'll do it may way. [Veronica turns around to face forward in her desk and continues writing.]
DANNY: How are you writing it?
VERONICA: I'm already summarizing it – I'm not doing it line by line.

In this brief interchange Veronica simplified a complex assignment for Danny, showing him that he could summarize the plot rather than "translate" line by line. Danny in turn provided an opportunity for Veronica to articulate her strategy and show her expertise. For a student who was most often on the receiving end of academic assistance this was powerfully affirming.

Many students seemed to welcome the opportunity to assist or to "play the expert." These roles were fluid. In the following interaction Danny assisted Veronica:

VERONICA: [said to no one in particular] I don't get it, I don't get it. [Danny comes over quickly to explain the assignment to her.]

The reciprocal nature of the peer assistance found in MOST contributed to the more flexible understanding of intelligence fostered by the program.

Sometimes students become known as experts in a particular subject, as we see in the following episode:

SANDRA: Mary, can you come over?
MARY: [loudly] I hate being loved!
SANDRA: You're not loved – you just know math.

Mary enjoyed being viewed as an expert in math by her peers. Throughout the course of my observations she made herself available to assist other students with their math work, and conspicuously mentioned to the class that her math teacher had recommended that she take a geometry class over the Summer at a prestigious local university.

Students' understandings of their own areas of expertise were also fluid. Often a student who had struggled in a particular subject would eagerly take an opportunity to demonstrate his or her expertise in that subject. In the following example, Jim, who mentioned to me early in the semester that he "wouldn't last in biology," was tutoring his classmates on scientific concepts:

STEVEN: [leafing through the textbook index] Nothing in here about free radicals.

JIM: Try "free floating electrons."

Jim has moved over to the group of girls who are working on science. He is perched on the edge of the desk directly facing Angie and Missy. He leafs through a binder and finds the definition that they need. He begins to carefully explain the concept to Missy and Angie and Veronica. Missy interrupts with questions, which Jim answers, without hesitation, explaining the same concept in a variety of ways to make sure it is understood. As the group continues to work together to prepare for the science test they go through their notebooks, looking at old notes and papers, checking for missing items. I hear Jim reminding them about earlier labs, explaining the concepts covered by the labs as they review.

By assisting one another with their work, MOST students reconstructed their identities as students on several levels. On a pragmatic level, "it helps if I have a fellow student to help me with it," as Brenna said, and it helps MOST become a place where, as Mary said, "there are a ton of people to help me out." On a more abstract level, students were able to push the boundaries of their self-images as students by acting as experts for one another, and could rebuild a sense of themselves as competent in academic areas in which they had previously experienced failure. In contrast with the competitive, individually oriented nature of the larger school which encouraged a more rigid view of intelligence, within MOST students worked collaboratively and were encouraged to see their academic abilities as fluid, expandable and of use to their peers.

Conclusion

At first glance, the support offered to the students in the MOST class I observed was quite concrete and utilitarian. Students gained needed time, access to resources, academic support from peers and teachers, a place to relax, and adults to push them when they faltered or slowed down. This support took place within the context of a learning environment in which working hard and doing well were accepted values. Equally important was a context that fostered a fluid understanding of academic competence. Students defined themselves as needing more time and assistance than some of their peers, but not in any way as their intellectual inferiors. This attitude was reinforced by the culture of peer assistance within the MOST class, the largely detracked nature of Mountain, and the easy flow of a variety of students in and out of the MOST classroom. In most cases this support enabled MOST students to attain a satisfactory degree of achievement in their academic classes.

The idea that support occurs within a particular sort of environment, and that it is the very nature of that environment which has a role in determining the success or failure of the support, may provoke useful discussion. Schools which are implementing tutoring, peer assistance, study centers, or other support-oriented programs may wish to discuss and examine the type of "learning environment" which might best allow students to utilize that support. Some questions for discussion might include the following: is the context stigmatizing? Are borders between this class and other classes rigid or permeable? Do the students have a personal connection with the teachers? Do students feel safe enough to take the risks entailed with receiving support? The idea is not to replicate the MOST program, but to consider the less tangible aspects of supporting "at risk" students.

Finally, I would argue that these students' voices are instructing us to pay attention to the "details" of school life. Does an assignment require access to a computer for writing and/or research? Are several large group projects due at the same time? Is this reading assignment a student's first encounter with Shakespearean language? Does a writing assignment ask students to work with new, abstract concepts? Such things matter to all students, and they certainly matter to those students who are struggling to succeed academically. Any reform designed to support "at risk" students should take into careful consideration the daily challenges those students face.

Raising expectations for students without providing the necessary assistance of time, resources, and expert adult attention, will only end in frustration for those targeted by the reform. All students have particular needs for learning. Just as students in honors and Advanced Placement classes receive special support, "at risk" students deserve to be in classes that are equally attentive to their needs. If support is provided within a context that nurtures a flexible understanding of competence and provides a counter-narrative to the individualistic competition found in the rest of the school such day-to-day assistance can be the difference between success and failure for "at risk" students in challenging school settings.

Notes

1 All names of people and places in this chapter are pseudonyms.
2 For other examples of bimodal schools in this volume see chapters by Morrell and Collatos, Silva, Rubin, Wing, Rodriguez, and Keiser and Stein.
3 The Cedar City public library provided after-school homework assistance for students.

Bibliography

Banks, J. (1994) *Multiethnic Education: Theory and Practice*. Boston: Allyn and Bacon.
Erickson, F. (1986) Qualitative methods in research on teaching. In: M. Wittrock (Ed.), *Handbook of Research on Teaching*. New York: Macmillan, 370–94.

Erickson, F. (1994) Transformation and school success: the politics and culture of educational achievement. In: J. Kretovics and E. Nussel (Eds), *Transforming Urban Education*. Boston: Allyn and Bacon, 375–95.

Haberman, M. (1991) Pedagogy of poverty versus good teaching. *Phi Delta Kappan*, 75(1): 8–16.

Giroux, H. and Simon, R. (1992) Schooling, popular culture, and a pedagogy of possibility. In: K. Weiler and C. Mitchell (Eds), *What Schools Can Do: Critical Pedagogy and Practice*. Albany: State University of New York Press, 293.

Jagers, R. and Carroll, G. (2002) Issues in educating African American children and youth. In: S. Stringfield and D. Land (Eds), *Educating At-risk Students*. Chicago: National Society for the Study of Education, 49–65.

Ladson-Billings, G. (1995) *The Dreamkeepers: Successful Teachers of African American Children*. San Francisco: Jossey Bass.

Land, D. and Legters, N. (2002) The extent and consequences of risk in U.S. education. In: S. Stringfield and D. Land (Eds), *Educating At-risk Students*. Chicago: National Society for the Study of Education, 1–28.

MacLeod, J. (1987) *Ain't No Makin' It: Leveled Aspirations in a Low-income Neighborhood*. Boulder: Westview.

MacLeod, J. (1995) *Ain't No Makin' It: Aspirations and Attainment in a Low-income Neighborhood*, second edition. Boulder: Westview.

McPartland, J., Balfanz, R., Jordan, W. and Legters, N. (2002) Promising solutions for the least productive American high schools. In: S. Stringfield and D. Land (Eds), *Educating At-risk Students*. Chicago: National Society for the Study of Education, 148–70.

Oakes, J. (1985) *Keeping Track: How Schools Structure Inequality*. New Haven: Yale University Press.

Oakes, J. (1992) Detracking schools: early lessons from the field. *Phi Delta Kappan*, (73)6: 448–54.

Padron, Y., Waxman, H. and Rivera, H. (2002) Issues in educating Hispanic students. In: S. Stringfield and D. Land (Eds), *Educating At-risk Students* Chicago: National Society for the Study of Education, 29–48.

Page, R. (1987). Lower-track classes at a college-preparatory high school: a caricature of educational encounters. In: G. Spindler and L. Spindler (Eds), *Interpretative Ethnography of Education: At Home and Abroad*. Mahwah, NJ: Lawrence Erlbaum Associates, 91–117.

Slavin, R. (2002) The intentional school: effective elementary education for all children. In: S. Stringfield and D. Land (Eds), *Educating At-risk Students*. Chicago: National Society for the Study of Education, 111–27.

Sleeter, C.E. (Ed.) (1991) *Empowerment Through Multicultural Education*. Albany: State University of New York Press.

Stringfield, S. and Datnow, A. (2002) Systemic supports for schools serving students placed at-risk. In: S. Stringfield and D. Land (Eds), *Educating At-risk Students*. Chicago: National Society for the Study of Education, 269–88.

Wink, J. (1997) *Critical Pedagogy: Notes From the Real World*. New York: Longman.

Conclusion

The dilemmas and possibilities of student-centered school reform research

Beth C. Rubin and Elena M. Silva

> Don't just look at students for answers – look at what we do, how we act.
>
> (Cushman, 2003: 1)

The research presented in this book provides us with a rich assortment of school reform casestudies gathered from the unique perspective of students. Conveying both the dilemmas and possibilities of equity-geared reforms, these studies serve as a "data set" of ten distinct examples of students' experiences with school reform. Together, these casestudies help us achieve a fuller understanding of how and why certain reforms are most promising for the least successful students.

The first part of this conclusion offers our key "findings" from this collection of studies. These findings offer some basic assertions about the dilemmas and possibilities of achieving equity through school change and highlight five particular elements of reform that stand out as most promising. In the second section of this conclusion we discuss the dilemmas inherent in taking a student-centered research perspective and how to best further this research agenda.

What students are telling us: findings from the collection

The casestudies in this book examine both the disappointments and successes of various equity-geared reforms. Taken as a collection, these studies remind us that no single discrete reform can effectively close the achievement gap that persists in today's large desegregated high schools. Through the candid words of students, these studies compel us to recognize the broader societal context of schooling and the need for a restructuring agenda that is attentive and connected to the social, cultural and economic realities of students' lives.

Highlighting the complexities, contradictions and potential of reforms, the authors of these casestudies offer insight into how educators, administrators, reformers and policy-makers might bring the adult world of reform closer to the student experience. The authors in the first half of the volume poke holes in some of today's most popular reforms, illustrating how disconnected many reforms are from the students they aim to affect. These studies compel educators, researchers and policy-makers to ask critical questions about how and in whose best interests reforms are developed and implemented. The authors in the second half of the collection portray reforms that more closely connect with the lived experiences of students, particularly the students struggling most with school. These studies uncover students' need for basic supports, skills and opportunities that are relevant to their present lives and that prepare them to achieve their future aspirations.

From the perspective of the students whose voices are featured throughout this volume, successful student-centered, equity-based reforms do the following:

- Bridge the gap between adult teachers and adolescent students and support close relationships between peers. These relationships serve to both encourage and push students, as in the examples of the El Puente Academy for Peace and Justice, the Technology Academy at Berkeley High School, and the MOST program at Mountain High School.
- Create smaller structures for more personalized learning and teaching and a greater sense of belonging among students, as in the Futures Project at James Madison High School, El Puente, and the Technology Academy.
- Provide curricula and opportunities that encourage critical awareness of self, school and society, as in the Futures Project, and the Civics and Government Institute at Montclair High School. Such curricular and participatory reforms empower awareness and action without forcing or reinforcing static notions of gender, race and class, as occurs in some single-gender academies, some identity-based courses, and some student-inclusion and detracking efforts.
- Match the rhetoric of high standards with the day-to-day supports students need to meet those standards, as in the Futures Project and the MOST program, and unlike the Cedar High detracking effort and the geometry portfolio assessments.
- Provide basic skills, support and resources to complete and transition beyond high school as in the MOST program, El Puente, and the Technology Academy, including the necessary networks and connections to provide access to and opportunity in higher education, such as in the Futures Project.

The overarching tone of many of these findings is strikingly simple, yet no less powerful. We find that day-to-day interactions are important to kids. It is clear that there is no monolithic "student experience" – kids' lives are varied and diverse. Race, class, and gender all seem to be important to kids' lives in school, although not always in ways that can be easily predicted. We see that schools are, perhaps even principally, social spaces for young people. Again and again it is shown that students want to feel a sense of connection to and admiration for the adults in their lives, to feel that someone with more experience is looking out for their best interests. It seems that high school students, on the edge of adulthood, desire learning that helps them to better understand themselves and the world around them, and feels like it is leading them somewhere productive. These assertions seem basic, even obvious, but are valuable nonetheless.

The burden and promise of student-centered research

Research that centers on the student perspective and experience promises a better and richer understanding of how students experience their schools and the vast array of school improvement efforts. At the same time, putting students at the center of a research agenda and analysis carries with it certain burdens and responsibilities. As adult researchers, we face inevitable conflicts over how to collect, interpret and represent students and student experience. The studies included in this collection represent a variety of approaches to introducing and including the student perspective, and they offer some important considerations and lessons about student-centered research.

An obvious and unavoidable tension in researching and writing about students and "student voice" is that we do so from an adult vantage point. While we may try to represent students and their experiences as genuinely as possible, we can portray the experiences, opinions and thoughts of students only from our perspective as adult researchers. After months and sometimes years spent as teachers, advocates and counselors to these young people, many of us developed close relationships and deep commitments to supporting and empowering these students. Thus it is difficult but quite necessary to acknowledge that our analysis of these students' words and worlds remains at least one step removed from their own.

With this limitation in mind, it is equally important that we strive for a cogent and contextualized analysis of students' words and experiences. It is not sufficient to merely promote student voice through the presentation of student stories and testimonials, nor is it helpful to privilege student insights as the ultimate solution to the problems of school reform. Rather, we must recognize that students' ideas and experiences, as varied and complex as those of adults, require a thorough and rigorous analysis that respects but does not romanticize students and student voices.

Student-centered research is at the crux of the conflict between representing young people as underdeveloped and voiceless victims of oppression or as powerful and skilled agents of change and resistance. Fine and Weis remind us to recognize and challenge these common theoretical dichotomies:

> These "choices" [are] carved out as the presumably only appropriate alternatives ... Simple stories of discrimination and victimization, with no evidence of resistance, resilience, or agency, are seriously flawed and deceptively partial, and they deny the rich subjectivities of persons surviving amid horrific social circumstances. Equally dreary, however, are the increasingly popular stories of individual heroes who thrive despite the obstacles, denying the burdens of surviving amid such circumstances.
>
> (Fine and Weis, 1996: on line)

Indeed, it may be easier and at times more provocative to portray students as the victims and champions of schooling. Yet, in the effort to confront deeply-entrenched inequities in today's schools, it is far more important to challenge these conventional characterizations and uproot old notions that the student experience is uniform and static and that students are incapable or unwilling to participate in "adult" reforms.

The authors of these studies approached their research and analysis with this shared agenda but from decidedly different angles. We employed a variety of research methodologies, from participant observation at multiple school sites to collaborative action research within a single school. Over varying time periods, from several months to several years, some of us followed students in and out of school and across contexts, while others centered their research on a particular classroom or program. As a collection, they represent the numerous strategies of student-centered reform studies.

As part of an emerging body of student-centered research (Cook-Sather, 2002; Fielding, 2001; Shultz and Cook-Sather, 2001; Rudduck and Flutter, 2000; Olsen et al., 2000; Wasley et al., 1997; Oldfather, 1995), this collection provides a window into the lives and experiences of students in today's large, diverse and often divided high schools. It is not our intent to celebrate student voice and agency as the key to any school reform or the remedy for any school's problems. Rather, we aim to better understand popular, equity-based school reforms from a perspective that is too often assumed, undermined or altogether ignored in the implementation and assessment of school change practices. In doing so, we reveal a small but essential piece of the larger puzzle of school reform.

A youth-centered perspective on detracking reform reveals the difficulties inherent in attempting to remedy widespread racial and socioeconomic inequalities through classroom-based reform. This approach to studying school reform is overlooked, but is critical, both for teachers implementing equity-geared reforms and researchers hoping to contribute to the school reform literature.

As teachers and other educators and school reformers struggle to create more equitable educational settings for students from racially and socio-economically diverse backgrounds, it is vital to examine the enactment of such practices by the intended beneficiaries – the students. The under-standings to be reached through observing and soliciting the perspective of students as they move through daily life in schools are invaluable. These perspectives enrich both the theory and practice of education. It provides teachers with a valuable window into how their practices are experienced by students, as well as helping them to look beyond their own classrooms for the causes of and solutions for pressing inequities. For researchers, looking at student perspectives reveals how school reform impacts the targets of that reform – the students – and creates a more complex picture of how a reform moves from theory to reality. Ericson and Ellett aptly describe the need to bridge the efforts of reformers with the experiences of students:

> In pursuing the goals of educational reform over the past several decades, educational policy makers have focused on teachers, administrators, and school structures as keys to higher educational achievement. Yet ... students are as causally central as educators in bringing about higher educational achievement.
>
> (Ericson and Ellett, 2002: 1)

We believe this to be true, and hope this collection will be part of an ongoing attempt to bring students' voices and perspectives into the mainstream of school reform research.

Bibliography

Cook-Sather, A. (2002) Authorizing students' perspectives: toward trust, dialogue, and change in education. *Educational Researcher*, 31(4): 3–14.

Cushman, K. (2003) *Fires in the Bathroom.* New York: The New Press.

Ericson, D.P. and Ellett, F.S. (2002) The question of the student in educational reform. *Education Policy Analysis Archives*, 10(31). Retrieved on line July 2 from: http://epaa.asu.edu/epaa/v10n31/.

Fielding, M. (Ed.) (2001) Special issue on student voice. *Forum*, 43(2).

Fine, M. and Weis, L. (1996) Writing the "wrongs" of fieldwork: confronting our own research/writing in urban ethnographies. *Qualitative Inquiry*, 2(3): 251–74.

Oldfather, P. (Ed.) (1995) Learning from student voices. *Theory into Practice*, 34(2).

Olsen, L., Nai-Lin Chang, H., De la Rosa Salazar, D., Dowell, C., Leong, C., McCall Perez, Z., McClain, G. and Raffel, L. (2000) *Turning the Tides of Exclusion*. Oakland, CA: California Tomorrow.

Rudduck, J. and Flutter, J. (2000) Pupil participation and pupil perspectives: carving a new order of experience, *Cambridge Journal of Education, 30:* 75–89.

Shultz, J. and Cook-Sather, A. (Eds) (2001) *In Our Own Words: Students' Perspectives on School*. Lanham, MD: Rowman and Littlefield.

Wasley, P., Hampel, R. and Clark, R. (1997) *Kids and School Reform*. San Francisco: Jossey-Bass.

Index